SpringerBriefs in Economics

SpringerBriefs present concise summaries of cutting-edge research and practical applications across a wide spectrum of fields. Featuring compact volumes of 50 to 125 pages, the series covers a range of content from professional to academic. Typical topics might include:

- A timely report of state-of-the art analytical techniques
- A bridge between new research results, as published in journal articles, and a contextual literature review
- A snapshot of a hot or emerging topic
- An in-depth case study or clinical example
- A presentation of core concepts that students must understand in order to make independent contributions

SpringerBriefs in Economics showcase emerging theory, empirical research, and practical application in microeconomics, macroeconomics, economic policy, public finance, econometrics, regional science, and related fields, from a global author community.

Briefs are characterized by fast, global electronic dissemination, standard publishing contracts, standardized manuscript preparation and formatting guidelines, and expedited production schedules.

Wanxue Lu

Post-Asian Financial Crisis Reforms in Thailand

A 20 Year Retrospective on the Banking Industry

Springer

Wanxue Lu
Graduate School of Economics
Kyoto University
Kyoto, Japan

ISSN 2191-5504 ISSN 2191-5512 (electronic)
SpringerBriefs in Economics
ISBN 978-981-97-3770-3 ISBN 978-981-97-3771-0 (eBook)
https://doi.org/10.1007/978-981-97-3771-0

This Springer imprint is published by the registered company Springer Nature Singapore Pte Ltd.
The registered company address is: 152 Beach Road, #21-01/04 Gateway East, Singapore 189721, Singapore

Preface

This book critically examines the Asian Financial Crisis, a pivotal event in the contemporary Asian economic landscape, over two decades after its onset. It explores the aftermath, scrutinizing the lessons learned and opportunities missed. Focusing on Thailand, where the crisis originated, this volume provides an in-depth analysis spanning 20 years. It delves into the financial reforms, market restructuring, and evolution of business practices and commercial banking performance post-1997, offering insights into the transformative impact of this significant economic upheaval.

The study delves into the tumultuous period of the Asian Financial Crisis, where numerous financial entities and commercial banks in Thailand faced bankruptcy, underwent government-driven restructuring, temporary nationalization, or were acquired by foreign institutions. Prompted by recommendations from international financial bodies, Thailand embarked on significant financial reforms aimed at reorganizing and deregulating its banking sector to foster transparency, competitiveness, and self-regulation. Central to this narrative is the "Financial Master Plan," initiated in 2004, along with pivotal regulatory modifications affecting foreign investments. The monography thoroughly examines these reforms, focusing on their distinctive features and consequential impact on Thailand's commercial banking sector post-crisis.

By examining significant alterations in ownership structures and shifts in the competitive market landscape, this research aims to assess the impact of financial reforms on the commercial banking sector. It conducts a detailed analysis of the changes within the banking industry, focusing on aspects such as corporate governance, business practices, and alterations in ownership and profit-cost dynamics. These facets are explored in the context of the financial reforms implemented post-crisis, highlighting how these reforms have reshaped the banking sector's operational and structural framework.

Furthermore, this book investigates the tangible effects of these regulatory changes at the organizational level, exemplified through a detailed case study of a Thai family-owned business group. It explores the transformation in family control dynamics, management restructuring, and business performance, thereby shedding light on how such reforms have altered operational mechanisms. This analysis offers an insightful view into the complex interplay between family-run businesses in emerging economies and the evolving socioeconomic environment, highlighting the intricate balance between entrepreneurship and regulatory changes.

The contents of this book were written in Kyoto during the COVID-19 pandemic, as a culmination of regular field surveys in Bangkok since 2014. The emergence of the pandemic triggered widespread panic and deep sense of uncertainty, an experience that remains vivid in my memory. It was during this period of global turmoil that I resonated profoundly with the words of George Gordon Byron: "The best prophet of the future is the past." This belief, that a historical review equips us with the wisdom and confidence to anticipate and shape our future, was the driving force behind my decision to revisit the Asian Financial Crisis.

As of early 2024, the global economy is characterized by a blend of uncertainty and measured hope. Numerous countries are grappling with the challenge of high inflation, prompting central banks to increase interest rates, a move that could decelerate economic growth. The risk posed by substantial public and private debts is exacerbated by the possibility of continued rate hikes. Furthermore, the patchy recovery from the COVID-19 pandemic contributes to regional disparities. Ongoing geopolitical tensions and trade conflicts further compound market instability and disrupt global supply chains. This intricate economic scenario, laden with the potential for crisis, underscores the importance of understanding past financial upheavals and reforms. A retrospective analysis, such as this study of the Asian Financial Crisis, offers crucial insights for navigating today's complex economic environment.

Lastly, I would like to extend my gratitude to Kosuke Mizuno, Shinsuke Nagaoka, Go Yano, Tomohiro Machikita, Miki Hamada, and Satoshi Shimizu for their valuable insights. My most profound acknowledgment goes to Fumiharu Mieno, a mentor who has significantly influenced my academic journey and helped me establish my own scholarly style. His guidance was crucial in integrating my financial engineering background with Southeast Asian studies, thereby refining my research methods and enhancing my practical understanding of the region.

I extend further thanks to Sukanda Lewis, Nualnoi Treerat, Saithip Konggiatnarong, Thanyalak Vacharachaisurapol, and Nattapong Puttanapong for their invaluable support and insights during the field survey phase. Gratitude is also due to the Ministry of Education, Science, Sports, and Culture of Japan (MESSC) for their support, denoted by the Scientific Research No. 21K20074, and the financial support provided by the Global Collaborative Research program at the Center for Southeast Asian Studies, Kyoto University.

Kyoto, Japan
January 2024

Wanxue Lu

Contents

About the Author

Wanxue Lu is an Assistant Professor in the Faculty of Economics, Kyoto University. She earned her M.A. in finance and a Ph.D. in Southeast Asian area studies, both from Kyoto University. With a research tenure at the Institute of Asian Studies at Chulalongkorn University in Thailand, and engagements in research projects at the Institute of Developing Economies (IDE-JETRO) and the Asia Pacific Institute of Research, her extensive experience has not only endowed her with a nuanced understanding of the financial dynamics in Asia, but also integrated her into a vibrant network of policymakers and industry professionals. Her scholarly output, including her analyses and documentation of financial reforms following the Asian Financial Crisis, offers profound insights into the complexities of Southeast Asian financial markets, proving essential for both academic and practical applications in understanding and navigating this region's economic environments.

List of Figures

List of Tables

Chapter 1
Introduction

Abstract This introduction examines the overall evolution of the organizational structure of Thailand's financial system and the transformation of the commercial banking sector by comparing key market characteristics before and after the Asian Financial Crisis, serving as a foundation for analyzing the post-Asian Financial Crisis financial reforms. The analysis reveals that, in contrast to the pre-crisis era characterized by a closed market structure, minimal foreign participation, and family-run operations in large banks, the commercial banking market has increasingly incorporated foreign capital and foreign banking entities. Traditional family founders of these banks have seen a reduction in their ownership control. In light of this market reorganization, the study scrutinizes the resulting changes in ownership structures and banking practices, aiming to evaluate the effectiveness of financial reforms and policies implemented in the post-crisis period.

1.1 Research Background and Problem Description

Throughout the history of the contemporary Asian economy, there have been few events as impactful as the Asian Financial Crisis (AFC). Current literature on AFC in the region often place emphases on the causes and impacts of the crisis itself. Nevertheless, analyses on the post-crisis financial reforms, positioned as diagnosis and remedies of governments, and their effectiveness and impacts on the financial system in the long run are still little understood. Over two decades have passed since the crisis. What has occurred since then? What lessons have we learned, or perhaps failed to learn? This study seeks to offer a longitudinal and evidence-based empirical analyses on the repercussions of financial regulatory reforms implemented in the wake of the AFC, examining the multifaceted impacts on the commercial banking sector in Thailand, where the crisis originated.

Having been typified as "bank-centric," the financial sector's expansion played a pivotal role in fueling Thailand's rapid economic ascent from the 1980s to the early 1990s. The vitality of the financial system is commonly perceived as a bellwether for the nation's overall economic trajectory. Yet, deficiencies such as subpar corporate

W. Lu, *Post-Asian Financial Crisis Reforms in Thailand*,
SpringerBriefs in Economics, https://doi.org/10.1007/978-981-97-3771-0_1

governance, inefficient lending practices, and widespread corruption in this sector were considered as key contributors to the AFC of 1997, casting a significant shadow over Thailand's economic landscape.

In response to directives from leading international financial institutions, Thailand initiated sweeping reforms in its financial sector, primarily targeting the banking industry. These reforms were designed to overhaul and liberalize the banking system, with an emphasis on enhancing transparency, fostering competitive practices, and promoting self-regulation. A cornerstone of these efforts was the "Financial Master Plan," which was set in motion in 2004. This plan was complemented by significant regulatory adjustments, particularly in relation to foreign investment, marking a critical turning point in Thailand's financial regulatory landscape.

Consequently, the past two decades have seen Thailand's banking sector grappling with intensified challenges from foreign entities, particularly those from East and Southeast Asia. Moreover, this competitive landscape was further shaped by the 2014 ASEAN Banking Integration Framework (ABIF), conceived as part of the preparations for the 2015 ASEAN Economic Community. This framework is anticipated to accelerate foreign competition in Thailand's commercial banking sector and simultaneously open avenues for domestic banks to expand their footprint in Southeast Asia.

In the context of both domestic regulatory reforms and international influences, Thailand's banking sector has undergone substantial transformations. Distinguished from collections of past events; through a thorough 20-year retrospective analysis of Thailand's post-AFC financial regulatory reforms and their complex effects on the commercial banking sector, this study is a lens through which the intricate relationships between regulatory changes, market dynamics, and organizational behavior are explored and understood.

This monograph aims to methodically examine the alterations in market structure and ownership dynamics within the banking sector, following the post-AFC financial reforms. The objective of this study is to conduct a critical analysis of the effects of post-crisis financial regulatory reforms, specifically aiming to elucidate the underlying mechanisms of policy impact at the micro-level.

This introduction chapter provides a historical overview of Thailand's commercial banking sector, framing it within the broader context of the country's financial system. This serves as a foundation for analyzing the post-Asian Financial Crisis financial reforms. The chapter outlines the research background, defines the scope of the study, and clarifies the terms and entities involved. Furthermore, it conducts a detailed exploration of the development of Thailand's commercial banking system, with a focus on significant market shifts post-2000. This investigation leads to the formulation of the study's central research problem and objectives.

1.1.1 *Organization Structure Evolution of the Financial Sector*

As delineated on the Bank of Thailand's Financial Institutions System homepage, the system of financial institutions is fundamental to the health of the economy. It serves a critical function in facilitating the flow and allocation of funds, alongside providing payment and settlement services. Consequently, the sustenance of economic growth necessitates a financial system that is both robust and efficient, as well as inherently stable.

Broadly, a financial system has several components: a financial control system, financial institutions, a capital market, a financial regulatory system, and the overall financial environment. In the realm of Thailand's financial markets, banks, as depository financial intermediaries, have historically assumed a preeminent role in fundraising activities. In 1998, total bank loans surged to 1.7 times the national GDP, representing 80% of the overall financial market, overshadowing commercial banks, which peaked at 1.3 times the GDP, indicating the "bank-centric" market structure of Thailand's financial sector.

Recent years, however, have witnessed a marked shift with the burgeoning of the stock and bond markets, elevating the stature of the capital market. By 2015, the stock market constituted 34% and the bond market 26% of total fundraising, signaling a decline in the banking sector's predominance, which accounted for a 40% share. Post-AFC, the financial market in Thailand has gradually evolved towards a more diversified fundraising landscape.

This section details changes in the financial market environment with respect to (1) the capital market, (2) the regulatory system, and (3) the financial institutions to illustrate the transformation of Thailand's commercial banking sector in recent years.

(1) Since the AFC, the capital market in Thailand has experienced accelerated growth, as displayed in Fig. 1.1. The equity market capitalization increased from 34% of GDP in 1997 to 96% of GDP in 2015. It constituted 34% of the total size of the financial system in 2015, which includes the equity market, the bond market, and total bank credits.

    Meanwhile, the bond market expanded from 11% of GDP in 1997 to 73% in 2015, which accounted for 26% of the total size of the financial system. According to statistics from the Bank of Thailand (BOT), short-term corporate financing through the bond market has grown rapidly since the mid-2000s, suggesting changes in corporate financing patterns in recent years.

    Despite the rapid development of the capital market, the banking sector maintains the largest market share of over 40%; Thailand's financial system is still considered "bank-based" for this reason.

(2) In collaboration with the Securities and Exchange Commission (SEC) and the Office of Insurance Commission (OIC), the BOT takes charge of the financial risk assessment and regulations to strengthen financial stability. These three

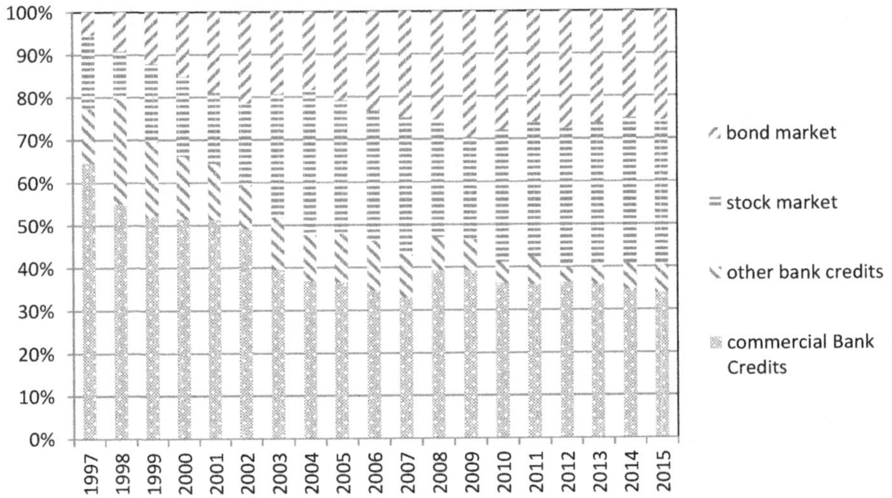

Fig. 1.1 The changes in Thailand's financial system from 1997 to 2015. *Source* Bank of Thailand, IMF, Asian Bonds Online. *Note* According to the definition and classification by IMF, domestic money banks comprise commercial banks and other financial institutions that accept transferable deposits, such as demand deposits

regulators constitute most of the financial supervision and regulation system in Thailand.

As a central bank, the BOT fulfills the roles of issuing banknotes, implementing financial policies, managing and controlling foreign exchange, and supervising the financial institutions. According to the "Bank of Thailand Act B.E. 2485" as amended by "B.E. 2551", the BOT is charged with the responsibility to supervise the financial status, analyze the financial performance, and improve the risk management system of the financial institutions, to promote financial institutions' stability.

Figure 1.2 illustrates the organizational structure of the BOT in detail. The Financial Institutions Policy Committee (FIPC) is the center within the BOT that conducts the supervision and examination of the financial institutions. Despite the supervisory and regulatory authority of the Ministry of Finance (MOF) over the BOT, the independence and regulatory power of the BOT over financial institutions was strengthened considerably by the "Bank of Thailand Act B.E. 2551" as amended in 2008.

(3) The BOT classifies Thai financial institutions into two categories: (1) depository corporations, including commercial banks, special financial institutions (SFIs), saving corporative and credit unions, finance companies, and money market mutual funds, and (2) non-depository corporations, such as mutual funds, credit card and personal loan companies, insurance companies, leasing companies, government pension fund, securities companies, and agricultural cooperatives.

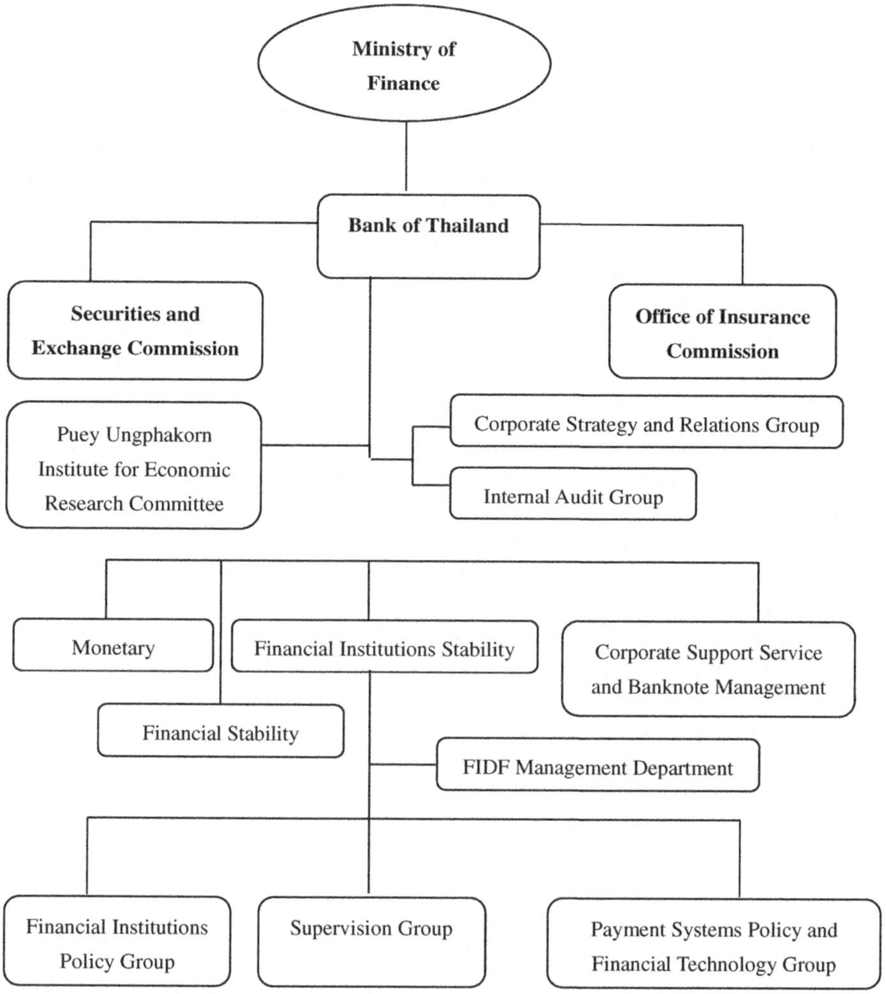

Fig. 1.2 The main organizational chart of the financial regulatory system. *Source* Ministry of Finance, Thailand. Bank of Thailand

Since the AFC of 1997, Thailand's financial institutions have undergone substantial structural transformation. Of the 176 financial institutions operational immediately before the crisis, 91 were finance and securities companies, occupying a predominant position within the market. Following a series of closures and mergers initiated in 1998, their numbers dwindled to 51 by 2017, and their contribution to the total market assets diminished to a mere 1%.

As of 2016, depositary corporations, encompassing 1,498 entities and holding 69.03% of the total assets, predominantly govern the financial sector in Thailand.

Commercial banks along with SFIs emerge as the principal entities within this category. Conversely, the non-depositary segment, comprising 7,039 entities, manages 30.97% of the sector's assets, prominently through mutual funds and insurance companies. Despite the numerical superiority of non-depositary entities, their control over assets markedly trails behind that of depositary institutions. This sector exhibits a wide spectrum of institutions including banks, cooperatives, insurance companies, and mutual funds, each distinctly influencing the aggregate asset distribution. This data underscores the diverse institutional landscape of Thailand's financial sector, highlighting the substantial disparity in asset control between depositary and non-depositary entities (Bank of Thailand, 2016a).

However, for this study, to be more specific regarding the observation and examination of the commercial banking sector, the financial institutions are divided into three categories as defined below:

(1) Non-bank Financial Intermediaries: this category includes the financial institutions but excludes commercial banks and SFIs, such as insurance companies, leasing companies, finance companies, credit card, personal loan and nano finance companies, and the different types of cooperatives.
(2) Commercial Banks: the Financial Institution Business Act B.E. 2551 of 2008 classifies commercial banks in Thailand into four categories: fully licensed commercial banks, foreign bank branches, retail banks, and subsidiaries of foreign banks. However, in this study, "commercial banks" refers to the fully licensed commercial banks, retail banks, and subsidiaries of foreign banks, and does not include foreign bank branches.
(3) Government-owned Specialized Financial Institutions (SFIs): this category comprises eight state-owned institutions. Specifically, the Government Saving Bank (GSB), the Government Housing Bank (GHB), the Bank for Agriculture and Agricultural Cooperatives (BAAC), and the Islamic Bank of Thailand (IBT) are the so-called Special Banks (SB); the rest fall under "Other Specialized Financial Institutions" (OSFI): the Small and Medium Enterprise Development Bank of Thailand (SME Bank), the Export–Import Bank of Thailand (EIB), the Secondary Mortgage Corporation (SMC), and the Thai Credit Guarantee Corporation (TCGC).

The SFIs accounted for 16.8% of total financial sector assets in 2002, dropping to 15.3% in 2016. The GSB, GHB, and BAAC have a relatively large share of the SFIs' total assets. These government-affiliated financial institutions, also known as policy-based financial institutions, have played a crucial role in the implementation of financial reforms since the AFC. For instance, the SFIs contributed significantly in the implementation of the "populist policy" that was pursued by the Thaksin administration[1] (2001–2006) with the aim to improve the accessibility of financial services to underserved communities and small and medium-sized enterprises.

As delineated by Menkhoff and Suwanaporn in 2007, the SFIs function as pivotal extensions of the government, facilitating economic and social development alongside the implementation of specific policies. They offer a diversified portfolio of financial services, including housing, small and medium enterprise (SME) credits, export–import financing, and microcredits, strategically targeting underserved sectors such as low-income groups. This approach significantly enhances access to financial resources for populations typically excluded from conventional commercial banking services.

Due to the unique ownership structure (state-owned) and the policy-based management style of SFIs, this research excludes them from the commercial banking sector and focuses on commercial banks as defined in Category (2) above.

1.1.2 The Transformation of the Commercial Banking Sector Before and After the AFC

Before the AFC, Thailand's commercial banking sector exhibited several major characteristics.

(1) First, the sector used to be a highly closed market. In terms of domestic entry, the Thai government permitted only two new banks to enter the market in the four decades since the 1950s: One is the Thai Military Bank Public Company Limited that was established in 1957. Following the AFC, it merged with the DBS Thai Danu Bank in 2004 and changed its name to TMB Bank in 2005. The other is Asia Trust Bank, which was established in 1965. It experienced significant financial distress afterwards and was purchased by the state-owned Krung Thai Bank.

    In terms of foreign entry, the financial regulations on foreign investment in the commercial banking sector were extremely strict before the AFC, even during the financial liberalization process in Thailand from the early 1980s to the mid-1990s. It is well known as the "No Exit, No Entry" policy.

(2) The commercial banking sector was a highly concentrated market. For a long period before the crisis in 1997, the market share of the top five large-sized banks—Bangkok Bank, Siam Commercial Bank, Krung Thai Bank, Kasikornbank, and Bank of Ayudhya—was in the range of 60–70%.

(3) The commercial banking sector used to be well known for its family-run business style. The ownership control and/or management control of most commercial

[1] Thaksin Shinawatra (Thai: ทักษิณ ชินวัตร, born July 26, 1949), a Thai and Montenegrin businessman and politician, was the Prime Minister of Thailand from 2001 until he was overthrown in a military coup on September 19, 2006. His party was outlawed, and he was barred from political activity. The Thaksin government launched programs to reduce poverty, expand infrastructure, and promote small and medium-sized enterprises and universal healthcare coverage.

banks were dominated by the founding families or several cooperative families before the AFC. For instance, three of the top five commercial banks—Bangkok Bank, Kasikornbank, and Bank of Ayudhya—were all family-run enterprises which were affiliated to the financial conglomerates owned by the founding families.

To capture the major characteristics of the banking market and analyze the transformation before and after the AFC, this subsection documents the development of the commercial banking sector. Table 1.1 depicts the changes in the number of commercial banks and branches from 1990 to 2014.

There were 15 commercial banks and 14 foreign bank branches in Thailand until the AFC. The closed banking system was considered positively related to the high level of concentration in the banking market. The structure was criticized as having undermined the efficiency of resource allocation. It resulted in insufficient market competition and a lack of motivation to improve financial accessibility, especially in respect of banking services for those in rural areas. The financial reforms following the AFC emphasized this issue.

Deregulation and Active Market Entry

Following the AFC, the Thai commercial banking sector experienced a long process of reorganization, with financial aid (with strict conditions) from the World Bank and the IMF. Some of the commercial banks that experienced financial difficulties received a series of public capital injections, a few were nationalized, while others were acquired by foreign banks. The general landscape of the banking market changed drastically.

Along with the implementation of financial reforms by the Thaksin administration from 2001, there was a wave of financial companies upgrading to retail banks or fully licensed commercial banks. In addition, the financial authority implemented the "Financial Sector Master Plan" from 2004, to guide the financial reforms introduced after the crisis to strengthen market competition conditions and improve financial accessibility. Consequently, the total number of commercial banks continued to decline until its lowest level of 12 in 2004. In contrast, the total number of foreign bank branches increased rapidly after the crisis.

Increasing Foreign Participation

A phenomenal increase in foreign investment in the banking sector drew considerable attention and became a distinguishing characteristic in the development of the market following the AFC. On the one hand, the total foreign ownership shares of commercial banks increased significantly under the Thaksin reforms. On the other hand, there were two instances of a significant upsurge in foreign bank entry that followed the AFC and the global financial crisis of 2008. In addition, three more foreign banks from

Table 1.1 Number of commercial banks and branches

Year	Number of commercial banks sector			Number of branches of big 4 banks				
	Commercial bank	Foreign branch	Branch[a]	Bangkok bank	Krung Thai bank	Kasikornbank	Siam commercial bank	Branches No. of big 4 to total branches (%)
1990	15	14	2,286	353	359	327	226	55.34
1991	15	14	2,457	383	388	349	239	55.31
1992	15	14	2,581	386	402	374	253	54.82
1993	15	14	2,700	396	409	385	271	54.11
1994	15	14	2,838	415	414	403	292	53.70
1995	15	14	3,055	453	435	426	323	53.58
1996	15	14	3,167	456	432	424	345	52.32
1997	15	20	3,319	476	464	443	362	52.58
1998	14	21	3,281	481	581	447	382	57.63
1999	13	21	3,853	526	643	533	496	57.05
2000	13	21	3,767	547	617	532	478	57.71
2001	13	20	3,683	570	610	530	477	59.38
2002	13	18	3,668	591	617	499	483	59.71
2003	13	18	3,748	616	621	497	501	59.63
2004	12	18	3,911	648	619	496	563	59.47
2005	16	18	4,249	685	643	499	692	59.28
2006	17	17	4,729	722	695	582	793	59.04
2007	18	17	5,110	792	761	629	872	59.77
2008	18	16	5,492	868	832	688	949	60.76
2009	17	15	5,806	913	884	805	987	61.82
2010	17	15	5,976	935	962	826	1,019	62.62
2011	16	15	6,201	975	1,022	832	1,094	63.26
2012	16	15	6,440	1,024	1,091	841	1,142	63.63
2013	16	14	6,715	1,072	1,161	869	1,173	63.66
2014	18	13	6,999	1,115	1,196	1,126	1,197	66.21
2015	19	12	7,040	1,138	1,214	1,121	1,209	66.51
2016	19	11	6,998	1,157	1,213	1,110	1,170	66.45

Source Bank of Thailand; *Commercial Banks in Thailand*, various versions

Note [a] The number of branches includes the number of foreign branches incorporated abroad but does not include the number of overseas offices of commercial banks incorporated in Thailand, that consist of overseas branches, overseas sub-branches and overseas representatives

China, Japan, and Australia entered the market around 2014–2015, in the regional financial integration trend that followed the establishment of the ASEAN Economic Community (Nomura, 2015).

Table 1.2 presents a detailed description of the financial information on commercial banks and foreign bank branches in 2016, including indicators of total assets, deposits, bank loans, gross non-performing loan ratio to total loans, return on assets, return on equity, and the total number of bank branches.

In 2016, there were 14 commercial banks, 1 retail bank, and 4 foreign bank subsidiaries, besides 11 foreign bank branches. Bangkok Bank, Siam Commercial Bank, Krung Thai Bank and Kasikornbank remained the top 4 major banks, as they had been in the previous few decades in terms of bank size, market share on total deposits, and bank credits. Bank of Ayudhya was bought by a Japanese bank in 2013 and kept its position as the fifth largest bank in Thailand, with total assets exceeding 1500 billion baht.

In addition, in the past decade, regional foreign banks, mainly from Japan, China, Singapore, and Malaysia, took over the leading role of foreign bank players in the market from traditional western multinational banks.

As displayed in Table 1.3, foreign bank branches accounted for 9% of the total assets of all commercial banks and foreign bank branches, and for about 7 and 6% of total loans and total deposits respectively, in 2016.

Constantly High Market Concentration

Even with such a dramatic change, the ratio of the number of branches of the top 4 largest banks to the total number of branches remained nearly unchanged, as shown in Table 1.2, which implies their constantly high level of market share.

Consistent with the high concentration in terms of the branch number ratio, the top 5 banks accounted for 77% of both the total assets and the total loans of all the commercial banks and reached a share of 79% of total deposits in 2016, as calculated in Table 1.4. If the foreign bank branches are also considered, the top 5 banks accounted for 70% of the total assets of all the banks and had the same market share of around 73% of total deposits and loans.

Excluding the period of turmoil of 1997–1998, Fig. 1.3 presents the change in market share of the top 4 banks relative to commercial banks' total assets, and the evolution of the Herfindahl–Hirschman Index. As one of the major characteristics of the commercial banking sector before the crisis, the oligopolistic market structure had not improved substantially since the crisis.

Overall, the market share of the top 4 banks maintained an average level of around 65% until 2014. The ratio even remained above 60% at its lowest level, despite the obvious decline in 2004–2005 due to increasing bank players as companies upgraded from financial companies to banks.

In addition, a similar trend is observed in the change of the Herfindahl–Hirschman Index (HHI). The HHI fluctuated between small scales from 0.12 to 0.14 in the period

Table 1.2 Landscape of the commercial banking sector in 2016—commercial banks

ID	Bank name	Total assets (million baht)	Deposits (million baht)	Loans (million baht)	Gross NPL/ total loans (%)	Return on assets (%)	Return on equity (%)	Branches
	Commercial bank							
1	Bangkok Bank (BBL)	2,838,799	2,116,659	1,777,103	3.2	1.0	7.8	1157
2	Siam Commercial Bank (SCB)	2,661,442	2,021,454	1,850,637	2.7	1.6	13.6	1170
3	Krung Thai Bank (KTB)	2,614,798	1,975,157	1,734,199	3.9	1.1	11.5	1213
4	Kasikornbank (KBANK)	2,467,252	1,798,440	1,589,192	3.2	1.4	12.1	1110
5	Bank of Ayudhya (BAY)	1,805,967	1,102,914	1,302,638	1.8	0.9	8.8	658
①	Sum of top 5	12,388,258	9,014,624	8,253,769	3.0	1.2	10.8	5308
6	Thanachart Bank (TBANK)	906,868	677,807	632,310	1.9	1.3	10.3	593
7	TMB bank (TMB)	820,172	599,021	568,335	2.5	1.0	9.7	453
8	United Overseas Bank Thai (UOBT)	451,743	324,081	308,972	2.6	0.8	7.4	153
9	CIMB Thai (CIMBT)	295,623	183,878	193,189	6.0	(0.4)	(5.0)	92
10	Tisco bank (TISCO)	260,742	155,951	213,994	2.0	1.4	13.4	57
11	Kiatnakin bank (KKP)	220,312	110,209	167,442	5.2	2.5	13.9	67
12	Land and Houses Bank (LHB)	209,695	149,639	138,051	1.8	1.2	14.3	133
13	Standard Chartered Bank Thai (SCBT)	190,701	52,180	32,284	5.6	0.2	1.1	18

(continued)

Table 1.2 (continued)

ID	Bank name	Total assets (million baht)	Deposits (million baht)	Loans (million baht)	Gross NPL/ total loans (%)	Return on assets (%)	Return on equity (%)	Branches
14	Industrial and Commercial Bank of China (Thai) (ICBCT)	158,151	92,024	93,797	1.3	0.9	5.5	20
	Retail bank							
15	Thai Credit Retail Bank (TCRB)	39,334	32,905	32,887	4.2	0.8	8.2	88
	Foreign bank subsidiary							
16	Bank of China (Thai) (BOC)	43,946	21,996	21,164	3.6	0.1	0.3	9
17	Sumitomo Mitsui Trust Thai bank (SMT)	29,260	8,607	19,904	0.0	(0.4)	(0.6)	1
18	ANZ Bank (Thai). (ANZ)	28,242	996	9,077	0.0	(0.4)	(0.6)	1
19	Mega International Commercial Bank (MICB)	20,212	11,675	15,287	1.8	1.2	4.3	5
	Sum of commercial banks	16,063,259	11,435,593	10,700,462	3.0	1.2	10.0	6,998
	Ratio of top 5 to the total above	**77.12%**	**78.83%**	**77.13%**				**75.85%**
	Ratio of top 5 to ALL	**69.91%**	**73.21%**	**72.64%**				**75.73%**

Source Bank of Thailand; *Commercial Banks in Thailand*, various versions

1999–2014. The high degree of market concentration kept this trend throughout the entire reorganization process and financial reforms that ensued after the crisis.

Table 1.3 Landscape of the commercial banking sector in 2016—foreign bank branches

ID	Bank name	Total assets (million baht)	Deposits (million baht)	Loans (million baht)	Gross NPL/ total loans (%)	Return on assets (%)	Return on equity (%)	Branches
	Foreign bank branch							
1	Mizuho bank	547,642	377,318	247,677	0.2	n.a.	n.a.	1
2	Sumitomo Mitsui bank	334,672	165,408	213,933	0.1	0.9	2	1
3	The Hongkong and Shanghai bank	225,163	105,691	65,164	0.2	1.2	7.4	1
4	Citibank	214,056	135,186	84,710	2.5	2	15.7	1
5	Deutsche bank	80,304	24,917	18,180	0.4	0.2	0.6	1
6	BNP Paribas	65,612	10,904	5,850	0	0.4	2.2	1
7	Bank of America	62,537	28,121	4,900	0	0.3	1.9	1
8	JP Morgan Chase bank	59,067	10,330	1,521	0.1	−0.3	−1.7	1
9	Oversea-Chinese bank	38,478	7,655	8,286	3.9	0.5	9.2	1
10	RHB bank Berhad	19,248	2,676	9,221	2.5	0.2	0.2	1
11	Indian overseas bank	11,328	8,879	3,347	9.5	1	1.5	1
③	Sum of foreign bank branches	1,658,107	877,085	662,789	0.5	0.6	2.4	11
④	Sum of all banks	177,213,666	12,312,678	11,363,251				7009
	Ratio of foreign branches to ALL total	**9.36%**	**7.12%**	**5.83%**				**0.16%**
	Ratio of top 5 to ALL	**69.91%**	**73.21%**	**72.64%**				**75.73%**

Source Bank of Thailand; *Commercial Banks in Thailand*, various versions

Decreasing Ownership of Founding Families

As mentioned above, another major feature of the commercial banking sector before the crisis was that the funding families maintained a high ratio of shareholdings and kept dominant control over the banking management. This family-run business style was considered key to improving bank lending performance and market share, due to the many banking transactions with a considerable number of enterprises affiliated to family-run business groups.

Table 1.4 The development of 19 domestic commercial banks from 1997–2016

Bank	Total assets in 2016		The banks used to be in operating		Total assets in 1997		Foreign ownership share				Background
	Rank	1 Billion bahts/market share	The banks established after 1998	The banks established before AFC	Rank	1 Billion bahts/market share	2001	2005	2010	2014	
Bangkok Bank	1	2,838.8 16.0%		Bangkok Bank	1	1,408.6 18.9%	31.8	48.3	43.6	35.0	Decentralized equity type, 3 of 15 Board of Directors are from Sophonpanich family, including the Chairman
Siam Commercial Bank	2	2,661.4 15.0%		Siam Commercial Bank	4	717.2 9.6%	27.5	55.5	34.8	37.3	Known as the "Royal Bank"
Krung Thai Bank	3	2,614.8 14.8%		Krung Thai Bank	3	792.7 10.7%	1.2	19.9	21.9	18.1	
				First Bangkok City Bank	7	316.1 4.2%					Nationalized in Feb. 1998, merged with Krung Thai Bank in Nov. 1998
				Bangkok Bank of Commerce	11	190.6 2.6%					Nationalized in Feb. 1998, merged with Krung Thai Bank in Nov. 1998
Kasikorn Bank	4	2,467.3 13.9%		Thai Farmers Bank	2	795.4 10.7%	33.6	49.0	49.0	49.0	Became state-owned after AFC, changed its name in 2003
Bank of Ayudhya	5	18,060.0 10.2%		Bank of Ayudhya	5	493.9 6.6%	11.1	32.0	47.2	72.1	Merged by MITSUBISHI UFJ FINANCIAL GROUP in 2013
			GM Money Retail Bank								Established in Jan. 2006, and transfer its assets to Ayudhya Bank in 2007
			AIG Retail Bank								Established in Mar. 2007, and transfer its assets to Ayudhya Bank in 2009
	6	906.9						0.0	49.0	49.0	

(continued)

Table 1.4 (continued)

Thanachart Bank		5.1%								Established in Apr. 2002, and took Bank of Nova Scotia as strategic partner with 24.99% shareholdings in 2007
			Siam City Bank	8	272.1 3.7%	0.0	25.0	0.0		Nationalized in 1998, then merged with Thanachart Bank in 2011
			Bangkok Metropolitan Bank	9	190.6 2.6%	0.0				Nationalized in 1998, then merged with Siam City Bank in 2002
TMB Bank	7	820.2 4.6%	Thai Military Bank	6	389.5 5.2%	0.9	39.6	36.1	39.0	Merged DBS Thai Danu Bank and Industrial Finance Corporation of Thailand in Sep. 2004, and changed its name in 2005
			Thai Danu Bank	12	130.3 1.8%	58.1				Bought by DBS in 1999, then merged with Thai Military Bank in 2004
United Overseas Bank (Thai, UOB)	8	451.7 2.5%				78.8	98.6	99.7	99.7	
			Radanasin Bank			75.0				Established in 1998, merged with Leam Thong Bank later, and then bought by UOB in 1999 (UOB Radanasin Bank)
			Bank of Asia	10	156.6 2.1%					Bought by ABN-AMRO in 1998 and sold again to UOB in 2005
			Leam Thong Bank	15	51.9 0.7%					Nationalized in 1998, then merged with Radanasin Bank later
CIMB Bank (Thai)	9	295.6 1.7%				0.0	6.0	97.2	96.8	CIMB bought Bank Thai in 2009
			Bank Thai			75.0				Union Bank of Bangkok merged with other finance companies to form a new bank in Dec. 1998
			Union Bank of Bangkok	14	73.3 1.0%					Nationalized in 1998, then reorganized as Bank Thai
TISCO Bank	10	260.7 1.5%					44.5	48.2	48.1	Established in 2004, and unlisted in 2009
	11	220.3					42.9	43.2	32.7	Established in 2005

(continued)

Table 1.4 (continued)

Kiatnakin Bank		1.2%								
Land and Houses Bank	12	209.7					N.A.	N.A.	0.9	Established as retail bank in Dec. 2005, and upgraded to commercial bank in 2011
		1.2%					N.A.	N.A.		
Standard Chartered (Thai)	13	190.7				75.0	99.8	100.0	100.0	S.C.Nakornthon Bank and S.C.B Thai Branch was integrated in 2005
		1.1%								
			Nakornthon Bank	11	73.8					Nationalized in 1998, and then bought by Standard Chartered Bank in 1999 (S.C.Nakornthon Bank)
					1.0%					
Industrial and Commercial Bank Of China (Thai)	14	158.2					38.4	97.4	97.7	Merged ACL Bank in Aug. 2010
		0.9%								
			ACL Bank							Established in Dec. 2005, and bought by ICBC in 2010
Bank of China	15	43.9								Upgraded from a foreign branch to a subsidiary in Aug. 2014
		0.2%								
Thai Credit Retail Bank	16	39.3						N.A.	N.A.	Established in Jan. 2006
		0.2%								
ANZ Bank (Thai)	17	28.2								Upgraded to a foreign bank subsidiary in 2015
		0.2%								
Sumitomo Mitsui Trust Bank (Thai)	18	23.3								Upgraded to a foreign bank subsidiary in 2015
		0.2%								
Mega International Commercial Bank	19	20.2					N.A.	N.A.	N.A.	Upgraded to International Commercial Bank of China in 2005, and changed its name in 2006
		0.1%								

Source Revised by the author based on Table 6.1 in Mieno and Lu (2020) and Appendix Table 1 in Lu (2018), utilizing data from Bank of Thailand, Stock Exchange of Thailand, *Commercial Banks in Thailand* (1997–2016), ORBIS database
Note Market share is calculated as a bank's total assets to all commercial banks' assets, foreign bank branches included. The banks in grey zone do not exist now

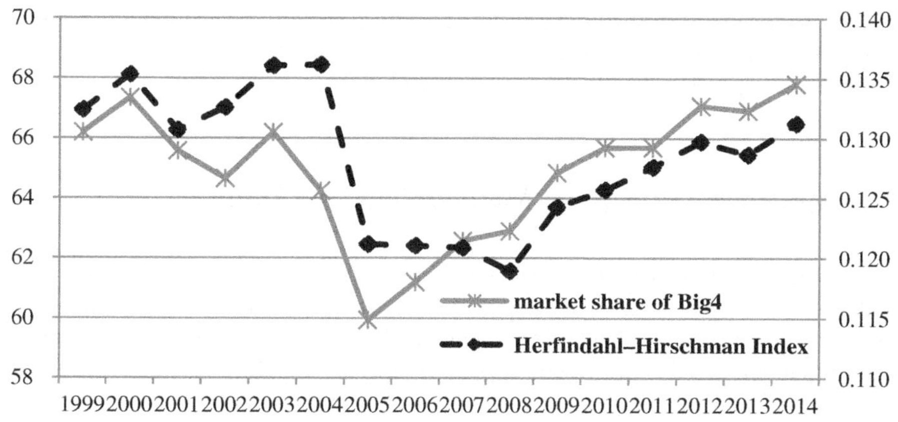

Fig. 1.3 Market concentration of commercial banking sector. *Source* Bank of Thailand, *Commercial Banks in Thailand*, various versions

However, it is also regarded as the very cause of compromised financial controls and failed screening systems of banks. It was considered to have contributed significantly to a large scale of relationship lending—special loans at interest rates significantly lower than market rates—and even to illegal transfers of profits to companies that were affiliated to the same family-run business group. This indigenous structure of highly centralized ownership and the family-run banking management style were among the primary targets of the financial reforms that followed the AFC.

During the process of reorganization of the commercial banking sector, several founding families lost a large proportion of their shareholdings; some of them even withdrew from the banking market entirely. The ownership structure of commercial banks experienced a drastic change following the crisis.

Table 1.4 provides details on ownership structure changes of commercial banks for 1997–2016, including the share of foreign ownership ratio, banking licenses, and backgrounds to the major events in the banks' development history.

For the large and medium sized banks, most founding families lost a large proportion of their shareholdings, with the exception of Siam Commercial Bank, which had a very stable and outstanding major shareholder (Bureau of the Crown Property and Group). Mergers and acquisitions by foreign banks led to the complete withdrawal of some traditional founding families of medium and small sized banks.

Meanwhile, as shown in Table 1.4, except for the Krung Thai Bank, which was a state-owned commercial bank, each of the other large-size banks had a ratio of foreign ownership of more than 30%. Commercial banks typically have a relatively high ratio of foreign ownership presently (large and medium sized banks especially), which suggests another significant feature of ownership structure in the commercial banking sector.

Despite the majority shareholding changes since the AFC, a few founding families still hold key positions in banks' management teams and boards of directors, which will be investigated in detail in the chapters to follow.

1.2 Research Objectives, Methodology and Data

Along with the implementation of financial reforms, the commercial banking sector underwent a long process of reorganization, which resulted in a drastic change in the overall landscape in Thailand following the AFC. The increase in foreign participation and the decreasing ownership by traditional founding families have also impacted banking business practice and performance considerably.

Given such a changing financial environment at home and abroad, this study aims to evaluate the financial reforms following the crisis and to analyze the impact of the regulatory changes on market transformation and the banks' management and performance for the period of two decades after the AFC. This section presents the objectives of this study in more concrete terms.

First, this study aims to examine the market reorganization process and the evolution of ownership structure of the commercial banking sector to analyze the effects of regulatory reforms and deregulation since the AFC.

In addition, the commercial banking sector has experienced a significant increase in foreign bank players and foreign investment in local banks since the AFC. As noted above, one major objective of the financial reforms following the AFC was to promote market competition to improve operation efficiency, risk management, and overall performance. Thus, on the one hand, this study aims to examine the changes in the competitive market environment at a macro level to evaluate the impact of the financial reforms. On the other hand, the study attempts to examine the impacts of foreign capital entry on operation efficiency, default risk, and profit structure of commercial banks at a micro level.

With many traditional founding families losing ownership control of banks, and the foreign ownership share maintaining a steady level, the resulting change in ownership structure will have implications for banking corporate governance, and hence banking performance. Thus, this study aims to investigate the impacts of ownership evolution on corporate governance at bank level through case studies, with an especial focus on the influence on banks' management control.

Thus, the study is proceeded as follows: First, the study conducts a descriptive analysis of the changes in regulation and ownership structure by reference to ownership changes in individual banks; observations cover all the existing fully licensed commercial banks, retail banks, and foreign bank subsidiaries.

Second, by means of a quantitative analysis from a macro perspective, the study investigates the transformation of the market structure and competitive environment to analyze the consequent impacts on the business practice and profit-cost structure of commercial banks.

Third, this study performs an empirical analysis through bank-level panel data on commercial banks from 1999 to 2014, to examine the impacts on banking performance from a micro perspective. The dataset includes local private banks, state-owned banks, joint-venture banks, and foreign bank subsidiaries, constituting an average of more than 95% of the total assets of the commercial banking sector. The data in this research are from multiple sources: the Bank of Thailand, Stock Exchange of Thailand, Bank Scope, ORBIS, annual reports of individual commercial banks, and interviews.

Finally, a case study of Kasikornbank is used to explore and interpret the mechanism of policy impacts through which ownership evolution affects banking governance and performance at the organizational level, from the perspective of management, business practice and financial performance. This research is conducted through documentary searches during fieldwork and interviews with management and research personnel in commercial banks (e.g., Bangkok Bank, Kasikornbank) and other related institutions, such as the Stock Exchange of Thailand and the Thai Bond Market Association.

1.3 Composition of the Study

According to the research objectives and approaches above, this study comprises seven chapters organized as follows.

The introduction chapter reviews the overall organization evolvement of Thailand's financial system and the transformation of the commercial banking sector, through a comparison of the major market characteristics before and after the Asian Financial Crisis. The scale and definition of research objects, the research objectives, the methodology, and the dissertation composition are presented in this section.

Chapter 2 examines the "Financial Sector Master Plan" at each stage, and the main financial acts, which concludes the transformation of financial regulations. Furthermore, it conducts a comprehensive investigation into the evolution of commercial banks' ownership structure at bank level throughout the Thaksin Administration and the post-Thaksin periods.

Chapter 3 documents the change in the regional financial landscape in East and Southeast Asian countries and positions the role of the Thai commercial banking sector in the region.

Chapter 4 investigates the effects on the overall market structure and competitive conditions of ownership evolutions in the banking sector and conducts an examination of the impacts on banking performance and business model.

Chapter 5 examines the impact of foreign capital entry on the cost and profit structure of commercial banks in Thailand through an empirical analysis, using bank-level panel data for the period 1999–2014. It distinguishes between market-level impacts and individual bank-level impacts.

Chapter 6 describes the family-run business model, and its ownership structure changes through a case study of Kasikornbank after the AFC, to examine how the impacts of post-AFC financial reforms have been materialized at an organizational level. It investigates the impact of the model on management structure and analyzes management reforms and their impact on banking performance.

Chapter 7 concludes this study and outlines the policy implications.

Chapter 2
The Financial Sector Reform and the Change in the Ownership Structure of the Commercial Banks

Abstract This chapter provides an analytical discourse on the evolution of ownership structures within commercial banks at the bank level since the Asian Financial Crisis, along with the ensuing financial reforms. It offers a detailed critique of the "Financial Sector Master Plan" across its various phases and the pivotal financial legislation, deducing a significant shift in financial regulations aimed at augmenting market efficiency, stability, and competitiveness. This shift is notably evident in the deregulatory measures concerning foreign investment. The analysis further includes a descriptive review of the changes in ownership structures within individual commercial banks following the regulatory reforms, during and after the Thaksin Administration era. The findings indicate a notable decline in ownership by traditional founding families, accompanied by a sustained increase in foreign participation in the banking sector post-Asian Financial Crisis. The entry and escalated activity of foreign banking entities have been pronounced since the international financial turmoil following the collapse of Lehman Brothers.

2.1 Introduction

In the 1980s and 1990s, Southeast Asian nations, including Thailand, were at the forefront of financial liberalization, characterized by extensive deregulation in financial services and liberalized capital flows. In Thailand, considerable strides were made towards financial deregulation from the late 1980s onward. The Bank of Thailand (BOT) implemented various deregulatory policies affecting interest and foreign exchange rates, aiming to elevate Bangkok to the status of a key financial hub in Asia, on par with cities like Hong Kong and Singapore. Furthermore, the BOT established the Bangkok International Banking Facilities, an offshore market designed to attract foreign capital. It also embarked on deregulating portfolio management and broadening the operational scope of financial institutions to improve their efficiency and stimulate competition within the financial sector.

W. Lu, *Post-Asian Financial Crisis Reforms in Thailand*,
SpringerBriefs in Economics, https://doi.org/10.1007/978-981-97-3771-0_2

The financial liberalization and deregulation initiatives were conducted in the absence of a comprehensive legal oversight framework, a deficiency now widely acknowledged as a contributing factor to the Asian Financial Crisis (AFC) in 1997.

Furthermore, as outlined in the preceding chapter, Thailand's commercial banking sector was characterized by a limited and oligopolistic nature, with most large banks being operated as family-run businesses primarily controlled by their founding families. This conventional family-centric ownership model in large commercial banks faced criticism for promoting weak corporate governance, fostering nepotistic lending practices, and enabling corruption. These issues are also recognized as having played a substantial role in the AFC.

In the immediate aftermath of the crisis, Thailand's economy was among the hardest hit by the AFC, leading to financial aid from the World Bank and the IMF. This aid came with stringent conditions, mandating tight monetary policies and comprehensive structural reforms. These reforms led to an extensive overhaul of the commercial banking sector, encompassing government-led capital injections, temporary state ownership of banks, and acquisitions of struggling banks by foreign entities.

Consequently, the reforms and restructuring processes often resulted in the dilution of control by business groups and their founding families over their banking subsidiaries. Conversely, the role of foreign capital, particularly in the banking sector, was notably amplified.

Thailand's economy began its recovery around 2002–2003, aligned with the execution of further restructuring and reforms, encapsulated in the "Financial Sector Master Plan". During this period, the commercial banking sector witnessed substantial changes in its ownership structure, alongside notable improvements in governance and performance.

One of the principal elements in the evolution of the Thai banking sector's ownership was the significant increase in foreign presence following the AFC in 1997. The proportion of foreign ownership in the commercial banking market reached its zenith at approximately 45% in 2007, and since then, it has stabilized, fluctuating around the 40% mark.

Additionally, there has been a notable shift in the makeup of major foreign banking entities in Thailand. The initial surge of foreign bank involvement, primarily through mergers and acquisitions, occurred post-AFC and saw a gradual decline leading up to 2002. Until the global financial crisis of 2008, institutional investors from Western countries, exemplified by Standard Chartered Bank from the UK and ABN-AMRO Bank from the Netherlands, were at the forefront of foreign investment in Thailand's banking sector.

Post-2008, the trend shifted, with banks from ASEAN countries, as well as from neighboring nations like Japan, China, and Australia, emerging as the primary international players in the sector. As of 2017, among Thailand's 19 commercial banks, 9 were foreign owned, with 7 originating from East and Southeast Asia. In the four-year period leading to 2017, 4 new banks from these areas entered the Thai banking market.

Alongside the inauguration of the ASEAN Economic Community (AEC) in 2015, central banks from ASEAN member nations also ratified the "ASEAN Banking Integration Framework (ABIF)", aiming at fostering regional financial integration. This initiative is expected to further encourage the entrance of foreign banks, predominantly from East and Southeast Asia.

Over the past 20 years since the AFC, the Thai banking sector has undergone significant transformations as a result of financial reforms, shifting away from the regulatory frameworks and ownership structures previously implicated in the crisis. This chapter delves into the restructuring and financial reforms of Thailand's commercial banking sector, analyzing from the perspective of individual banks, with a particular focus on the evolution of their ownership (Yutani, 2014).

The rest of this chapter is organized as follows: Sect. 2.2 considers the macroeconomic development in Thailand since the AFC and discusses the financial reforms with a focus on the "Financial Sector Master Plan." Sections 2.3 to 2.6 describes the reorganization of the commercial banking sector, capturing the transformation of ownership structure at each stage. Conclusions are presented in Sect. 2.7.

2.2 Financial Regulatory Reforms Post-Asian Financial Crisis

2.2.1 Macro-economic Environment in Thailand

In the immediate aftermath of the AFC, backed by financial assistance from the World Bank and the IMF, extensive regulatory reforms were undertaken to rectify the shortcomings of the financial sector. This period saw some struggling commercial banks receiving injections of public funds, while others underwent nationalization or were taken over by larger banks during the tenures of the Chavalit Yongchaiyudh[1] and Chuan Leekpai[2] governments. The Thai economy continued to struggle until 2002, but from 2003, there were encouraging signs of recovery from the crisis.

The Thaksin administration, which assumed power in 2001, dedicated considerable efforts to tackling the substantial non-performing loans. To revitalize the domestic economy, it also promoted the "Dual Track" policy, which focused on stimulating domestic demand and enhancing export growth. Up until the military coup in

[1] Chavalit Yongchaiyudh (Thai: ชวลิต ยงใจยุทธ), was Thailand's 22nd Prime Minister from 1996 to 1997. He was also a retired army officer. From 1986 to 1990 he was the Commander-in-chief of the Royal Thai Army (RTA), and Supreme Commander of the Royal Thai Armed Forces from 1987 to 1990. In 1990, he founded the New Aspiration Party which he led until 2002.

[2] Chuan Leekpai (Thai: ชวน หลีกภัย, Chinese: 呂基文), was the Prime Minister of Thailand from September 20, 1992 to May 19, 1995 and again from November 9, 1997 to February 9, 2001. He is also known as a third-generation Thai Chinese of Hokkien descent.

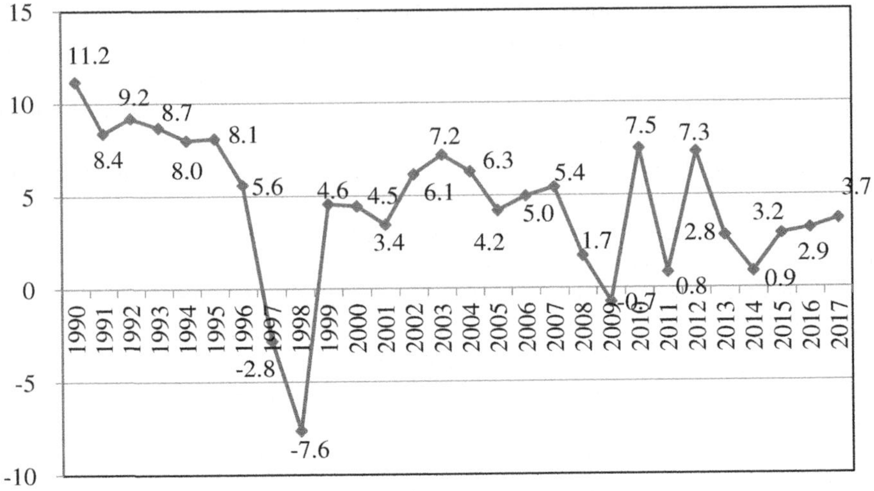

Fig. 2.1 The change in real GDP growth rate in Thailand from 1990 to 2017 (%). *Source* Key Indicators, World Bank

2006, which led to the fall of the Thaksin administration, Thailand's economy experienced significant recovery, with an average annual GDP growth rate surpassing 5%.

The Thai economy, however, faced a sharp downturn due to capital outflows and the global market slump during the 2007–2008 global financial crisis. This decline is evident in mid-2009, as depicted in Fig. 2.1, with the GDP growth rate falling into negative territory. Despite this setback, the economy began to rebound soon after, influenced by events like the May 2011 coup d'état and the flooding in the Bangkok region, which inflicted significant damages on foreign-owned businesses, notably Japanese automobile manufacturers.

Since 2012, Thailand's economic growth has been slower compared to other ASEAN nations, partly due to political instability. Notably, the extensive anti-government demonstrations against Yingluck Shinawatra[3] administration in late 2013 and the coup d'état in May 2014 had detrimental impacts on the country's economy.

General Prayuth Chan-ocha[4] orchestrated a coup against Yingluck Shinawatra's government in 2014, and then led the National Council for Peace and Order from

[3] Yingluck Shinawatra (Thai: ยิ่งลักษณ์ ชินวัตร), was Thailand's first female Prime Minister and its youngest in over 60 years and was removed from office on May 7, 2014 by a controversial Constitutional Court decision. She is a member of the Pheu Thai Party who became the 28th Prime Minister of Thailand following the 2011 election. Also, she holds the distinction as the world's first female of Chinese descent to have led the government of a UN member state.

[4] Prayuth Chan-ocha (Thai: ประยุทธ์ จันทร์โอชา), is a retired Royal Thai Army officer and the head of the National Council for Peace and Order (NCPO), a military junta, and concurrently serves as the Prime Minister of Thailand. The council, of which he appointed himself head, along with other junta members, has the power to name the prime minister and control prime ministerial positions.

2014 to 2019. Under his military government, economic policies were geared towards fostering growth through enhanced public investment and bolstering the export and tourism industries. This approach has led to a steady recovery of Thailand's economy in recent years, with significant contributions from the burgeoning tourism sector and expanded infrastructure investments.

In 2016, the military government launched the Thailand 4.0 initiative, a strategic plan to transform the Thai economy into a more innovative and value-based system. This initiative aims to propel Thailand from a middle-income to a high-income nation.

2.2.2 Financial Sector Master Plan: Phase I

The early 2000s saw a substantial transformation in Thailand's financial landscape, driven by the financial reorganization process. In the aftermath of the AFC, with support from the World Bank and the IMF, the Thai government implemented a range of reforms aimed at improving the oversight of the financial market and ensuring the stability of the financial system. In January 2004, the Thaksin administration, in collaboration with the Ministry of Finance (MOF) and the BOT, initiated the "Financial Sector Master Plan Phase I" (FSMP Phase I). This plan served as a roadmap and set of guidelines for medium-term, inclusive reforms of the financial system.

The BOT's FSMP Handbook (2006), FSMP Phase I details the first phase of the FSMP, set for rollout from 2004 to 2008, with three core objectives for transforming the Thai financial system:

(A) Universal Access: To ensure that all economically viable individuals and enterprises gain access to fundamental financial products and services at fair pricing.
(B) System Competitiveness: To foster a financial ecosystem that is competitive, efficient, stable, and inclusive, meeting the needs of both sophisticated and unsophisticated participants.
(C) Customer Protection: To promote fairness and safeguard customers through stringent adherence to corporate governance by financial institutions, alongside providing comprehensive information and advice to empower informed financial decision-making (BOT, 2006; Takayasu, 2008).

To summarize, in FSMP Phase I, the Thai financial authorities set out to prioritize (1) broadening financial access, (2) boosting operational efficiency and encouraging competition in the market, and (3) enhancing corporate governance along with customer protection. Consequently, an analysis was conducted on the specific strategies implemented under FSMP Phase I to assess their influence on the banking sector.

One of the key initiatives for widening financial access involved implementing measures to improve fundamental financial infrastructure, particularly targeting low-income demographics. Inspired by international precedents, Thai financial regulators proposed the creation of APEX institutions.[5] These entities are designed to optimize financial intermediation by directing funds from donors to microfinance providers operating in local communities.

Research in this field suggests that the development of permanent and sustainable microfinance institutions (MFIs) is more effective for expanding services to underprivileged groups than simply increasing the number of MFIs. APEX institutions, governed by stringent regulations, channel funds to those local MFIs that meet established standards in management quality and service delivery, thereby promoting the emergence of enduring and effective microfinance services.

Furthermore, the Thai financial authorities implemented incentives to encourage commercial banks to extend services to low-income populations. The Bank for Agriculture and Agricultural Cooperatives (BAAC), initially focused on agricultural financing, was recommended to widen its service range to cater to rural low-income communities. The introduction of E-bank initiatives aimed to facilitate easier access to financial services for low-income groups, simplifying the requirements for opening a deposit account. For instance, according to the BOT, E-bank allows customers to open an account with just their life insurance, needing only basic documentation like proof of income, identification, and a small deposit of US$ 8.

Beyond these measures to enhance financial access for low-income individuals, the Thai financial regulators also established a new banking license category named "retail bank". This initiative is geared towards improving financial services for individual retail customers and small and medium enterprises (SMEs). Retail banks, with a more accessible minimum equity capital requirement of 250 million Baht and constraints on engaging in foreign exchange and derivative financial products, are authorized to perform almost all activities typical of fully licensed commercial banks.

The above measures focused on extending financial access to underserved communities and SMEs are integral to the Thaksin administration's approach, often referred to as the "populist economic policy".

To realize Vision 2 of their financial strategy, the MOF and the BOT overhauled the commercial banking license framework. Under this reform, the variety of licenses available to depositary financial institutions was streamlined from six to four types: while commercial bank and foreign bank branch licenses were maintained, licenses for International Banking Facilities, restricted banks, finance companies, and Credit Foncier Companies were consolidated into retail bank and foreign bank subsidiary licenses.

Between 2004 and 2007, eight financial entities and foreign bank branches transitioned to retail banks and foreign bank subsidiaries. This expansion increased the total count of commercial banks from 13 in 2002 to 17 in 2006, ostensibly promoting more vigorous market competition.

---

[5] APEX institutions are second-tier or wholesale organizations that channel funding (grants, loans, and guarantees) to multiple microfinance institutions. Funding may be provided with or without supporting technical service, according to a global partnership "Consultative Group to Assist the Poor" (CGAP).

Additionally, the Thai financial authorities liberalized foreign investment guidelines in banking. This change enables foreign financial institutions to open up to four more branches and broaden their operational scope. Such deregulations are expected to spur further financial innovation and introduce new international entities into the market. Concurrently, domestic financial institutions are expected to benefit from the spill-over effects of the financial technology and management expertise of foreign financial institutions.

Moreover, the introduction of the "One-presence" policy requires financial conglomerates to maintain only a single deposit-taking institution, significantly altering the previous norm where conglomerates could own commercial banks, International Banking Facilities (IBFs), and financial companies at the same time (Imaizumi, 2007). This policy serves two main objectives: firstly, to curb regulatory arbitrage, which could occur when a business group operates several deposit-taking institutions; secondly, to consolidate these entities, anticipated to bolster profitability through economies of scale (BOT, 2006). This shift resulted in a profound transformation of the overall financial market structure.

These measures are also reflective of the economic policy ethos under the Thaksin administration. To dismantle the oligopolistic banking market and enhance competitive dynamics, the government prioritized the introduction of additional banking players and the promotion of the stock and bond markets' growth.

2.2.3 Financial Sector Master Plan: Phases II and III

Under the FSMP Phase I, several financial companies were elevated, broadening their banking operations. Concurrently, the emergence of new retail banks and foreign bank subsidiaries played a pivotal role in enhancing financial accessibility. Furthermore, the introduction of the "One-presence" policy was intended to augment the profitability of these institutions. These internal reforms, alongside the transformation in the financial market structure, were significantly influenced by the seismic shifts in international financial markets triggered by the 2008 global financial crisis.

In response to these evolving dynamics, the BOT, MOF, and the Economic Cabinet of Thailand jointly endorsed the Financial Sector Master Plan Phase II (FSMP Phase II) in November 2009. Spanning from 2010 to 2014, FSMP Phase II concentrated on fostering operational efficiency and intensifying market competition to effectively navigate both local and global challenges. According to the BOT, the enactment of FSMP Phase II was strategically aligned with attaining specific objectives for Thailand's financial system as below:

(A) Efficiency Enhancement: To boost the efficiency of financial institutions, thereby reducing the cost of financial services to support economic growth.
(B) Strength and Resilience: To build a robust financial system capable of enduring global financial market fluctuations.

(C) Diversification: To expand the range of financial intermediation services, making them accessible to broader segments of the population.
(D) Fairness and Transparency: To ensure the provision of financial services is conducted transparently and equitably (BOT, 2009).

In pursuit of the Financial Sector Master Plan Phase II's (FSMP Phase II) goals, authorities identified three primary areas of focus. First, enhancing the operational efficiency of financial institutions. Post FSMP Phase I, the efficiency of the financial system had moderately improved, evident from the resilience shown by financial institutions during the 2008 global financial crisis.

However, to complete the transformation toward a modern banking system, and faced with intensified market competition at home and abroad, financial institutions have made further efforts through various measures, resulting in high overall operational costs. To be more concrete, more investment has been focused on the introduction of professional talents, innovation on information technology, and the improvement of financial infrastructure, such as ATMs and branch networks. In addition, the legacy of non-performing loans (NPL) and non-performing assets (NPA) dating back to the AFC remains a burden on the financial sector.

Moreover, the ongoing impact of NPL and NPA originating from the AFC persists as a significant challenge for the sector. In response, BOT has actively sought to refine financial regulatory amendments, aiming to curtail operational expenses while preserving financial stability and integrity. Complementing this, various strategies were deployed to expedite the resolution of NPLs and NPAs. Notably, commercial banks received authorization to collaborate with private entities for the disposal of foreclosed properties. Additionally, the establishment of the "NPA Information Center" represents a strategic move to enhance the efficiency of NPA disposals, demonstrating a coordinated effort to mitigate the long-standing issue of distressed assets in the financial system.

The second focal area under the FSMP Phase II was the fortification of the financial intermediary role and the augmentation of financial accessibility. This was achieved partly through regulatory easing, which allowed for an expanded scope of financial business activities and eased market entry. Consequently, this led to the conversion of foreign bank branches into subsidiaries and the entry of new foreign banking institutions from neighboring countries into the Thai market. The BOT observed that this diversification of market players was instrumental in elevating the quality of financial services.

Furthermore, aligning with the objectives of FSMP Phase I, the BOT placed considerable emphasis on the cultivation of specialized financial institutions (SFIs). These SFIs have played a crucial role in amplifying financial accessibility, particularly for low-income individuals and small businesses, by providing a wide array of financial services tailored to these groups. In addition, the development of comprehensive credit information and credit rating systems was another strategic initiative undertaken by financial authorities. These systems were designed to enhance microfinance services, thereby facilitating broader financial inclusion, especially for underserved segments of the population. This comprehensive approach underlines the commitment to not only expand financial services but also to ensure their accessibility and suitability for all segments of society.

The third pivotal element of the FSMP Phase II centered on fostering a resilient and sound financial system, a goal that aligns closely with and supports the enhancement of operational efficiency. As per the BOT, a critical strategy in this pursuit was the development of an advanced risk management system of financial institutions (BOT, 2009). This entailed bolstering prudential regulations for effective risk control, upgrading the information technology infrastructure for supervisory systems, and crafting sophisticated tools for risk monitoring. Such measures were envisioned to lay the foundation for a robust and reliable financial system across the nation.

Building on the momentum of these financial reforms, May 2016 marked the launch of the Financial Sector Master Plan Phase III (FSMP Phase III), set to be executed from 2016 to 2020. This phase was designed with the ambition of molding Thai financial institutions into entities that are more competitive, inclusive, connected, and sustainable (BOT, 2016). The rationale behind FSMP Phase III was to adeptly navigate the shifting financial landscapes both locally and globally, and to facilitate Thailand's economic growth amidst the burgeoning era of regional economic integration. This phase represented a forward-looking approach, aiming to adapt and thrive in a rapidly evolving financial and economic environment.

2.2.4 *Improvement of Legal Bases*

In accordance with the implementation of the Financial Sector Master Plan, the BOT has undertaken a comprehensive suite of regulatory reforms with a strategic focus on managing various types of risks, including strategic, credit, market, liquidity, and operational risks within commercial banks. These reforms are integral to reinforcing the overall stability of the banking sector.

A key aspect of these reforms has been the enhancement of corporate governance and risk management within financial institutions. This has involved stringent measures to improve NPL provisioning regulations, thereby ensuring better handling of potential credit losses. Additionally, the BOT has been a proponent of adopting the International Accounting Standard Basel II, a global framework that strengthens bank capital requirements by increasing bank liquidity and decreasing bank leverage risk. Furthermore, the development of sophisticated risk-based stress tests and the introduction of various prudential guidelines have been crucial in enabling financial institutions to better assess and prepare for potential adverse conditions.

Since 2007, Thai monetary authorities have also enacted three new legislative acts to fortify the financial system's management framework. These acts represent significant steps in evolving the regulatory landscape to ensure more robust and effective management of the financial sector, aiming to foster a resilient and sound financial environment in Thailand.

(A) The "Amended Bank of Thailand Act B.E. 2551" prioritizes ensuring the stability of Thailand's financial system as its primary aim. To achieve this, the Act focuses on reinforcing the BOT's operational independence, transparency in its processes, and accountability in its actions. One of the key provisions of this Act is the clarification of the process and term of appointment for the Governor of the BOT, thereby establishing a more structured and autonomous governance mechanism.

Furthermore, the Act confers upon the BOT augmented capacities in the realm of asset management. This enhancement is pivotal in enabling the BOT to more effectively oversee and navigate the complexities of the financial markets. Additionally, the Act introduces improvements in the mechanisms for enforcing monetary policies. These enhancements are designed to ensure that the BOT can implement monetary strategies more efficiently, thereby contributing to the overall stability and responsiveness of the financial system in Thailand. This comprehensive approach underscores the Act's role in fortifying the regulatory and operational framework of the central bank

(B) "The Financial Institution Business Act B.E. 2551" (FIBA, 2007) was enacted to replace the earlier Commercial Banking Act B.E. 2505 and the Act on the Undertaking of Finance Business, Securities Business, and Credit Foncier Business 2522, marking a significant evolution in Thailand's financial legislative landscape. This Act was designed to clearly outline the respective roles of the MOF and the BOT in crafting a more effective regulatory framework and strengthening the supervisory system over financial institutions. Under FIBA, the MOF is authorized to grant new licenses to commercial banks, while the BOT assumes enhanced responsibilities in overseeing all financial institutions and conglomerates.

A pivotal aspect of FIBA is its emphasis on aligning Thai financial regulations with international standards, notably the International Accounting Standard Basel II and Basel III. The adoption of these standards, beginning with Basel II at the end of 2008 and followed by Basel III since 2013, marks a significant step towards bolstering the stability and resilience of Thailand's financial institutions. FIBA sets forth specific business regulations for the banking sector, such as imposing limits on large exposures, establishing minimum standards for capital adequacy ratios, and defining entry requirements for the banking market. With Basel III, Thai commercial banks are required to maintain a capital adequacy ratio of at least 8.5%, a Core Tier I ratio of no less than 4.5%, and a Tier II ratio exceeding 6.0%.

To create a more competitive and effective banking system, FIBA also modifies the foreign ownership limits in financial institutions, raising the threshold from 25 to 49%, subject to approval by the BOT. Furthermore, with the MOF's approval and the BOT's recommendation, foreign ownership can surpass 49%. This policy shift aims to infuse the Thai banking sector with additional capital, advanced expertise, and refined skills in marketing and banking management, facilitating a more dynamic and globally integrated financial environment in

Thailand. This approach reflects a strategic move to enhance the capacity and global competitiveness of the Thai financial sector.

(C) "The Deposit Protection Agency Act B.E. 2552" was introduced as a reformative measure to supersede the blanket deposit guarantee scheme established in response to the AFC. This Act represents a strategic shift aimed at ensuring greater fairness and bolstering customer protection within the Thai financial system. A key feature of this legislation is the empowerment of the Deposit Protection Agency with specific responsibilities critical to safeguarding depositor interests.

Under this Act, the Deposit Protection Agency is entrusted with the task of compensating depositors in instances where a financial institution's license is revoked, thereby providing a safety net to depositors against the potential losses due to institutional failures, similar to those experienced during the crisis.

Additionally, the Act designates the Deposit Protection Agency as the liquidator for such distressed financial institutions. This role involves managing the dissolution and asset distribution of failed banks, ensuring an orderly and fair process. These provisions reflect a concerted effort to enhance the stability and trustworthiness of the Thai banking system, offering a more robust framework for customer protection and financial integrity in the wake of the challenges experienced during the AFC. This approach underscores Thailand's commitment to maintaining a secure and equitable financial environment for its citizens.

In summary, the series of financial reforms undertaken in Thailand has been strategically focused on addressing and rectifying systemic flaws and structural challenges within the financial sector. Key areas of these reforms include reducing the high concentration in the banking market to enhance competitive dynamics, fortifying the risk management framework, and refining the operational mechanisms of the BOT. These initiatives have had a profound and transformative impact on Thailand's commercial banking sector.

As a result of the implementation of the Financial Sector Master Plan and the accompanying amendments to financial legislation, there have been marked shifts in the ownership structures of individual commercial banks and in the broader banking market landscape since the AFC. These shifts represent significant changes in the way the banking sector operates, with implications for competitiveness, stability, and regulatory compliance. The nature and extent of these changes, and their impact on Thailand's banking sector, are further analyzed in the subsequent section, shedding light on the evolving face of the Thai banking industry in the post-reform era.

2.3 Market Reorganization: Before Versus After the AFC (Until 2001)

During the 1997/1998 AFC, Thailand faced profound financial turmoil. In response, alongside receiving international financial support from entities such as the World Bank and the IMF, the Thai government implemented a comprehensive suite of financial reforms. These reforms had two main facets: on one hand, a number of financially distressed commercial banks were either infused with public capital or temporarily brought under state control. On the other hand, several small and medium-sized commercial banks became acquisition targets for foreign banking institutions. This dual approach led to a significant transformation in the commercial banking sector's landscape, a process extensively chronicled in Appendix 1.

The upcoming sections provide a descriptive analysis focused on the shifts in the ownership structure within the banking sector. This analysis seeks to evaluate the influence of the financial reforms on the structure of the banking market and to discern the primary characteristics of ownership evolution over time. Conducted at the individual bank level, this analysis is segmented into four distinct phases, tracing the trajectory of changes since the AFC. This analytical framework is crucial for understanding how the financial reforms reshaped the Thai banking sector, highlighting the dynamics of ownership change and their implications for market competition and stability.

This section presents a comparative analysis of the ownership structures of Thai commercial banks before and after the AFC, illustrating the marked transformations that ensued in the aftermath of the crisis. As per Table 1.3 in Chap. 1, by 2016, the landscape comprised 19 commercial banks and 11 foreign bank branches. The licensing among these commercial banks varied, with 14 holding full licenses, one operating as a retail bank, and four functioning as foreign bank subsidiaries. Notably, before the AFC, the Thai commercial banking sector was often described as insular, maintaining a consistent structure of 15 commercial banks and 14 foreign bank branches since the 1960s. This stability was largely due to the rigid "No Exit, No Entry" policy, which effectively limited market dynamics and competition.

The dominant entities in this stable market were the "Big 4" banks—Bangkok Bank, Siam Commercial Bank, Krung Thai Bank, and Kasikornbank (renamed from Thai Farmers Bank in 2002). As detailed in Chap. 1, the sector was not only characterized by its oligopolistic nature and restricted market access but also by its inclination towards family-run businesses, significantly shaping the industry's evolution.

Specifically, focusing on the ownership of these leading banks, Krung Thai Bank was state-owned, while Siam Commercial Bank, often referred to as the "royal bank," was under the ownership of the Bureau of the Crown Property and Group. Bangkok Bank, historically the largest in Thailand, was established in 1944 by Chin Sophonpanich, a Chinese-Thai whose family hailed from Guangdong province, China—a region renowned for producing the Teochew Group, a globally recognized community of successful overseas ethnic Chinese merchants. Similarly, Kasikornbank, founded by Choti Lamsam in 1945, was owned by the Lamsam family, a prominent

Hakka group in Thailand. These family-run banks, particularly those with Chinese-Thai roots, played a significant role in shaping the characteristics and evolution of Thailand's banking sector, reflecting the intricate interplay of cultural and economic factors in the industry's development.

The majority of the other 11 banks in Thailand's commercial banking sector were also predominantly family-run businesses or closely linked to family business groups. Many of these founding families had Chinese-Thai roots. For example, the Bank of Ayudhya had been under the stewardship of the Ratanarak family since 1958, a period coinciding with significant domestic economic reforms. The Ratanarak family is counted among the three most influential business families in Thailand, alongside the Sophonpanich and Lamsam families. Nakornthon Bank, founded in 1933 by the Wanglee family, is another example of a prominent bank established by a Thai family of Teochew Chinese descent.

A distinctive trait of the business practices of overseas ethnic Chinese merchants is their focus on fostering strong mutual trust within their networks. This approach significantly shaped the ownership structure in Thailand's commercial banking sector, particularly during its rapid growth phase in the early 1960s. During this time, the primary focus was on accumulating initial capital. To ensure financial stability and cultivate trust, founding families often brought in reliable and well-reputed business partners to participate in the bank's ownership.

For instance, Chuan Ratanarak, the principal owner of the Bank of Ayudhya, was also a major shareholder in Siam City Bank from the 1960s to the 1980s, a bank that was later influenced by the Mahadamrongkut family and the Kanjanapas family through cross-shareholding arrangements. The Bangkok Metropolitan Bank, established by the Tejapaibul family in 1950, held stakes in other banks like the Bank of Asia and First Bangkok City Bank, exemplifying the prevalent cross-ownership structure that reinforced cooperation within these family-run businesses (Moore, 2017).

However, the AFC precipitated significant shifts in the major shareholders of these banks. Post-crisis, some founding families either exited the banking industry due to financial insolvency or strategically pivoted their core business away from banking to other sectors. In contrast, some families retained their dominant positions. These changes in the landscape of major shareholders, both before and after the AFC, are comprehensively detailed in Table 2.1, illustrating the dynamic evolution of Thailand's commercial banking sector in response to economic challenges and strategic realignments.

2.3.1 The Banks That Survived the AFC

According to the data presented in Appendix 1, a total of seven commercial banks successfully navigated through the AFC and sustained their operations. With the exception of Siam City Bank, which underwent a merger with Bangkok Metropolitan Bank in April 2002, the survivors were predominantly the top six largest banks in

Table 2.1 The transformation of business status and major shareholders in the commercial banking sector: 1996 versus 2001

ID	Year	Bank name	Opening year	Total assets (MB)	Employees	Branches	Founding families (FF)/largest shareholders (LS)
1	1996	Bangkok bank	1944	1,155,109	26,218	456	FF: Sophonpanich family
	2001	Bangkok bank		1,249,031	18,705	570	LS: HSBC banks (UK)
2	1996	Krung Thai bank	1966	715,995	16,561	432	Government
	2001	Krung Thai bank		976,510	15,233	610	Government
3	1996	Thai farmers bank	1945	646,007	15,740	424	FF: Lamsam family
	2001	Thai farmers bank		774,385	10,472	530	LS: state street and trust company (US)
4	1996	The Siam commercial bank	1906	541,417	12,904	345	Bureau of the crown property
	2001	The Siam commercial bank		716,049	10,412	477	Bureau of the crown property
5	1996	Bank of Ayudhya	1945	414,879	11,339	313	Ratanarak family
	2001	Bank of Ayudhya		438,560	9,092	403	Ratanarak family
6	1996	The Thai military bank	1957	333,994	8,400	289	Thai defense forces
	2001	The Thai military bank		367,452	6,925	364	Government
7	1996	First Bangkok city bank	1934	252,146	3,691	83	Siriwattanapakdee family
	2001	n.a.		n.a.	n.a.	n.a.	*1
8	1996	Siam city bank	1941	234,145	6,110	161	Srifuengfung and Mahadamrongkut family
	2001	Siam city bank		298,892	4,167	210	*2
9	1996	Bangkok metropolitan bank	1950	191,550	5,806	149	Tejapaibul and Siriwattanapakdee family

(continued)

Table 2.1 (continued)

ID	Year	Bank name	Opening year	Total assets (MB)	Employees	Branches	Founding families (FF)/largest shareholders (LS)
	2001	Bangkok metropolitan bank		191,157	3,509	177	*3
10	1996	The Bangkok bank of commerce	1944	185,575	5,384	148	Tantipipatpong family
	2001	n.a.		n.a.	n.a.	n.a.	*4
11	1996	Bank of Asia	1939	126,508	2,570	79	Phatrapraisit family and Euachukiat
	2001	Bank of Asia		159,372	2,636	118	*5
12	1996	The Thai Danu bank	1949	119,598	3,434	81	Tuchinda family and other 6 families
	2001	(DBS Thai Danu bank)		99,019	1,773	62	*6
13	1996	The union bank of Bangkok	1949	64,610	2,880	97	Chonwichan family
	2001	(Bank Thai)		271,338	2,476	79	*7
14	1996	Nakornthon bank	1933	64,471	2,028	59	Wang Lee family
	2001	(Standard chartered Nakornthon bank)		69,920	1,562	46	*8
15	1996	The Laem Thong bank	1948	41,117	1,023	37	Chansrichawla family
	2001	(UOB Radanasin bank)		54,929	1,139	37	*9

Source Stock Exchange of Thailand; Bank of Thailand; "Varieties of Capitalism in Southeast Asia", Joel David Moore, 2017; "The fifth tiger: A study of Thai development policy", pp. 267–268, Robert J. Muscat, 1994

Note *1. Merged with Krung Thai Bank in 1998

*2. Being ordered to be offered for sale in 1998, transfer to BOT, merged BMB in 2002

*3. Being ordered to be offered for sale in 1998, transfer to BOT, was merged by SCIB in 2002

*4. Transfer good assets to Krung Thai Bank, transform itself into an asset management company in 1998

*5. Acquired by ABN-AMRO (Netherlands) in 1998

*6. Acquired by DBS (Singapore) in 1999

*7. Merged with other finance companies as Bank Thai in 1998

*8. Acquired by Standard Chartered in 1999 as Standard Chartered Nakornthon Bank

*9. Merged with UOB (Singapore) in 1999

Thailand. These included three banks associated with the major Chinese-Thai family business groups and three others that were either state-owned or had affiliations with the royal family and the military. This period also witnessed a notable transformation in their ownership structures, primarily characterized by a substantial increase in foreign ownership shares.

In particular, apart from Krung Thai Bank and The Thai Military Bank, the other leading banks in this group experienced a significant influx of foreign capital. For instance, foreign investment in Bangkok Bank escalated from 17.9% in 1997 to 31.8% in 2001, while Thai Farmers Bank saw its foreign ownership increase from 16.4% in 1997 to 33.6% in 2001. Notably, this trend of heightened foreign investment was more pronounced in the larger banks, as compared to their smaller and medium-sized counterparts. This shift towards greater foreign ownership in the aftermath of the crisis underscores a strategic reorientation within the Thai banking sector, reflecting a move towards greater international integration and a response to the globalized financial landscape that emerged following the crisis.

2.3.2 The Banks That Merged After the AFC

In the aftermath of the AFC, eight commercial banks that were operational prior to the crisis underwent significant mergers. This included First Bangkok City Bank and Bangkok Metropolitan Bank, which merged with other domestic banks. Bangkok Bank of Commerce reallocated its viable assets to Krung Thai Bank, while The Union Bank of Bangkok consolidated with various finance companies, culminating in the establishment of "Bank Thai" in 1998. The other four banks, which were smaller and medium-sized, merged with foreign banks based in Singapore and the UK. This wave of mergers signaled a comprehensive shift away from the traditional family-run business approach that had long characterized Thai commercial banks.

To sum up, from a broader transformational perspective, this era is distinguished by two major trends: the relinquishment of ownership control by the original founding families and a remarkable surge in foreign capital infusion. Foreign entities entered the Thai banking landscape through two predominant avenues. Smaller and medium-sized banks, severely affected by financial distress during the crisis, were often subjects of mergers and acquisitions (M&A) by foreign banks. In contrast, direct investments predominantly targeted the larger, more established banks. This dual approach not only diversified the ownership structure of Thai banks but also introduced new dynamics and competitive elements into the sector, reflecting a significant evolution in the banking industry's overall strategic and operational landscape.

2.4 Deregulation and Opening Market Access Under the Thaksin Administration (2001–2006)

Following a period of instability and subsequent adjustments post-crisis, the Thai economy began to exhibit positive recovery signs around 2001–2002. During the tenure of the Thaksin administration (2001–2006), a new wave of economic reforms was introduced, characterizing a strategic shift in Thailand's economic policy. The government implemented a "dual track policy" which simultaneously aimed to stimulate domestic demand, particularly in rural regions, and to attract foreign investment, while also placing a strong emphasis on export promotion.

In the realm of financial reforms, the Thaksin administration's strategy was to create an open financial market, bolstered by rigorous prudential oversight. A key aspect of these reforms was addressing the substantial burden of non-performing loans that had been a legacy issue since the crisis. Additionally, the reforms highlighted the critical need for deregulating the foreign investment regulatory landscape and improving financial accessibility within the domestic market. These initiatives led to profound changes in the ownership structure of the Thai banking sector during this phase. The easing of foreign investment regulations opened doors for increased international participation in the banking sector, while efforts to enhance domestic financial access contributed to diversifying the banking landscape and promoting a more inclusive financial environment. This period marked a significant transformation in the Thai banking sector, reflecting the intersection of domestic economic strategies and global financial integration.

2.4.1 Partial Foreign Equity Participation Versus Green Field Entry/Acquisition

In response to heightened market competition and the need for internal restructuring following the crisis, Thailand's large-sized commercial banks actively sought substantial foreign investments to enhance their capital base. This period saw all major banks experiencing a surge in foreign participation. Notably, this included Thai Military Bank and the state-owned Krung Thai Bank, which had previously seen only modest increases in foreign ownership post-AFC. Meanwhile, Bangkok Bank and Kasikornbank consistently maintained a high level of foreign participation, hovering around 48 and 49%, respectively. A standout case was Siam Commercial Bank, which witnessed the most substantial foreign investment influx, at times surpassing 50% and reaching a peak of 60.8%. Among the medium-sized banks, foreign ownership shares in Bank of Ayudhya and Siam City Bank also rose significantly, exceeding 30 and 25%, respectively.

Figure 2.2 presents a dual perspective on foreign entry, measured both at the market and individual bank levels. At the market level, calculated as the annual ratio of the number of foreign banks to the total number of banks, the data suggests a

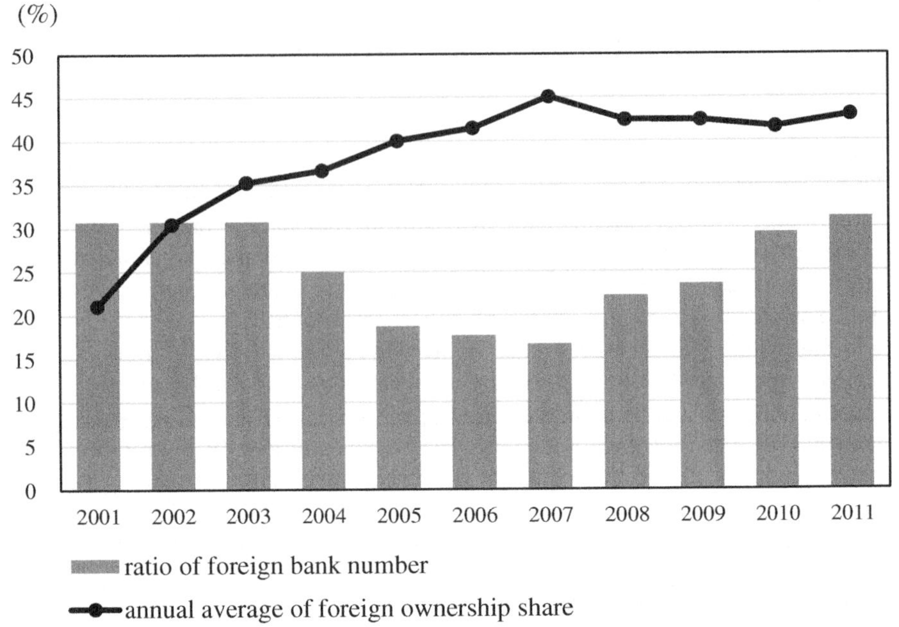

Fig. 2.2 The change of foreign entry and its patterns: Thaksin versus Post-Thaksin Period. *Source* Bank of Thailand, Stock Exchange of Thailand. *Note* Foreign ownership share is calculated as the weighted annual average of every commercial bank's foreign ownership, weighted by the bank's total assets

trend of foreign entry predominantly through mergers and acquisitions (M&A) or upgrades from foreign bank branches to subsidiaries. At the bank level, measured as the annual average ratio of foreign ownership share, the trend indicates a pattern of direct foreign investment in local banks.

Notably, under the Thaksin administration's financial reforms, the share of foreign ownership nearly doubled, increasing from 21% in 2001 to 41% in 2006. However, the number of foreign banks, in terms of their share of the total number, declined from 31% in 2001 to 18% in 2006. This decline, juxtaposed with the rising foreign ownership share, suggests a shift in foreign investment strategies, possibly indicating a move towards larger stakes in fewer banks, rather than a broader spread across many institutions. This trend reflects a nuanced evolution in the foreign investment landscape within the Thai banking sector, aligning with broader market consolidation and strategic investment approaches in the post-crisis period.

Apart from the easing of regulations by financial authorities on foreign shareholding limits, mergers and acquisitions (M&A) and transitions from foreign bank branches to foreign bank subsidiaries significantly influenced foreign entries into the market.

In 2005, Standard Chartered Nakornthon Bank was integrated into its parent company, establishing it as a wholly foreign-owned commercial bank. Additionally, the Bank of Asia, after being acquired by ABN-AMRO (Netherlands) in 1998, merged with UOB Radanasin Bank, resulting in the creation of another fully licensed, foreign-owned commercial bank, UOB Bank (Thai). That same year, the International Commercial Bank of China (Thai) transitioned from a foreign bank branch to the first foreign bank subsidiary in the Thai banking sector, subsequently rebranding as Mega International Commercial Bank in 2006.

Concurrently, two other foreign banks, DBS (Singapore) and ABN-AMRO (Netherlands), which had entered the market in the previous period, withdrew their investments from Thailand in 2004 and 2005, respectively. Notably, DBS (Singapore) had acquired Thai Danu Bank in 1999 to form DBS Thai Danu Bank and later merged with Thai Military Bank and Industrial Finance Corporation of Thailand in 2004.

Compared to the previous phase characterized by active entry of foreign banks, this period witnessed a limited influx of new foreign bank players into the banking market. The total asset share held by foreign banks decreased from 6.5% in 2002 to 5.1% in 2006, and their number reduced from four to three during the same period.

In summary, under the financial reforms implemented by the Thaksin administration, there was minimal entry of foreign banks. In contrast, direct foreign investment played a significant role, primarily targeting large banks. In other words, the increasing foreign involvement indicated a trend towards profit-seeking through direct investment in the banking sector, rather than aiming for a long-term strategic position in the Thai banking market, typically represented by the entry of foreign banks.

2.4.2 Promoting a Diverse Array of Domestic Banking Participants

In the context of domestic banking institutions, the regulatory authority sanctioned the entry of multiple new banks into the market. A novel category of bank license, termed "retail banking license", was introduced, primarily targeted at enhancing financial inclusivity for marginalized groups and Small and Medium-sized Enterprises (SMEs). This move was in alignment with the wealth redistribution strategy fervently adopted by the Thaksin administration.[6]

---

[6] Besides commercial banks, the specialized financial institutions (SFIs) played a positive role in the redistribution of wealth and the expansion of domestic financial access during this period. The top three major SFIs, Government Savings Bank (GSB), Bank for Agriculture and Agricultural Cooperatives (BAAC), and Government Housing Bank (GHB) contributed tremendously to the household and cooperative loan sectors from 2002. By improving the credit information system and the credit rating system, the SFIs were able to provide microfinance services for low-income groups and small business groups at a larger scale compared with the previous stage. In addition,

Between 2002 and 2006, in addition to the entry of the foreign bank subsidiary Mega International Commercial Bank, four new entities were authorized as fully licensed commercial banks: Thanachart Bank (2002), TISCO Bank (2004), Kiatnakin Bank, and ACL Bank (both in 2005). Furthermore, licenses were granted to four retail banks: Land and Houses Retail Bank (2005), GE Money Retail Bank (2006), The Thai Credit Retail Bank, and AIG Retail Bank (early 2007).

The composition of commercial banks experienced a notable shift, moving from a stable configuration of 15 banks before the AFC to 13 banks in 2001, and subsequently expanding to 17 banks by 2006. However, the overall influence on the markedly concentrated market structure was limited. This was primarily due to the fact that the newly incorporated banks were predominantly small to medium in size. As illustrated in Fig. 1.4 in previous chapter, this dynamic indicates a slight reduction in the collective market share of the four largest banks, from 66% in 2001 to 61% in 2006.

Concurrently, the financial regulatory authority placed significant emphasis on the development of an efficient risk management system. This initiative was a crucial part of the preparatory measures for the adoption of Basel II standards, initiated in 2008. The Bank of Thailand, acting as the financial supervisory authority, engaged in close collaboration with the banking sector. Together, they dedicated efforts towards the advancement of risk management tools and financial methodologies for risk assessment and mitigation. This also included a focused assessment of capital adequacy to effectively address the inherent risks in banking operations.

2.4.3 The Impacts on Ownership Structure

In the post-restructuring phase leading up to 2006, the ownership structures of commercial banks evolved dynamically, particularly among the large-scale banks that withstood the crisis. This period was marked by significant changes involving 3 foreign banks and their subsidiary, the entry of 4 new commercial banks, 2 retail banks, and the medium-sized Siam City Bank and Bank Thai. The top 6 commercial banks, in particular, experienced detailed ownership alterations.

First, state-owned Krung Thai Bank underwent a series of mergers with various financial institutions, while First Bangkok City Bank selectively acquired the profitable assets of Bangkok Bank of Commerce post-crisis. The government-operated "Financial Institution Development Fund (FIDF)" emerged as the predominant shareholder, owning a stake exceeding 50%. Concurrently, the majority shareholders of Siam Commercial Bank and Thai Military Bank, which integrated with DBS Thai Danu Bank in 2004, maintained their controlling interests.

Furthermore, the ownership transitions of the remaining three banks garnered increased scrutiny due to their affiliation with the three prominent Chinese-Thai

the total number of ATMs per 100,000 adults and bank accounts per 1000 adults have been rising rapidly in recent years.

family business conglomerates. Table 2.2 delineates a comparative overview of the ownership frameworks of these banks.

Diverging from its peers, Bangkok Bank embarked on comprehensive modernization reforms well ahead of the AFC. Bangkok Bank's shareholdings underwent significant redistribution, moving away from being predominantly owned by its founding family. Post-AFC, the Stock Exchange of Thailand (SET) and the Thai NVDR Company emerged as the two largest shareholders, collectively holding between 10 and 20% of the shares, and remained as the bank's primary shareholders. Established in 2000, the Thai NVDR Company, predominantly (99.9%) owned by the SET, specializes in the acquisition and disposition of equity in publicly listed companies.

Nonetheless, the founding family maintained their influential positions on the board of directors, including the Chairmanship. Chatri Sophonpanich held the position of Board Chairman from 1999 until a recent period. His son, Chartsiri Sophonpanich, has served as the President of Bangkok Bank since 1994, and his brother, Charn Sophonpanich, has been a board member since the 1980s. These three members of the Sophonpanich family have a longstanding history of involvement on the board of Bangkok Bank, spanning the period before and after the AFC. Their continued presence in key roles on both the board and executive team indicates an enduring influence over the bank's governance by the Sophonpanich family.

Kasikornbank exhibits a similar trend. Post-AFC, it significantly increased foreign investment, with the Thai NVDR Company emerging as its predominant shareholder

Table 2.2 Ownership structure of selected commercial banks in 2005–2006

Bank name	Bangkok bank	Kasikornbank	Bank of Ayudhya
Principal shareholder	SET	Thai NVDR	Thai NVDR
Major foreign shareholders	HSBC (Singapore)	State street bank and trust bank company	GL asset
	State street bank and trust company for London	Chase nominees	Nortrust nominees (UK)
	Barclays bank	HSBC	State street bank and trust bank company for Australia
	The bank of New York	HSBC (Singapore)	
	State street bank and trust company	Mellon Bank	
Number of foreign shareholders in the top 10 largest shareholders	6	8	3
Chairman of the board	Chatri Sophonpanich	Banyong Lamsam	Krit Ratanarak
Other family board members	Chartsiri Sophonpanich (president)	Banthoon Lamsam (president)	None
	Charn Sophonpanich	Sujitpan Lamsam	

Source Bank of Thailand, Annual report of each bank, ORBIS

since then. From 2002 to 2006, the Kasikornbank board included three members from its founding family. The Chairman, Banyong Lamsam, is the progeny of Choti Lamsam, the 1945 founder of Kasikornbank. Banthoon Lamsam, initially President and later CEO, is the offspring of Bancha and Sam-angwan Lamsam, and nephew to Banyong Lamsam. Pridiyathorn Devakula, Sam-angwan's half-brother and a former governor of the Bank of Thailand under the Thaksin Administration, is another family connection. Additionally, Sujitpan Lamsam, Banthoon's aunt, has been part of the board since 1998.

In the case of Bank of Ayudhya, its Chairmanship was held by Krit Ratanarak until 2006. Krit, the son of founder Chuan Ratanarak who established the bank in 1945, sustained his leadership position through the aftermath of the AFC.

Meanwhile, major foreign shareholders predominantly consisted of globally renowned Western financial institutions, including HSBC, State Street Bank, and other similar entities. Around 2006, foreign shareholders comprised a significant portion of the top 10 largest shareholders in both Bangkok Bank and Kasikornbank, with shares amounting to 60 and 80% respectively.

To encapsulate the dynamics of these three major banks, which are integral to Chinese-Thai business conglomerates: despite the surge in foreign investment and a reduction in familial shareholdings, the founding families retained their pivotal roles on the boards and in executive positions. This scenario underscores their sustained influence over the banks' management, juxtaposing the growing foreign participation with the enduring family control.

2.5 Changing Financial Environment at Home and Abroad (2006–2011)

During the tenure of the Thaksin Administration, financial reforms led to a marked expansion of domestic banking players and heightened foreign participation, indicative of a trend towards greater market liberalization. However, the landscape shifted dramatically with the coup d'état on September 19, 2006, orchestrated by the Royal Thai Army, resulting in the overthrow of the Thaksin Government. General Sonthi Boonyaratglin, erstwhile Commander-in-Chief of the Royal Thai Army, assumed state leadership and declared martial law across the nation. This coup, unfolding against a backdrop of intense political instability, had swift and profound consequences on Thailand's financial sector, particularly affecting the Thaksin Administration's financial reform initiatives.

Furthermore, the international financial scene was rocked by the 2008 Lehman Brothers collapse, commonly referred to as the Lehman Shock. The conjunction of these domestic and global financial upheavals in the post-Thaksin era profoundly reshaped the landscape of Thailand's commercial banking sector, influencing both market dynamics and ownership structures.

2.5.1 Capital Enrichment of Large and Medium-Sized Banks

The financial regulatory body altered its earlier policies favoring retail bank development. GE Money Retail Bank, inaugurated in 2006, terminated its operations in January 2007. AIG Retail Bank, initially an upgrade from AIG Consumer Financial Company in March 2007, was subsequently acquired by Bank of Ayudhya in April 2009. Land and Houses Retail Bank, initiated in 2005, was granted authorization to evolve from a retail bank into a fully licensed commercial bank by December 2011. This era saw a decline in retail bank numbers, plummeting from four at the beginning of 2007 to just one by the end of 2011, with Thai Credit Retail Bank being the only remaining entity.

In stark contrast to their relatively muted role during the Thaksin Administration, the larger and mid-sized commercial banks experienced substantial business expansion and capital enhancement. This growth was facilitated through strategic M&As and the incorporation of foreign investments as key partners. Consequently, the market dominance of the Big 4 banks escalated from 61% in 2006 to 66% in 2011, returning to their pre-Thaksin levels of market influence.

In September 2007, Bank of Ayudhya acquired a significant investment from GE, which constituted a 33% ownership stake, thus establishing GE as its primary shareholder. GE, a renowned multinational conglomerate, is celebrated for its proficiency in retail banking services and corporate governance standards. This alliance augmented Bank of Ayudhya's capabilities in cooperative and SME loan banking, complemented by its comprehensive national branch network, thereby markedly advancing its retail banking segment. Additionally, this collaboration with GE fostered capital growth, elevating the bank's capital adequacy ratio beyond 20% and making it the most robust in capital adequacy among Thailand's commercial banks.

The partnership precipitated a leadership shift, with Krit Ratanarak, the leader of the Ratanarak family business empire, stepping down from his chairman role in 2007, succeeded by Veraphan Teepsuwan. Despite this change, the Ratanarak family continued to exert significant influence through substantial shareholdings in Bank of Ayudhya. Two entities connected to the Ratanarak family, BBTV Statelvision Company and BBTV Asset Management Company, remained as two of the top ten shareholders.

The April 2009 merger with AIG Retail Bank further amplified Bank of Ayudhya's retail banking division, solidifying its status as a leading player in Thailand's domestic retail banking sector.

In a notable parallel development, the Bank of Nova Scotia initially purchased a 25% interest in Thanachart Bank in July 2007, later escalating its share to 48.99% by February 2009, which approached the maximum limit allowed for foreign ownership under regulatory standards. This investment positioned the Bank of Nova Scotia as a key shareholder, with it acquiring four board positions and multiple executive appointments.

Further, in the final quarter of 2011, a significant merger occurred: Thanachart Bank, then ranked as Thailand's 7th largest bank, combined forces with Siam City Bank, the 8th largest. This consolidation boosted Thanachart Bank's total assets to over 878 billion THB by the end of 2011, thereby leapfrogging TMB Bank to secure the 6th position in the banking sector. Throughout the Siam City Bank integration process, spanning 2010 to 2011, the Bank of Nova Scotia injected a total capital of C$ 650 million. This strategic collaboration resulted in a joint management structure for Thanachart Bank, shared between the Bank of Nova Scotia and Thanachart Capital Public Company (TCAP). TCAP, a part of the Thanachart financial group, continued as the majority shareholder of Thanachart Bank with a 50.92% share.

2.5.2 The Rising Role of Regional Foreign Bank Players Since the Lehman Shock

Following the Lehman Shock, which precipitated an economic downturn in the USA and a debt crisis in the EU, there was a notable shift in Thailand's commercial banking landscape. Banks from East and Southeast Asia became increasingly prominent, supplanting the previously dominant role of Western multinational financial institutions.

In a prime example, CIMB Bank, a fully owned subsidiary of Malaysia's second largest banking group, CIMB Group, ascended to become the principal shareholder of BankThai. This was achieved through the purchase of a 42.13% share from the then-largest shareholder, the Financial Institution of Development Fund (FIDF), in November 2008. CIMB Bank further solidified its position by raising its stake to a majority 92.04% through a tender offer in January 2009. Subsequently, in May 2009, BankThai underwent a rebranding to CIMB Thai Bank Public Company Limited, symbolizing its full integration into the CIMB Group.

This strategic move was pivotal in the CIMB Group's expansion plans, which targeted establishing the bank as a top-three major player in the ASEAN region by 2015. Moreover, this acquisition heralded the onset of a trend, marking the beginning of a wave of foreign bank entries from regional countries into Thailand's commercial banking sector, which stood as one of the most rapidly evolving markets in Southeast Asia.

The next new foreign bank player was from China, the Industrial and Commercial Bank of China (ICBC), a premier lender within China and one of the global giants in commercial banking. Following its dual stock market listings in Shanghai and Hong Kong in October 2006, ICBC embarked on a series of cross-border acquisitions. In a strategic move in April 2010, ICBC acquired ACL Bank, securing a 19.26% stake from Bangkok Bank, a 30.6% share from the Thai Finance Ministry, and additional shares through a tender offer for equity and preference shares.

Despite ACL Bank being a smaller entity in Thailand, its possession of a universal commercial banking license offered ICBC a strategic platform for regional business expansion, particularly into the Greater Mekong Subregion (GMS). This acquisition represented ICBC's inaugural venture into Thailand and its second major move in Southeast Asia, following the acquisition of Indonesia's Halim Bank.

This development underscored a marked contrast in strategies between Western banks, which had slowed their M&A pursuits post-subprime mortgage crisis, and East and Southeast Asian regional banks. Banks like ICBC were increasingly engaging in international expansion, buoyed by robust cash reserves and substantial foreign currency assets, showcasing a dynamic shift in global banking trends.

In encapsulating the shifts in ownership structures: The annual average foreign ownership shares in commercial banks during this time saw a fluctuation between 40 and 45%. This was a notable change from the sharp escalation from 14% in 1997 to a peak of around 45% in 2007. The advent of the 2008 Global Financial Crisis signaled the cessation of a decade-long expansion in foreign ownership shares.

Nonetheless, the stagnation in the aggregate growth of foreign ownership shares did not deter the influx of foreign banking entities into the market. As depicted in Fig. 2.2, a pivotal shift occurred from the Thaksin Administration era to a new phase where mergers and acquisitions by regional foreign banks emerged as the primary mode of market entry. This trend was in concordance with their strategic objectives, particularly in anticipation of the forthcoming period of regional integration within Southeast Asia.

2.6 Acceleration of Intraregional Investment (2011–2016)

The Thai economy confronted a pronounced downturn in 2011, influenced by a confluence of adverse factors at both domestic and international levels. A severe flood crisis, the worst in half a century, engulfed northern, northeastern, and central Thailand from late July 2011 to mid-January 2012, inflicting significant human and economic losses, including a disruption to banking services in the afflicted regions. Simultaneously, the Thai economy grappled with repercussions from the global economic deceleration stemming from the Western debt crisis. Although 2012 saw a swift economic rebound, Thailand's economic stability remained under pressure from escalating household debt and ongoing political unrest, which adversely affected domestic consumption and investment activities.

On the political front, Yingluck Shinawatra, Thaksin Shinawatra's younger sister, achieved a resounding victory in the second half of 2011, becoming Thailand's youngest and first female Prime Minister. However, her tenure was abruptly interrupted by a coup d'état in May 2014, orchestrated by the Royal Thai Armed Forces, which dissolved the Senate and initiated a six-month political crisis. This led to the governance of the military junta, the National Council for Peace and Order (NCPO), which lasted until 2019.

On the international stage, the inaugural ASEAN Economic Community Blueprint (2008–2015) catalyzed strategic preparations among major regional financial entities, such as Malaysia's CIMB Group and China's ICBC, in anticipation of the upcoming

AEC era. Notably, several prominent banking groups commenced strategic expansions into regional markets, marking a pivotal shift in the Southeast Asian financial landscape.

The ASEAN Central Bank Governors endorsed the "ASEAN Banking Integration Framework (ABIF)" and its attendant Guidelines in December 2014, aimed at regional financial integration. This initiative was directed towards facilitating regional financial integration, allowing Qualified ASEAN Banks (QABs)—banks adhering to specific standards—to enjoy expanded access and operational flexibility in other ASEAN markets (ABIF, 2014).

December 2015 marked a significant milestone with the formal establishment of the ASEAN Economic Community, as an integral component of the ASEAN Community, signifying a new chapter in regional integration efforts. The endorsement of the second ASEAN Economic Community Blueprint 2025 at the 27th ASEAN Summit in Kuala Lumpur, Malaysia, in November 2015, further emphasized the ambition to deepen economic cohesion within the region.

This subsection delves into the latest dynamics in Thailand's commercial banking sector, taking into account a diverse array of influencing factors. These include natural disasters, domestic political upheaval, evolving global economic conditions, and the strides in regional integration. It aims to unpack how these multifaceted elements collectively shape the strategic direction and operational realities of Thailand's banking industry in this new era of regional connectivity.

In a significant shift in September 2012, GE Capital International Holdings Corporation (GE), which held the largest share in Bank of Ayudhya at 33%, initiated a divestment process by offloading 7.6% of its ordinary shares on the Stock Exchange of Thailand (SET). By November, GE opted to fully exit its stake, concluding its seven-year strategic alliance with the Ratanarak Group. The following year, 2013, saw the Bank of Tokyo-Mitsubishi UFJ (BTMU), the foremost commercial bank in Japan and a segment of the Mitsubishi UFJ Financial Group, solidify its presence in Thailand by acquiring a controlling 72% stake in Bank of Ayudhya. This acquisition entailed purchasing 25.33% from GE, complemented by a Voluntary Tender Offer for the remaining shares, thereby integrating Thailand's fifth-largest commercial bank as a consolidated foreign subsidiary and a key part of BTMU's international portfolio.

The integration process further evolved in January 2015 when BTMU's Bangkok Branch merged with Bank of Ayudhya, in adherence to the Bank of Thailand's "One Presence Policy." This consolidation boosted BTMU's ownership in Krungsri Bank (the rebranded name for Bank of Ayudhya since 2014) to 76.88%. This merger stands as the most extensive foray of a foreign bank into Thailand's commercial banking sector to date, and it also represents BTMU's largest investment in its Asian market expansion efforts.

In addition, another three foreign banks obtained commercial bank licenses in Thailand. The Bank of China (Thai) upgraded from a foreign bank branch to a foreign bank subsidiary in August 2014. The ANZ Bank (Thai) upgraded from a representative to a foreign bank subsidiary in June 2015. The Sumitomo Mitsui Trust Bank (Thai) upgraded from a representative to a foreign bank subsidiary in June 2015.

These upgrades are reflective of an increasing trend of foreign bank involvement in Thailand's banking sector. This trend is detailed in Table 2.3, which enumerates major foreign financial institutional investors who have established themselves as key strategic and core partners in the Thai commercial banking sector, each holding significant investments exceeding a 25% stake.

The landscape of foreign financial investment in Thailand's banking sector has undergone a significant shift. On the one hand, the primary foreign investors have transitioned from Western multinational financial groups to regional banks from ASEAN, Japan, China, among others. On the other hand, the Big 4 banks in Thailand have not integrated core foreign partners, a decision that has seemingly limited the impact on the traditional dominance exercised by major shareholders, especially the founding families. In terms of M&A activities, there is a noticeable trend where foreign bank activities predominantly target smaller banks, whereas major foreign financial institutional investors have a more pronounced presence in medium-sized banks. This evolving ownership landscape is exemplified in the case study of Krungsri Bank (formerly Bank of Ayudhya).

As noted earlier, Krungsri Bank has been a longstanding part of the Ratanarak Group, one of the three major Chinese-Thai business family groups. Following the AFC, the Ratanarak Group opted against government financial aid, instead successfully raising capital independently. In 2007, GE was introduced as a core partner, aimed at reinforcing capital adequacy, and enhancing business operations and performance.

However, the significant acquisition by BTMU through a Voluntary Tender Offer, which resulted in them obtaining a majority shareholding, stirred considerable debate about the ongoing management control by the Ratanarak Group. Even as BTMU emerged as the controlling shareholder, the Ratanarak Group maintained a stake in the bank. This case illustrates a pivotal shift in ownership and management control, transitioning from the traditional model dominated by founding families to a more diversified structure. This change is indicative of a broader transformation in Thailand's commercial banking industry, historically characterized by family-run enterprises.

The transition in ownership heralded a new era for Krungsri Bank, marked by the arrival of BTMU executives who brought with them a series of transformative reforms. These executives concentrated on refining the bank's organizational structure and operational workflows, aiming to boost efficiency and fortify risk management and regulatory compliance. Simultaneously, in pursuit of evolving Krungsri Bank into "a major ASEAN financial powerhouse", the BTMU leadership underscored the integration of cutting-edge financial technology and the fostering of innovation, ensuring that these advancements were implemented cost-effectively.

Furthermore, leveraging BTMU's extensive international business networks, Krungsri Bank was poised to explore broader opportunities in the global banking landscape. This transformation, embracing strong corporate governance and operational optimization, resonated with the financial regulators' aspirations of advancing market openness and integrating sophisticated foreign financial practices.

Table 2.3 The entry of major foreign financial institutional investors in the banking sector

	Bank code	Year of entry	Foreign financial institutional investors	Ownership of foreign shareholder in the left/bank status (in 2014)
1	BBL			
2	SCB			
3	KTB			
4	KBANK			
5	BAY	2007	GE capital international	33%
		2013	Bank of Tokyo-Mitsubishi UFJ	72%
6	TBANK	2007	Bank of Nova Scotia	25%
		2009	Bank of Nova Scotia	49%
7	TMB	2007	ING bank	25%
8	UOBT	1999	UOB	By acquisition of Radanasin Asia in 1999, then merged with Bank of Asia in 2005
9	CIMBT	2009	CIMB	By acquisition of BankThai in 2009
10	TISCO			
11	KKP			
12	LHB			
13	SCBT	1999	Standard chartered	By acquisition of Nakornthon bank in 1999
14	ICBCT	2010	Industrial and commercial bank of China	By acquisition of ACL bank in 2010
15	TCRB			
16	BOC	2014	Bank of China	Foreign bank subsidiary
17	SMT	2015	Sumitomo Mitsui trust bank	Foreign bank subsidiary
18	ANZ	2015	ANZ bank	Foreign bank subsidiary
19	MICB	2005	Mega financial holding company	Foreign bank subsidiary

Source ORBIS database, Bank of Thailand, Annual Report of each bank (1997–2015), *and Commercial Banks in Thailand* (1997–2015)

Note 1. The information on foreign ownership and shareholders is recorded at the end of 2014

2. The table lists the strategic foreign financial institutional partners with more than 25% shareholdings of the commercial banks ranked by banks' total assets

* All the bank codes are consistent with the bank name in the second column of Table 1.2 "The Landscape of Commercial Banking sector in 2016—Commercial Bank"

In summary, the ongoing process of regional financial integration in the early 2010s was marked by an influx of foreign banking entities into the market. The forthcoming chapters aims to offer an in-depth analysis of how these shifts in ownership have influenced the dynamics of the commercial banking sector.

2.7 Conclusions

In the wake of the AFC, Thailand's economy faced profound challenges, necessitating intervention and financial support from global institutions like the World Bank and the IMF. This aid, however, came with stringent conditionalities, pushing the country towards monetary restraint and widespread structural overhauls. In response, Thailand's financial authorities set in motion an ambitious reform agenda, spearheaded by the Financial Sector Master Plan Phases I and II, rolled out in the mid-2000s and early 2010s.

Within this challenging backdrop, the Thai commercial banking sector experienced sweeping and multifaceted transformations. The government's role became more pronounced with sustained capital infusions into the banking system, sometimes even extending to temporary state stewardship of certain banks. Concurrently, the sector saw a marked increase in foreign bank participation, primarily through mergers and acquisitions, heralding a significant restructuring of the banking market. This era also marked a diminishing presence of traditional family-led business groups in the banking sphere, denoting a pivotal shift in the patterns of ownership and control in Thailand's banking industry. This transition was reflective of the broader economic recovery efforts and the strategic redirection of the financial sector post-crisis.

Moreover, in the evolving landscape of Thailand's banking sector, the rise of foreign bank participation became increasingly significant, with institutions from neighboring nations, notably China and Japan, taking on increasingly prominent roles. This trend was further amplified in the wake of the Lehman Shock, indicating a deeper integration of Thailand's banking industry within the broader regional and global financial dynamics. By 2014, this shift was evident as foreign banks had garnered over 40% of the market share in Thailand, with their total assets comprising more than 15% of the entire industry. This marked a substantial change from the pre-crisis era, reflecting the sector's adaptation to the regulatory changes and integration within the global financial landscape.

Overall, this era of financial reforms post-crisis, characterized by the dwindling influence of traditional founding families and burgeoning foreign participation, precipitated marked changes in both the ownership structure and market organization of Thailand's commercial banking sector. This analysis is crucial for grasping the full scope and significance of the post-AFC regulatory adjustments in shaping the contemporary economic and financial terrain in Thailand.

The forthcoming chapter is set to document the evolving financial dynamics within East and Southeast Asia, establishing a contextual backdrop for understanding the Thai commercial banking sector's positioning in the region. This foundational overview will pave the way for the subsequent chapters, which are devoted to thoroughly dissect and comprehend the intricate and far-reaching consequences of the financial regulatory reforms implemented following the AFC.

Chapter 3
Thailand's Commercial Banking Sector in Regional Asian Markets

Abstract This chapter delves deeply into the intensified competitive pressures that Thailand's commercial banking sector faces from neighboring markets, tracing these pressures back to both economic and regulatory changes in those regions. It charts the evolution of the financial sectors within East and Southeast Asia and defines the Thai commercial banking sector's position within this evolving regional scenario. It also recognizes Thailand's substantial progress in broadening financial access among its populace relative to other countries in the region, a direct outcome of comprehensive financial reforms initiated in response to the Asian financial crisis. However, it notes that major Thai banks are identified as facing ongoing challenges in scaling their operations and extending their international footprint.

3.1 Introduction

In the aftermath of the 2008 global financial crisis, a notable influx of foreign banks into Thailand was observed. Concurrently, Thai commercial banks have increasingly pursued international business opportunities. This trend is situated within a broader context of regional financial integration, placing the Thai commercial banking sector in a more competitive and challenging position due to evolving financial dynamics in East and Southeast Asia.

From a domestic standpoint, the catastrophic floods in 2011 profoundly affected Thailand's banking industry. This natural disaster led to a pronounced downturn in the growth of overall retail loans, a trend that persisted with a progressive decrease in both SME and corporate loan growth rates from 2012 onwards. Concurrently, there was a notable accumulation of non-performing loans. A significant development during this period was the escalation in hire purchase loans, known as installment loans. This surge can be attributed, to a substantial degree, to the "first car policy" enacted by the Yingluck Administration (2011–2014), which was designed to invigorate the automotive industry by offering incentives to individuals purchasing their first car.

W. Lu, *Post-Asian Financial Crisis Reforms in Thailand*,
SpringerBriefs in Economics, https://doi.org/10.1007/978-981-97-3771-0_3

These layered financial strains exerted immense pressure on Thai commercial banks, particularly the larger institutions, to achieve the net profit targets expected by their investors. In response to these stringent domestic conditions, major Thai banks have been compelled to pursue novel business strategies in international markets, focusing particularly on expanding their presence and operations in regions offering promising growth opportunities.

Since late 2000s, Thai banks have increasingly focused their overseas expansion strategies on regional markets within East and Southeast Asia, notably Cambodia, Laos, Myanmar, and Vietnam (collectively referred to as the CLMV countries). This strategic focus can be partly attributed to the prevalent use of the Thai language in these nations, which significantly mitigates linguistic barriers and facilitates smoother business operations for Thai banks in the Indo-Chinese Peninsula. Moreover, the past decade has witnessed a surge in Thai corporate entities extending their operations into CLMV markets. This trend in corporate expansion has, in turn, spurred Thai banks to actively seek out opportunities in these countries, aligning their international expansion strategies with the growing presence of their domestic corporate clients in these markets.

From an international standpoint, the inception of the Association of Southeast Asian Nations Economic Community (AEC) in 2015 signified a pivotal shift towards heightened regional economic integration. In anticipation of this regional integration, central banks of the ASEAN member states ratified the "ASEAN Banking Integration Framework (ABIF)" in 2014. This framework was designed to cultivate a more cohesive and harmonized banking system, while concurrently liberalizing the sector. This was followed by the execution of multiple bilateral agreements. A critical component of these initiatives was the introduction of the "Qualified ASEAN Bank" (QAB) status, a designation allowing selected banks enhanced operational flexibility and access within the ASEAN region. These measures have substantially broadened the horizon for ASEAN commercial banks, offering them expanded prospects for international business development within the region (De Jesus and Torres, 2017).

For Thailand's commercial banks, international expansion, particularly within regional countries, is deemed an integral component of their strategic development, both presently and in the foreseeable future. This outward expansion is not only vital for understanding the role and stature of Thailand's commercial banking sector in regional markets but also serves as a platform to comparatively analyze their competitive advantages and disadvantages relative to their counterparts in other ASEAN countries. Moreover, it provides a lens through which the potential for business growth and development of Thai banks can be assessed in the context of regional economic dynamics.

Thus, this chapter is positioned as a supplement to clarify the domestic changes of the macrocosmic environment and overall market structure described in the last chapter. The chapter is organized as follows: Sect. 3.2 provides a comprehensive investigation of the transformation of the macrocosmic environment and market structure in East and Southeast Asia. Section 3.3 examines the competitive environment for Thai commercial banks from a bank-level perspective. Section 3.4 presents the conclusions.

3.2 The Transformation of Reginal Financial Environment

Beyond Thailand, the financial environments of East and Southeast Asian nations have undergone considerable transformation since the AFC. Figure 3.1 presents a comprehensive comparative analysis of the financial sector sizes in Thailand, the Philippines, Indonesia, Malaysia, and Singapore (collectively referred to as the top five ASEAN countries), alongside major East Asian economies (Korea, Japan, and China) for the years 1998, 2002, 2009, and 2015.

Until the late 2000s, the financial infrastructure in most of these East and Southeast Asian countries was predominantly bank-centric, except for Singapore, which featured a capital market-centric financial system. The AFC brought about extensive financial turmoil across the region. In response, substantial financial restructuring and reform were initiated, supported by aid from IMF and the World Bank. These reforms aimed at fortifying financial system stability and enhancing the efficacy of financial institutions. Concurrently, there was a marked acceleration in the development of bond and stock markets from the early 2000s, reflecting a shift towards a more diversified approach to capital generation.

More specifically, post the economic resurgence from the AFC around 2002, the bond market entered a phase of consistent growth. Nevertheless, it experienced a phase of relative stagnation beginning in 2009. In contrast, the stock markets in developing countries within the region, notably Thailand, the Philippines, and Indonesia, have seen impressive growth. In contrast to the notable expansion of the bond and security sectors, the banking sector's market share decreased until the global financial crisis, after which it began to exhibit a slow upward trend.

It has been observed that since 2009, the aggregate size of the stock and bond markets in these eight countries has consistently exceeded that of the banking sector. This development indicates a pivotal shift from traditional bank-centric markets to markets primarily driven by capital market activities during this timeframe.

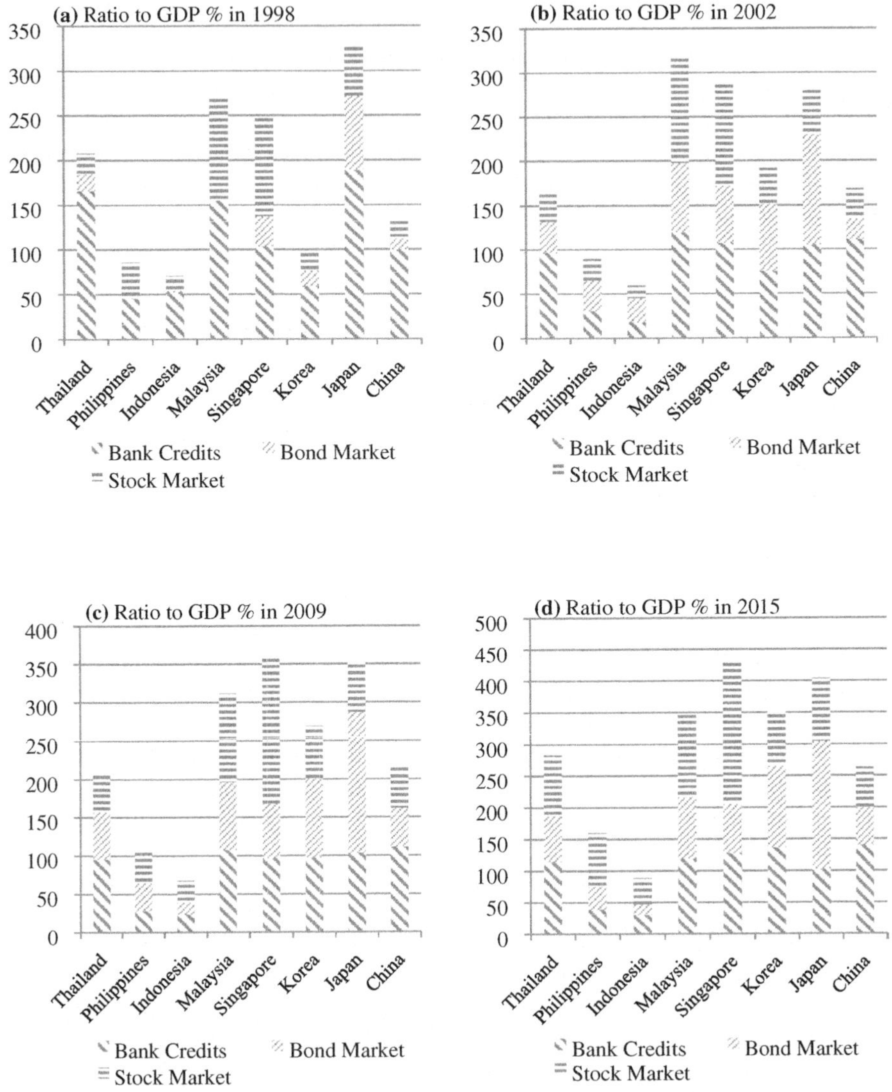

Fig. 3.1 The change in the financial sectors' scale in East and Southeast Asian Countries. *Source* MIF, ADB, Asian Bonds Online, calculated by the author. *Note* 1. Bank credit is calculated from domestic money banks, which comprise commercial banks and other financial institutions that accept transferable deposits

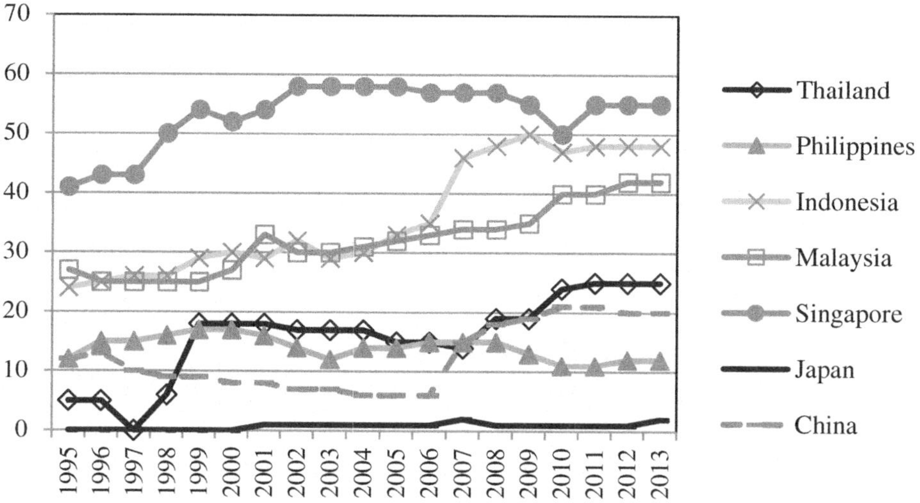

Fig. 3.2 The change of foreign bank number ratio (%)

The evolving dynamics in the financial market landscape necessitate a strategic redirection within the commercial banking sector. Increasingly, banks are directing their focus towards enhancing non-lending operations, such as investment services, fee-based financial products, and wealth management services. This strategic shift is propelled by the growing recognition that non-interest income—revenue streams originating from sources other than conventional interest earnings—harbors more significant growth potential in the prevailing financial environment. This trend reflects the broader shift in the financial sector, where capital market activities are playing an increasingly dominant role, prompting banks to diversify their revenue sources beyond traditional lending practices.

Simultaneously, these markets are witnessing heightened competition due to the expanding presence of capital markets, coupled with a notable increase in foreign bank entries. This influx of foreign banks represents a significant alteration in the operational milieu for commercial banks. Figure 3.2 illustrates this trend of foreign bank participation in the major East and Southeast Asian markets, underscoring the dynamic nature of the regional banking sector.

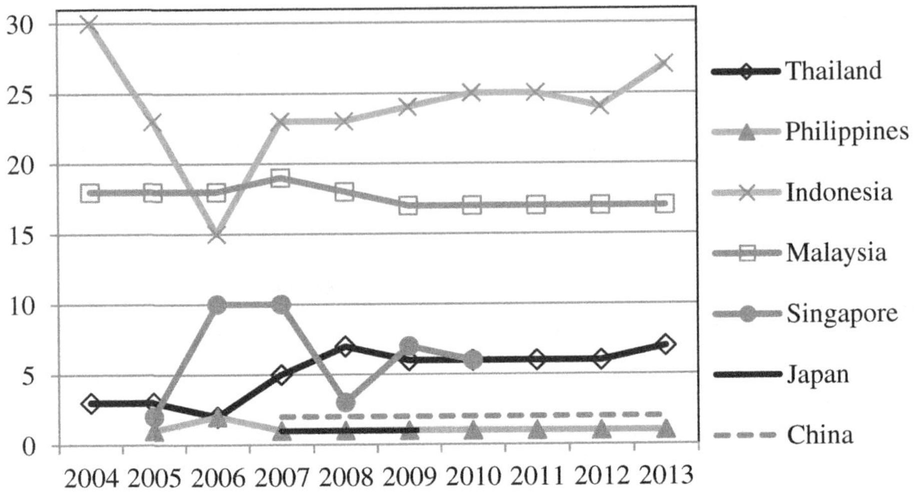

Fig. 3.3 The change of foreign bank asset ratio (%). *Source* World Bank. *Note* A foreign bank is defined as a bank with 50% or more of its shares owned by foreign investors

In the aftermath of the AFC, a significant reorganization occurred within the commercial banking sector of ASEAN countries. Part of this restructuring involved relaxing regulations on foreign bank entries, a move aimed at enhancing market competition. This policy shift resulted in a marked increase in the proportion of foreign banks operating in nearly all Southeast Asian countries. Notably, Thailand and Singapore experienced substantial increases in their ratios of foreign banks shortly after the crisis (Fig. 3.3).

The trend of rising foreign bank presence gained further momentum following the global financial crisis. Starting in the late 2000s, a wave of foreign banks from neighboring countries such as Japan, China, and Australia began entering the ASEAN banking markets. In a notable shift from historical patterns, prominent banks from Singapore, Malaysia, and Thailand have emerged as key players in this surge of foreign bank entries into ASEAN countries. This development signifies a departure from the previous dominance of major European and American banks, highlighting a regional realignment in the banking sector's international presence.

Indonesia and Malaysia exhibit notably higher levels of foreign bank involvement than other regional counterparts, as evidenced by both their foreign bank ratios and the ratios of total banking assets. In Singapore, renowned as the financial epicenter of the region, the ratio of foreign banks has consistently surpassed 50% since the 2000s. However, intriguingly, the share of total banking assets held by these foreign banks has been below 10% during the same timeframe. This stark disparity in asset distribution between foreign and domestic banks underscores the strength and development of Singapore's domestic banking sector. Thailand, experiencing a spike in foreign bank entries in the early 2000s, has since maintained a steady ratio of foreign bank assets following the global financial crisis.

In a broader perspective, the major ASEAN countries have seen a relatively heightened presence of foreign banks in recent years. The implementation of the ABIF in 2014 and the formation of AEC in 2015 are anticipated to open up further avenues for overseas business endeavors for key ASEAN banks in regional markets. This evolving landscape of foreign bank participation is expected to notably influence the dynamics of market competition, potentially altering the competitive balance within these financial markets.

3.3 Competitive Environment in Bank-Level

Concurrent with the increased foreign bank participation in recent years, ASEAN markets have also witnessed numerous mergers among domestic banks. These mergers have predominantly been orchestrated under government-led financial reform initiatives, a response to the AFC. This combination of internal restructuring and external market participation has reshaped the competitive landscape of these markets. Table 3.1 provides insight into this shift, presenting the market concentration levels in major ASEAN and neighboring countries. This is gauged by the ratio of total assets held by the top three largest commercial banks in each market.

Excluding Singapore, where the banking sector follows a different trajectory, the concentration levels in most countries in the mid-2010s were notably lower than those preceding 1997. In Malaysia, the market concentration peaked at 97–99% between 2006 and 2009, but this figure plummeted post-2011. Thailand, the Philippines, and Indonesia have maintained a consistent concentration level around 45% in recent years, a figure that aligns closely with the market concentrations observed in Japan and China. This data indicates a shift towards a less concentrated, more competitive banking environment in these nations, in contrast to the historical dominance of a few large players.

In Malaysia, a comprehensive financial master plan was enacted in response to the AFC. This plan led to a series of mergers involving small and medium-sized banks, effectively consolidating the banking sector from 27 banks, including four merchant banks, down to just eight commercial entities. This restructuring notably amplified the market share of major banks, such as the Overseas Chinese banks. Indonesia witnessed a parallel trend, where domestic bank mergers mirrored those in Malaysia.

Table 3.1 Concentration of top 3 commercial banks in regional countries (%)

	Thailand	Philippines	Indonesia	Malaysia	Singapore	Japan	China
1996	67.31	79.29	47.72	46.66	76.16	41.48	64.76
1997	69.14	77.62	50.02	53.9	64.7	47.65	66.19
1998	71.22	80.38	49.39	50.26	85.39	49.06	56.09
1999	49.03	87.34	63.12	36.44	95.99	31.76	54.79
2000	49.68	100	55.07	56.84	92.89	32.23	51.57
2001	48.43	100	56.14	61.73	95.95	34.96	58.15
2002	48.65	100	54.22	62.59	98.3	38.54	68.01
2003	49.23	98.73	51.32	69.61	100	36.54	68.88
2004	47.16	41.5	47.26	83.41	97.88	36.97	63.92
2005	44.16	41.22	42.84	94.59	94.77	37.19	62.46
2006	44.76	39.61	42.37	98.99	85.17	40.02	60.92
2007	45.83	47.19	42.35	97.53	84.95	38.27	50.43
2008	44.48	47.5	42.96	97.34	94.09	44.96	48.11
2009	46.14	46.67	44.11	97.01	88.78	44.65	47.29
2010	46.71	47.61	43.22	92.74	89.68	44.16	45.14
2011	45.66	40.59	42.07	53.55	89.91	43.4	43.28
2012	46.75	41.31	41.74	45.8	89.93	43.23	43.66
2013	46.84	43.36	41.03	48.91	86.66	43.6	44.04
2014	46.49	47.11	43.08	56.64	90.41	46.34	44.43

Source MIF, ADB

In contrast, Thailand's banking landscape diverged from this pattern. Despite the nationalization of several medium-sized banks, the overall count of commercial banks in Thailand expanded, bolstered by the entrance of both new domestic and foreign banking institutions. As detailed in the preceding chapter, significant foreign investments were channeled into Thailand's large-sized banks following the AFC. Consequently, the consolidation in market share among Thailand's top three banks remained relatively modest after the early 2000s. The data thus reflects a notable decline in market concentration specifically in Thailand and the Philippines, distinguishing these two countries within the regional banking sector's evolving competitive landscape.

Singapore, recognized as one of the foremost developed financial markets within ASEAN, saw its banking sector concentration ratio reach a pinnacle of 100% in 2003, subsequently stabilizing at approximately 90%. This high concentration ratio is indicative of the dominant market presence of Singapore's top three commercial banks.

Detailed in Table 3.2 are the top 20 commercial banks in ASEAN, ranked according to their asset sizes. The top three spots are firmly held by Singaporean banks, underscoring their formidable asset base in comparison to their regional

Table 3.2 Top 20 major banks in ASEAN in 2018

Ranking	World ranking	Bank name	Country	Total assets (1 million USD)
1	68	DBS Bank	Singapore	386,351
2	79	Overseas Chinese Banking Corporation (OCBC)	Singapore	339,506
3	92	United Overseas Bank (UOB)	Singapore	267,606
4	115	Malayan Banking Berhad (MayBank)	Malaysia	188,498
5	150	CIMB Bank	Malaysia	124,754
6	180	Public Bank	Malaysia	97,359
7	189	Bangkok Bank	Thailand	94,134
8	192	Siam Commercial Bank	Thailand	92,535
9	198	KasikornBank	Thailand	88,765
10	201	Krung Thai Bank	Thailand	87,338
11	213	Bank Rakyat Indonesia (BRI)	Indonesia	83,130
12	214	Bank Mandiri	Indonesia	83,016
13	268	RHB Bank	Malaysia	56,702
14	274	Bank Central Asia (BCA)	Indonesia	55,382
15	284	BDO UniBank	Philippines	53,448
16	293	Bank Negara Indonesia (BNI)	Indonesia	52,357
17	334	Hong Leong Bank	Malaysia	45,583
18	357	Metropolitan Bank & Trust Company	Philippines	41,673
19	428	Thanachart Bank	Thailand	30,892
20	432	AmBank	Malaysia	30,422

Source The Banker, Top 1000 World Bank, 2018

counterparts. Notably, DBS Bank alone possesses an asset scale nearly matching the combined assets of Thailand's Big 4 commercial banks. In the wake of targeted government-led acquisitions, three of Malaysia's major banks have ascended to positions within the top 10 as of 2018. Meanwhile, Thailand's Big 4 commercial banks are ranked between the 7th and 10th positions, reflecting their significant, yet comparatively smaller, scale within the regional banking landscape.

Despite the notable differences in their respective sizes, leading banks from Singapore and Malaysia have embarked on overseas business expansions much earlier and more assertively than their ASEAN peers.

As of 2017, Singapore's prominent banks, namely DBS Bank, Overseas Chinese Banking Corporation (OCBC), and United Overseas Bank (UOB), had established a widespread network of subsidiaries, branches, or representative offices across the ASEAN region, with the exception of Cambodia and Laos. Malaysia's top banks have mirrored this expansive approach. Maybank has ventured into all ASEAN countries, while CIMB Bank has extended its reach to a similar extent, except for the Philippine market.

In contrast, Thailand's banking sector, represented chiefly by Bangkok Bank, displays a more moderate level of regional penetration. Bangkok Bank stands out amongst Thai banks for its international endeavors, having established seven branches and a subsidiary in Malaysia, covering all regional markets except Brunei. This level of overseas presence is significantly more extensive than the other Big 4 banks in Thailand, which collectively maintain a regional network less than half the size of Bangkok Bank's.

The "ASEAN Economic Blueprint 2007" highlights that the overseas expansion strategies of ASEAN commercial banks are fundamentally aligned with the goals of AEC, a vision to create a region characterized by the free movement of goods, services, investment, skilled labor, and capital has catalyzed an upsurge in regional business activities and cross-border investments. Consequently, major banks in the region have been proactively establishing operations abroad, both to support their domestic clients who are expanding internationally and to further their own growth ambitions. This expansion is also a strategic move to provide accessible, high-quality financial services in these growing markets.

Moreover, major ASEAN commercial banks are leveraging overseas expansion as a key strategy to augment profitability. Faced with nearing saturation in their domestic markets, these institutions are exploring foreign markets to unearth new business opportunities and develop untapped markets. Post the global financial crisis, this strategy has been particularly evident among major banks from Singapore and Malaysia, which have intensified their business operations in Indonesia, the Philippines, and Thailand. Thai banks, in parallel, have directed their expansion efforts towards the CLMV markets since the early 2010s, a strategic pivot prompted by the deceleration in domestic SME and corporate loan growth.

Similar upsurges in foreign bank entries are also expected by the ASEAN financial authorities. The primary aim of fostering this increase is to intensify market competition and bring in cutting-edge financial technologies and management expertise. This is particularly crucial for enhancing financial accessibility in the region's less developed countries, such as Laos, Myanmar, and Cambodia. The infusion of foreign banks is seen as a catalyst for elevating the financial infrastructure and services in these areas, potentially leading to greater economic inclusion and development.

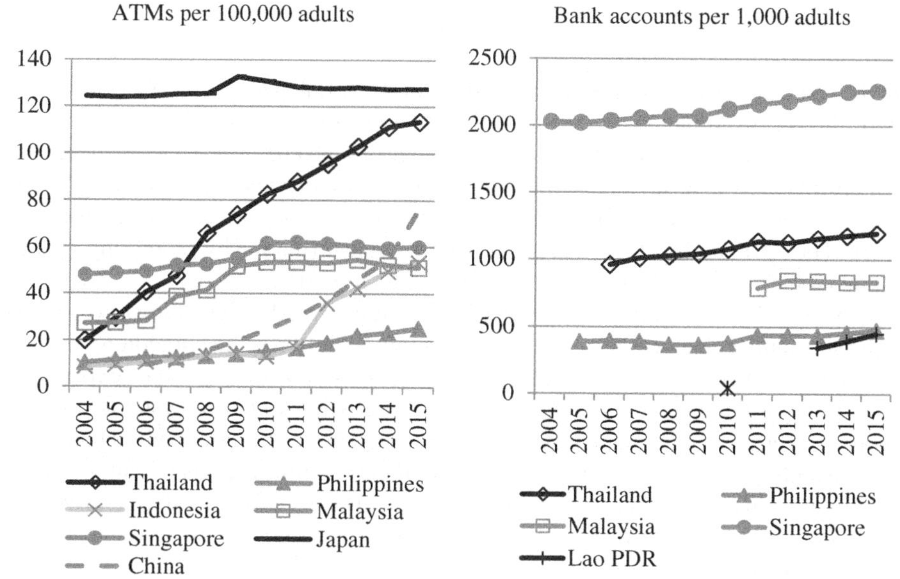

Fig. 3.4 The Change of Financial Accessibility in East and Southeast Asian Countries. *Source* MIF, World Bank

Figure 3.4 offers a comparative analysis of financial accessibility across major East and Southeast Asian nations. It does so by tracking changes in two key metrics: the number of Automated Teller Machines (ATMs) per 100,000 adults and the number of bank accounts per 1,000 adults. These indicators illustrate the extent of financial services penetration and availability, reflecting the level of financial inclusion in these countries.

The data reveal that Singapore, Thailand, and Malaysia stand out for their higher levels of financial accessibility within the ASEAN region. A striking example of this enhanced accessibility is seen in Thailand, particularly through the lens of the ATM per 100,000 adult's metrics. This measure saw a marked surge following the financial reforms initiated by Thailand's Thaksin Administration. These reforms, aimed at modernizing and expanding financial services infrastructure, significantly increased the availability of ATMs across the country. As a result, by the mid-2010s, Thailand's ATM density reached a level comparable to that of Japan, indicating a substantial advancement in its financial accessibility.

3.4 Conclusions

In the wake of the long-term financial restructuring initiated after the AFC, combined with the recent implementation of ABIF and the formation of AEC, the financial landscape in ASEAN countries has undergone profound changes. This restructuring, which involved a series of reforms aimed at stabilizing and strengthening financial systems, set the stage for a more integrated and collaborative financial environment. The ABIF and AEC further propelled this transformation by promoting greater financial harmonization and connectivity within the region.

On one side, the financial market structures within the ASEAN region have undergone substantial changes. A notable aspect of this evolution is the burgeoning growth of capital markets, with stock markets in particular demonstrating robust expansion. This trend signifies a pivotal shift from traditional bank-centric systems towards more market-centric financial models. As a consequence, Thai commercial banks are increasingly gravitating towards diversifying their revenue streams by emphasizing non-interest income businesses, such as investment services and fee-based products. This strategic shift is a response to the intensifying competition in conventional lending operations.

On the other side, there has been a noticeable rise in foreign bank participation in countries like Indonesia, Malaysia, and Thailand, a trend that gained momentum post the global financial crisis. This new landscape is characterized by the diminishing dominance of traditional Western financial institutions, supplanted by the growing prominence of major banks from Singapore, Malaysia, and Thailand. This regional shift aligns with the broader trajectory of financial integration within ASEAN, offering Thai commercial banks enhanced opportunities for overseas business. These opportunities are twofold: supporting domestic clients expanding or residing abroad and tapping into the potential of burgeoning economies in rapidly developing countries.

At the same time, Thai commercial banks are currently navigating a competitive landscape marked by the strong presence of sizable banking entities from Singapore and Malaysia. This competitive dynamic is underscored by a notable gap in the overall scale and reach of Thai banks compared to their larger counterparts in Singapore and Malaysia. The disparity in scale encompasses aspects like total assets, international network, and market penetration. Consequently, strategizing to effectively compete with these leading ASEAN banks has become an essential aspect of the operational and growth strategies for Thailand's major commercial banking institutions.

As is widely anticipated, especially by Thai financial authorities, the competitive pressure from larger ASEAN banks is not merely prompting Thai banks to refine their service offerings and enhance their operational efficiency. It also serves as a catalyst for these banks to embrace innovation and expand into new markets, crucial steps in ensuring their continued relevance and growth within the regional banking landscape.

One of the goals of the subsequent chapters is to examine the anticipated effects of this competitive environment on the Thai commercial banking sector.

This analysis will be conducted from multiple angles, encompassing macro-level (industry-wide trends and economic impacts), micro-level (individual bank performance and strategies), and organizational-level (internal management and operational dynamics) perspectives. This multi-faceted approach aims to provide a thorough understanding of how Thai banks are adapting and strategizing in response to the evolving competitive scenario at home and abroad.

Chapter 4
The Business Practice and Performance of Commercial Banks

Abstract This chapter examines the evolution of the overall market structure of the commercial banking sector at macro-level following the post-crisis financial regulatory reforms and assesses its implications for the competitive landscape and business methodologies. It first determines that, notwithstanding increased foreign participation, foreign capital has been primarily channeled into sizable banks, while foreign banking entities represent a comparatively minor share of the market, culminating in pronounced market concentration and the maintenance of an oligopolistic framework. Secondly, through an analysis of profit-cost structures and bank lending behaviors, the study deduces that larger banks maintain greater profit margins, operational efficiency, and interest rate spreads compared to their smaller and medium-sized counterparts, including foreign banks. The marginal rise in profits, interest spreads, and the minimal alteration in expenses among large banks underscore the insufficient advancements in fostering market competition and fortifying the robustness of the banking system.

4.1 Introduction

The Thailand's commercial banking sector has gone through a dramatic reorganization progress since the AFC. The commercial banks facing financial difficulties, have accepted capital injection by the government, or get temporal nationalized, or merged by foreign banks. Along with the Thaksin financial reform and the implementation of Financial Sector Master Plan Phase I and II, foreign participation in commercial banking sector has increased sharply.

Until 2014, the market shares of foreign participation exceed 40%, foreign banks account for more than 15% of total assets of the entire banking sector, 5 out of the whole 6 foreign banks are from East and Southeast Asia area, and another 3 foreign banks that were granted with full license in 2015 are all from regional countries.

W. Lu, *Post-Asian Financial Crisis Reforms in Thailand*,
SpringerBriefs in Economics, https://doi.org/10.1007/978-981-97-3771-0_4

Compared with the withdrawing trend of western multinational bank players that entered Thai market right after the AFC, the foreign bank entry from neighbor countries has been more high-profile. The bank players from China, Japan, and some ASEAN countries in particular, have an active participation since the Lehman Shock.

Under such a profound change of the overall financial landscape, there is a significant meaning to conduct a comprehensive observation on the market structure and the market competition condition, to capture the major characteristics of the changing market condition, and to analyze the subsequent impacts on business practice and the profit-cost structure of Thailand's commercial banks.

Through a comprehensive analysis of the market structure and competitive environment, this chapter conducts an examination of business practice and banking performance. Thus, the rest of this chapter is comprised as follows[1]: Sect. 4.2 investigates the transformation of overall market structure of Thai commercial banking sector. Section 4.3 examines the change of competitive conditions along with ownership evolutions. Section 4.4 conducts an investigation on business practice and banking performance of commercial banks. The conclusions are presented in Sect. 4.5.

4.2 The Transformation of Overall Market Structure

Since the AFC, the financial reorganization progress in Thailand has resulted in a tremendous change in the overall market structure and competitive environment. Along with a series of financial reforms, most of the foreign banks entered Thai market through the merge and acquisition (M&A) of the local commercial banks with getting full banking licenses. Besides, a large scale of foreign capital has flowed into the top level large-sized commercial banks since the AFC.

During the implementation process of Financial Sector Master Plan since second half of 2000s, a couple of foreign banks have got the approval from Bank of Thailand and Ministry of Finance to get the retail bank licenses or full commercial bank licenses. A new foreign entry boom has been observed since the Global Financial Crisis.

Another three foreign banks from Japan, China and Australia-New Zealand, have get the foreign bank subsidiaries licenses in the mid-2010s. Until 2016, 9 of the 19 commercial banks are foreign bank owned, except for Standard Chartered (Thai), the rest of them are all from neighboring Asian-Pacific countries. The detailed ownership structure of commercial banks in 2016 is summarized in Table 4.1.

Compared with the major shareholder composition from 1996 to 2001 in Table 2. 1 in the last chapter, Table 4.1 indicates a significant ownership structural change of domestic commercial banks. Firstly, among the 10 domestic commercial banks

[1] Parts of the data and analysis presented in this chapter have been updated and revised by the author, utilizing data and analysis from Lu (2018) and Mieno and Lu (2020) with the consent of all involved authors.

Table 4.1 The ownership structure of commercial banks in 2016

	Bank	Total assets in 2016		The principal stockholder			Foreign ownership share	Local/ foreign	Ownership details	Banking Licenses
		Million bahts	Market Share	Name	Share (%)	Country/ region				
1	Bangkok bank	2,838.8	17.7	Thai NVDR Co., Ltd.	33.41	USA	35.0	Local	Decentralized ownership	Commercial bank
2	Siam commercial bank	2,614.8	16.3	Bureau of the crown property and group	23.7	Thailand	37.3	Local	A subsidiary of Siam Commercial Bank Public Company Limited's financial conglomerate	Commercial bank
3	Krung Thai bank	2,661.4	16.6	Financial institutions development fund	55.1	Thai government	18.1	Local	State-owned	Commercial bank
4	Kasikornbank	2,467.3	15.4	Thai NVDR Co., Ltd.	26.8	Thailand	49.0	Local	A subsidiary of Kasikornbank financial conglomerate	Commercial bank
5	Bank of Ayudhya	1,806.0	11.2	Mitsubishi UFJ financial group	72.1	Japan	72.1	Foreign	Foreign bank owned (Japan; rebranded as Krungsri bank in 2014)	Commercial bank

(continued)

Table 4.1 (continued)

	Bank	Total assets in 2016		The principal stockholder			Foreign ownership share	Local/ foreign	Ownership details	Banking Licenses
		Million bahts	Market Share	Name	Share (%)	Country/ region				
6	Thanachart bank	906.9	5.6	Thanachart capital	51.0	Thailand	49.0	Local	Was 50.96% owned by Thanachart Capital PCL (TCAP), its parent company	Commercial bank
7	TMB bank	820.2	5.1	Ministry of Finance, Thailand	26.0	Thai government	39.0	Local	The Ministry of Finance of Thailand and ING Bank N.V. collectively owned more than 50% of its total shareholdings	Commercial bank
8	United overseas bank (Thai)	451.7	2.8	United overseas bank	99.7	Singapore	99.7	Foreign	Foreign bank owned (Singapore)	Commercial bank
9	CIMB Thai bank	295.6	1.8	CIMB group	96.8	Malaysia	96.8	Foreign	Foreign bank owned (Malaysia)	Commercial bank

(continued)

Table 4.1 (continued)

	Bank	Total assets in 2016		The principal stockholder			Foreign ownership share	Local/ foreign	Ownership details	Banking Licenses
		Million bahts	Market Share	Name	Share (%)	Country/ region				
10	TISCO bank	260.7	1.6	TISCO financial group	100.0	Thailand	0.0	Local	Conglomerates/ a subsidiary of TISCO financial group	Commercial bank
11	Kiatnakin bank	220.3	1.4	Thai NVDR Co., Ltd.	10.0	Switzerland	32.7	Local	Decentralized ownership	Commercial bank
12	Land and houses bank	209.7	1.3	LH financial group	100.0	Thailand	0.9	Local	Conglomerates	Commercial bank
13	Standard chartered (Thai)	190.7	1.2	Standard chartered bank	100.0	UK	100.0	Foreign	Foreign bank owned (United Kingdom)	Commercial bank
14	Industrial and commercial bank of China (Thai)	158.2	1.0	Industrial & commercial bank of China	97.7	China	97.7	Foreign	Foreign bank owned (China)	Commercial bank
15	Bank of China (Thai)	43.9	0.3	Bank of China	100.0	China	N.A.	Foreign	Foreign bank owned (China)	Foreign bank subsidiary

(continued)

Table 4.1 (continued)

	Bank	Total assets in 2016		The principal stockholder			Foreign ownership share	Local/ foreign	Ownership details	Banking Licenses
		Million bahts	Market Share	Name	Share (%)	Country/ region				
16	Thai credit retail bank	39.3	0.2	Thai Life insurance group	n.a.	Thailand	0.0	Local	Controlled by the Chaiyawan family with an aggregate indirect shareholding of 71.9%	Retail bank
17	ANZ bank (Thai)	29.3	0.2	N.A.		Australia–NZ	N.A.	Foreign	Foreign bank owned (Australia)	Foreign bank subsidiary
18	Sumitomo-Mitsui-Trust-Thai-bank	28.2	0.2	N.A.		Japan	N.A.	Foreign	Foreign bank owned (Japan)	Foreign bank subsidiary
19	Mega international commercial bank	20.2	0.1	Mega financial holding company	100.0	Taiwan	100.0	Foreign	Foreign bank owned (Taiwan)	Commercial bank

Source Revised by the author based on Appendix Table-1 in Lu (2018) and Table 6-2 in Mieno and Lu (2020), utilizing data from Bank of Thailand; *Commercial Banks in Thailand*, various versions; BankScope; annual reports of each bank (the banks that have a foreign ownership share less than 50%), most of them have a largest shareholder with a relatively high ownership share, except for Bangkok Bank and Kiatnakin Bank. To be more specific, a number of traditional major shareholders still keep their dominant shareholder position in the bank, such as Bureau of the Crown Property and Group in Siam Commercial Bank, Financial Institutions Development Found in Krung Thai Bank, and Thanachart Capital in Thanachart Bank. However, even in those commercial banks, the foreign ownership keeps a relatively high proportion.

Secondly, in terms of the nationality of principle shareholder and the foreign ownership share in each commercial bank, 11 of the 19 commercial banks have a foreign investor as its largest shareholder. To a certain extent, such a change indicates the ownership declining of traditional founding families.

Thirdly, a couple of domestic banks has accepted foreign institutional investors as a core strategic partner. For instance, Thanachart Bank has accepted the Bank of Nova Scotia as a major shareholder since 2007, with yielding four seats in the board of directors as well as some executive positions. Such an ownership change implies that instead of the decentralization of shareholdings, the major shareholders tend to cooperate with financial institutional partners to enhance capital management and improve banking performance.

The accruing foreign entry largely featured in the market transformation of "whole foreign bank sector" since the AFC. Apart from "banks incorporated in Thailand" shown in Table 4.1, foreign bank branches have operated in Thailand. Table 4.2 shows the list of them with total asset and the market share between 1997 and 2016. The number of foreign bank branches reduced from 20 branches in 1997 to 11 in 2016.

In terms of the relative bank size, the largest foreign bank branch Mizuho Corporate Bank and second largest foreign bank branch Sumitomo Mitsui Banking Corporation has occupied 3.1 and 1.9% market share respectively, which is equivalent to the middle-sized commercial banks United Overseas Bank (Thai) and CIMB Thai Bank.

The total market share of foreign bank branches has declined from 19.3% in 1997 to 9.1% in 2016, both due to the retreat of some western banks and the upgrade of some Asian banks from foreign bank branches to commercial banks. It has also been found that different from the active performance of Asian banks that described in Table 4.1, the western banks are inclined to operating as foreign bank branch, instead of upgrading to full-licensed commercial banks as the Asian banks did.

In examining the evolution of foreign bank involvement in Thailand since the Asian Financial Crisis, it is noted that by the end of 2016, the collective market share of foreign commercial banks—encompassing both fully-licensed foreign commercial banks and their non-fully licensed subsidiaries but excluding branches of foreign banks—grew from 0% in 1997 to 17.1% in 2016. Additionally, the aggregate presence of foreign banks, inclusive of foreign bank branches, expanded from 19.3% in 1997 to 26.2% in 2016. This analysis, taking into account the commercial banking sector's structure classified by licensing and ownership, reveals that the upgrading of

Table 4.2 The bank size and market share of foreign bank branches in 1997 and 2016

	1997	Total assets (million baht)	Share (%)		2016	Total assets (million baht)	Share (%)
1	The bank of Tokyo-Mitsubishi	215,216	2.9	1	Mizuho corporate bank	547,642	3.1
2	The Sumitomo bank	188,086	2.5	2	Sumitomo Mitsui banking corporation	334,672	1.9
3	The Dai-Ichi Kangyo bank	172,581	2.3	3	The Hong Kong and Shanghai banking corporation	225,163	1.3
4	The Sakura bank	159,065	2.1	4	CitiBank	214,056	1.2
5	The industrial bank of Japan	128,983	1.7	5	Deutsche bank	80,304	0.5
6	Citibank	119,539	1.6	6	BNP Paribas	65,612	0.4
7	The Hong Kong and Shanghai Banking Corporation	85,438	1.1	7	Bank of America	6,537	0.0
8	Standard charted bank	53,262	0.7	8	JP Morgan Chase bank	59,067	0.3
9	The Chase Manhattan bank	50,610	0.7	9	Oversea-Chinese banking corporation	38,478	0.2
10	Bank of America	50,585	0.7	10	RHB bank Berhad	19,248	0.1
11	ABN-AMRO bank	43,076	0.6	11	Indian overseas bank	11,328	0.1
12	Dresdner bank	38,646	0.5				
13	The Chase Manhattan bank	36,858	0.5				
14	Credit Agricole Indosuez	33,298	0.4				
15	Banque Nationale de Paris	27,396	0.4				
16	Oversea-Chinese banking corporation	9,736	0.1				
17	Bank of China	7,854	0.1				
18	The international commercial bank of China	7,701	0.1				

(continued)

Table 4.2 (continued)

	1997	Total assets (million baht)	Share (%)		2016	Total assets (million baht)	Share (%)
19	Bharat overseas bank	3,538	0.0				
20	Sime bank Berhad	2,186	0.0				
	Sum	1,433,654	19.3			1,602,107	9.1

Source Revised by the author based on Table 6-3 in Mieno and Lu (2020), utilizing data from Bank of Thailand, *Commercial Banks in Thailand*, various versions
Note The foreign bank total assets share is calculated as the ratio of all commercial banks total assets including foreign bank branches

foreign bank branches to full-fledged commercial banks has been a significant driver of this increased foreign presence.

Regarding market concentration, as measured by the market share of the Big 4 banks, there was a notable rise in concentration, with the Big 4's combined market share escalating from 49.9% in 1997 to 67.3% in 2016.

To sum up, during the past two decades after the AFC, the foreign banks has remains as small and middle-sized commercial banks. On the other hand, a large capital inflow by institutional investors were directed to large-sized commercial banks, resulting in which is large foreign ownership in them. Such a transformation has enlarged the gap between large-sized banks and the new bank players that represented by the foreign bank entrants. It is considered to result in a further concentrated banking market structure in Thailand, and a strengthening competition condition for the large-sized commercial banks.

4.3 The Market Competitive Environment

Such a market structural changes may pose the question on how the accruing foreign participation changed the market competition condition, as the participation are thought to influence business practice and performance of commercial banks.

Figure 4.1 shows the evolution of foreign participation by means of tracking three indicators of foreign presence for the past 25 years. Indicator (1) represents the foreign bank ratio of total assets. Indicator (2) is the weighted annual average ratio of each commercial bank's foreign ownership, which is weighted by relative bank assets. Indicator (3) represents the foreign bank ratio of total bank numbers. The foreign bank here is defined as the commercial banks that have a foreign ownership share more than 50%. Overall, there is barely any foreign banks getting the commercial bank license before 1997, due to the "No Exit No Entry" regulation. Along with the financial reforms since the AFC, the foreign bank ratio of total assets has increased

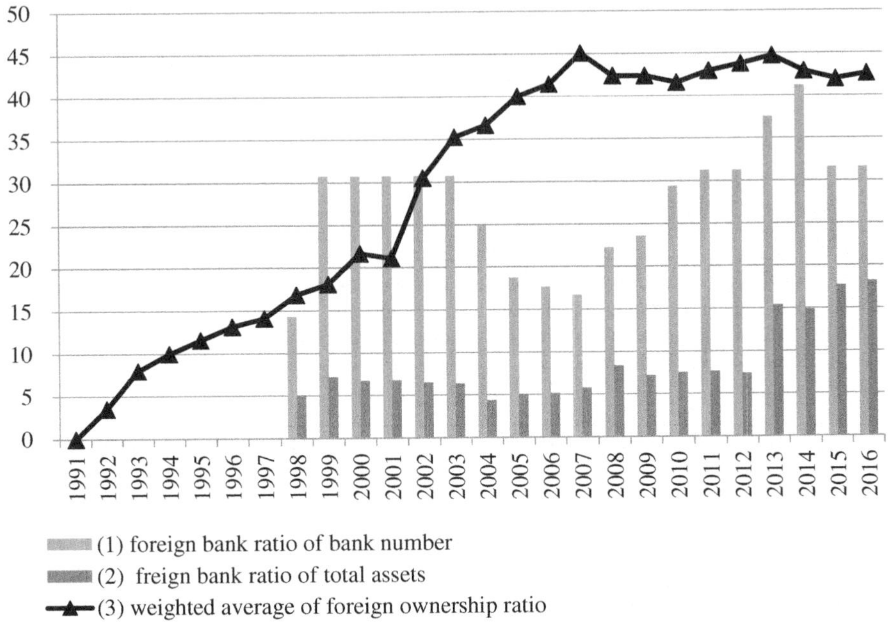

Fig. 4.1 The change of foreign ownership ratio. *Source* Updated by the author based on Fig. 2 in Lu (2018), utilizing data from Bank of Thailand, Stock Exchange of Thailand. *Note* (3) represents the annual average of foreign ownership for each commercial bank, weighted according to the bank's total assets

to 6% and the foreign bank ratio of total bank numbers has achieved about 30% in the early 2000s.

Along with the establishment of retail banks under Thaksin financial reform, the total commercial bank number increased from 12 banks in 2004 to 17 banks around 2006. Accordingly, the foreign bank ratio of total bank numbers had declined significantly during 2004 to 2006. On account of the relatively small size of new entered banks, the foreign bank ratio of total assets decreased slightly in this period. However, The Global Financial Crisis has been a turning point for foreign bank presence. Owing to the slowdown of US economy and the subprime debt crisis in Europe, many foreign investors has shifted focus to the rapid growing East and Southeast Asian Area.

In pace with the foreign investment deregulation under Financial Sector Master Plan Phase II, foreign bank players entered into Thai market with full banking licenses in forms of M&A or acquiring licenses as "foreign bank subsidiary". The most notable case is the merge and acquisition of Ayudhya Bank by Bank of Tokyo-Mitsubishi UFJ from Japan in 2013. It is the first M&A case by foreign banks towards the first-tier commercial bank in Thailand and is also the largest M&A case by foreign bank in terms of total amount since 1997.The foreign bank ratio of total assets has raised to 15% since 2013.

The weighted annual average ratio of foreign ownership (indicator (2)) has shown a stable and rapid growth until 2007 and retained around 40% to 45% since then. The foreign ownership achieved almost half of the entire market share. The accruing trend of foreign ownership is mainly resulted from a long period of accelerated foreign capital inflows in large-sized commercial banking market.[2] The foreign participation in the major large-sized banks has achieved a substantial proportion since the AFC. The foreign ownership ratio of Siam Commercial Bank used to exceed 50% in 2005 and kept at a high level more than one third afterwards, Bangkok Bank and KasikornBank had also kept a high foreign ownership share of more than 40% since 2005.

However, such a change of market competitive environment is a different picture from what Thai financial authorities expected which aimed to promote the entry of new bank players for improving market competition condition under two phases to the Financial Sector Master Plan.

As highlighted in Chap. 1, Fig. 1.3 depicts the evolution of the competitive landscape in the commercial banking sector over the past 25 years. The Herfindahl–Hirschman Index (HHI) shows a very slight change after the AFC, which reveals the market concentration condition has not witnessed any significant improvement in these years as expected. On the other hand, the total assets share of top 4 large-sized banks indicates a more detailed track of the transformation of market competitive environment. In spite of the decline of the total asset ratio of Big 4 banks during the financial liberalization process in early 1990s, the index had increased to 67% in 1999, due to the bankruptcy of some small and medium-sized banks in the crisis.

Along with the foreign bank entry boom that mainly passed through merging with the middle-sized banks, the index even declined to less than 60% in 2005, when a number of new bank players entered the market. However, the total assets ratio of Big 4 banks has kept on accruing in recent years and achieved 68% in 2014, which exceeded the recorded highest level since 1990s. These facts suggest that the new entrants have inserted very limited impacts on promoting market competition due to their relatively small bank sizes. On the contrary, the large amount of foreign investment that flow into large-sized banks resulted in a greater market concentration (Mieno and Lu, 2020).

To sum up, despite the foreign bank entry as middle-sized banks such as UOB and CIMB, most of the new bank players are in relatively small market shares. The large-sized banks have maintained management control and realized capital reinforcement through accepting accruing foreign investment, which further consolidate their monopolistic positions. Thus, the improvement of competition condition through market entries that represented by foreign banks, has not proceeded as expected.

[2] Of course, foreign banks' M&A of local medium-sized banks are thought to be the other components of the surge, although it seems a minor factor.

4.4 The Business Practice and Performance

The accruing foreign capital into banking sector and resulting strengthened market concentration as noted in Sect. 4.2 brought about significant changes to operation and performance. This section will firstly examine the transformation of macro financial environment, and secondly, the changes of commercial banking management and performance under such a business environment.

4.4.1 The Business Environment After the AFC

Regarding the evolution of gross capital flows for the past two decades, including inbound and outbound investment in Thailand, on one hand, the foreign investment towards banking sector reduced to minus after the AFC and recovered since 2003. In spite of a significant fluctuation of net inbound investment around Global Financial Crisis in 2008, the foreign direct investment has kept on accruing along with the accumulation of export-oriented manufacture.

On the other hand, domestic market has generally maintained a surplus of current account, as well as excess saving structure since the AFC. The foreign reserves have accumulated to a great extent, which strengthened the capability to cope with international speculative capital compared with the conditions during the AFC. Thai outbound investment has also drawn great attention due to its significant increase since the mid-2000s.

On the whole, the outbound investment has generally reached a balanced level to the inbound investment, the aspect of direct investment in particular. Thailand has gradually become a capital-exporting country in recent years on one hand and remained as a recipient country of direct investment.

Such a change of macro financial environment suggests the possibility that a demand for new advanced financial services occurs, associated with the accruing personal consumption or expanding outbound investment.

Figure 4.2 depicts the trend of total assets and loan deposit ratio of commercial banks. The total size of the sector has shrunk to a large extent after the crisis and rebounded since 2000. Along with the recovery of macro economy, the ratio of total bank assets to GDP has gradually declined to 86% in 2007, which implies the commercial banking sector's slower pace of recovery compared with the overall economy. However, the share of total bank size to GDP turned to a sharp pace of increase after 2007, which implies the trend of financial deepening since late 2000s.

On the other hand, the loan deposit ratio had declined sharply after the AFC, reached the bottom in 2001, and recovered gradually to 100% in 2010. Such a change implies the severe decline of financial intermediation function of commercial banking sector in the financial reorganization progress after the AFC.

To a certain degree, the recovery of loan deposit ratio since 2007 indicates the constant surplus of loanable funds in commercial banking sector, which suggests

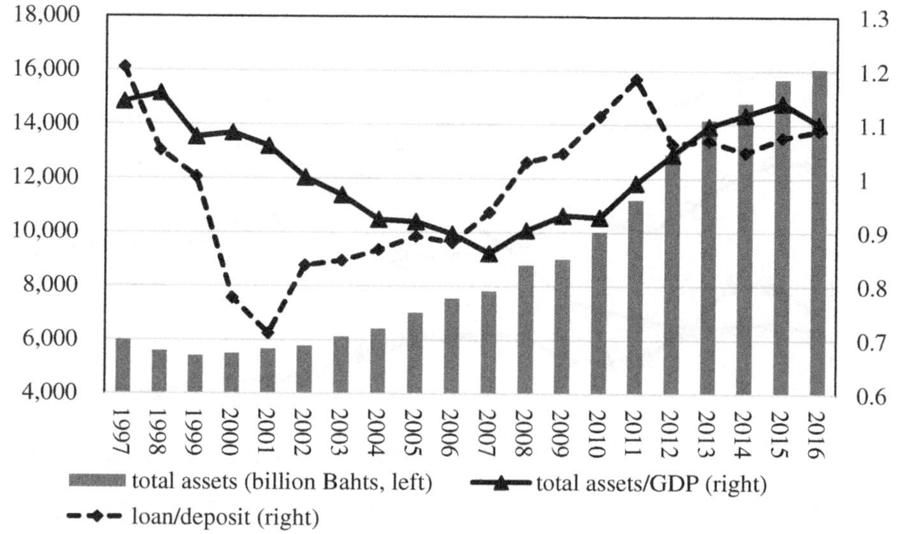

Fig. 4.2 The change of total assets and loan deposit ratio. *Source* Updated by the author based on Fig. 6 in Lu (2018), utilizing data from Bank of Thailand, Commercial Banks in Thailand, various versions, Bangkok Bank, BankScope

the major task of banks on the functional enhancement of bank credits, and on the further exploration of potential market demand for funds.

4.4.2 The Shift of Lending Behavior

Figure 4.3 depicts the change of banking credits that classified by industry. Firstly, while manufacturing sector largely contributed to the economic recovery from the AFC, the share of bank credit to this sector has declined from its peak of 31% in 1997 to 17% in 2014. Secondly, bank credit share to commerce sector including wholesale and retail business, a traditional client for commercial banks, had dropped continuously during 1990s into 12% in 2010 and gradually rebounded afterwards. Thirdly, the commercial banking sector has shifted the priority of credits to the sector of finance and personal consumption.

The decrease of bank credit share to manufacturing and commerce industry implies a significant change of business model in terms of the banking lending in the past two decades. Also, the share of bank credits to finance sector had dropped sharply in the period of financial reform under Thaksin government (2001–2006), and again increased after the global financial crisis.

The share of credit to financial sector and personal consumption sector increased from 11% in 2007 to 21% in 2014 and from 10% in 1997 to 27% in 2014, respectively. The sharp increase in these sectors is thought to be reflected by the expanding

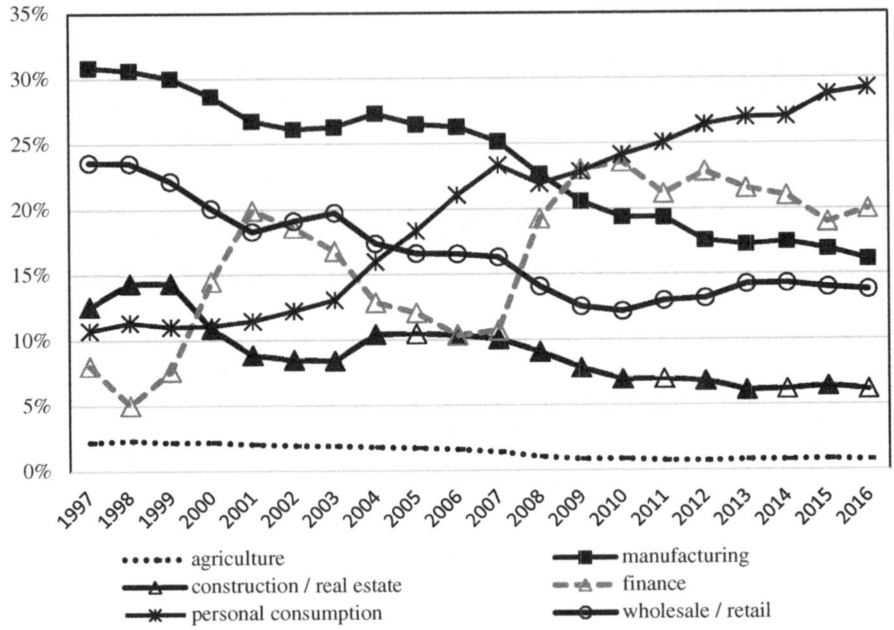

Fig. 4.3 The Change of Banking Credits Classified by Industry. *Source* Updated by the author based on Fig. 3 in Lu (2018), utilizing data from *Commercial Banks in Thailand*, Bangkok Bank

demand for housing loan and installment finance for smartphone and automobile consumption, online shopping, the credit card business.

As one evidence, according to a micro-level bank data in recent years, the hire-purchase loan kept a rapid growth during 2012 to 2014 along with the implementation of "first-car buyer scheme" by Yingluck administration. The policy benefits consumers with tax bonus to encourage the purchase or reservation of automobile, the low-income earners in particular. The middle-sized commercial banks such as Thanachart bank, Kiatnakin Bank, Tesco bank and Bank of Ayutthaya, have benefited enormously from this so-called "populist policy," which also resulted in the increase of non-performing loan at the same time.

4.4.3 The Profit–Cost Structure–General Structure

Under such a transformation of business environment for commercial banks, the financial performance has significantly changed, too. Figure 4.4 illustrates the change of profit–cost structure of commercial banking sector since 1997. After a long process of capital injection by the government, temporal nationalization and foreign banks' acquisition, the profit of commercial banking sector has turned to plus since 2002. It

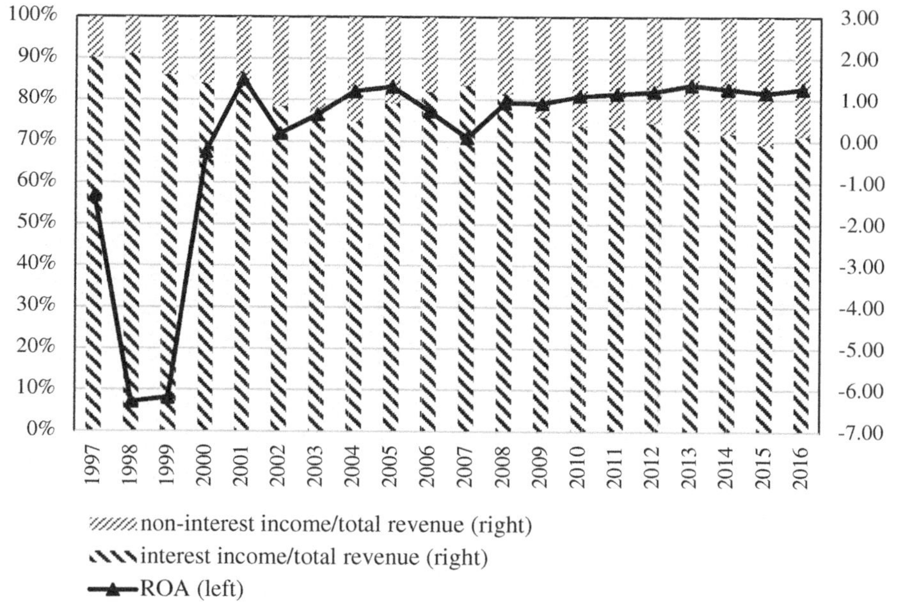

Fig. 4.4 **a** The profit structure of commercial banks 1997–2016. **b** The cost structure of commercial banks 1997–2016. *Source* Revised by the author based on Fig. 4 in Lu (2018), utilizing data from BankScope, Bureau van Dijk

indicates that since the year, the commercial banks have recovered from the crisis, and entered a new phase for the launch of new business.

In the profit–cost structure, the non-interest income ratio, which reflects the revenue from fees and commissions for banking services such as funds transfer services and securities sales, has not shown any significant change from the AFC to 2010. On the other hand, the ratio of interest income to total income kept on accruing until 2007–2008. It implies that commercial banks have continued to depend on net interest income as major profit source. The traditional lending operations still plays the leading role in banking business. In particular, along with the increasing domestic consumption, commercial banks have expanded business in various aspects of personal loan, hire purchase, housing loan and credit card. However, the non-interest income ratio has gradually increased since the Global Financial Crisis, along with the second upsurge of foreign bank entry after the AFC.

The net interest income showed a significant increase from 1.4–2.0% in early 2000s to 2.8–3.2% in late 2000s. As described in Chap. 2, one of the major goals of Financial Sector Master Plan Phase I was to improve the market competition condition through the enhancement of prudential supervision, and the promotion of new market entry. However, the market concentration condition was strengthened as indicated in the high total assets ratio of large-sized banks (Big 4). The increase of net interest income is consistent with the continuous high level of market oligopoly, which is considered to be related to the deterioration of market competition condition.

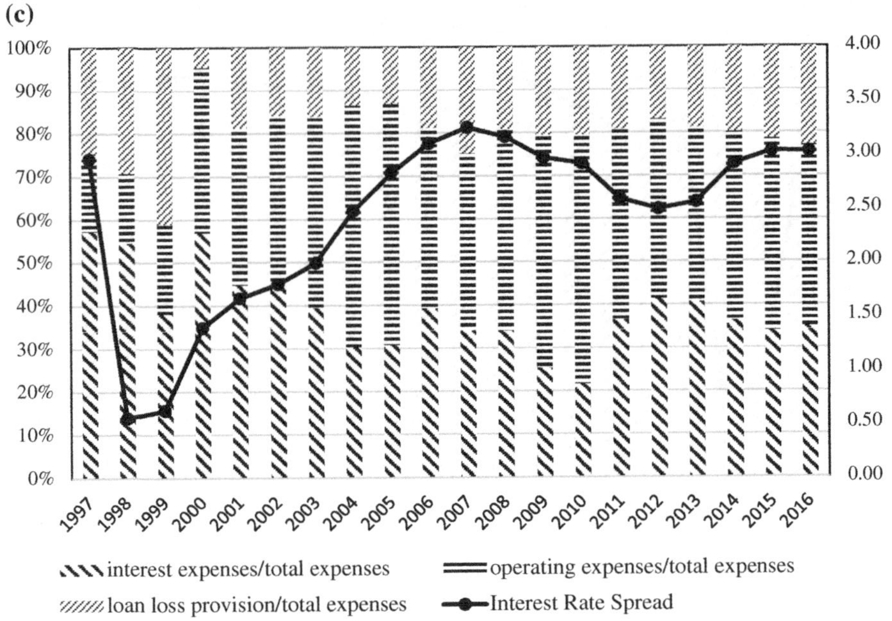

Fig. 4.4 (continued)

Furthermore, the operating expenses has fluctuated from 2.0–2.5%. As aforementioned, through the increasing foreign bank entry and deregulation on foreign investment since the AFC, the introduction of advanced financial technology, management skills and financial innovation to commercial banking market is highly expected by financial authorities. However, the poor improvement of operation efficiency suggests that the policy goal above has not been realized as expected.

4.4.4 The Profit–Cost Structure—Comparison by Ownership

Table 4.3 exploit major financial indicators in bank-level to make an explicit illustration on the change of banking performance. They capture the difference among major large-sized banks, representative middle-sized banks and small-sized banks on one hand; and to examine the difference between domestic banks and foreign banks.

Return on Assets

Table 4.3 illustrates the change of average Return on Assets of Big 4 banks (including Bangkok, Siam Commercial Bank, KasikornBank and Krung Thai Bank), the selected middle-sized foreign banks United Overseas Bank (UOB) and CIMB

Table 4.3 The change of return on assets of selected banks

Year	ROA				
	Average of Big 4 (%)	TMB (%)	Standard chartered bank (%)	United overseas bank (%)	CIMB (%)
1999	−6.7	−3.5	−0.8	−7.4	
2000	1.7	−7.5	−3.3	−2.6	
2001	0.1	0.2	−1.1	−2.4	
2002	0.1	0.0	0.7	−1.9	
2003	1.3	−3.7	1.2	1.1	
2004	1.6	0.1	1.2	0.5	
2005	1.9	1.1	1.4	0.5	
2006	1.6	−1.6	2.4	0.3	
2007	1.7	−7.1	1.4	−0.1	
2008	1.7	0.0	1.2	0.9	
2009	1.6	0.4	1.0	0.5	0.1
2010	1.7	0.6	1.1	0.9	0.7
2011	1.8	0.5	1.4	0.5	0.8
2012	1.9	0.2	1.6	0.8	0.7
2013	2.0	0.9	1.4	0.9	0.4
2014	1.6	1.2	0.7	0.6	0.3
2015	1.3	1.1	0.1	0.7	0.2
2016	1.3	1.0	0.2	0.8	−0.4

(since its entry in 2009), the selected middle-sized domestic bank TMB, and the small-sized foreign bank Standard Chartered Bank (SCBT), which entered banking market in an early stage.

It has been found that the average ROA of Big 4 banks is generally 1% higher than foreign banks, such as UOB, CIMB and SCBT. In addition, the difference between the almost same middle-sized domestic bank TMB and foreign bank UOB is not significant. Both TMB and UOB show a lower profit ratio than the small-sized bank SCBT.

Among the foreign banks, SCBT shows a better performance on banking profitability than UOB and CIMB, especially during the period before the global financial crisis. This difference of ROA has been shrunken to a large extent since 2008. As explained in last chapter, after the global financial crisis, one important change of commercial banking market is active foreign bank entry from neighbor countries. These ASEAN and East Asian foreign banks have enhanced the on-going preparation for the upcoming AEC era, expanded customer base in the region, and placed more attention on the improvement of performance and competitiveness.

In general, it has been found that the large-sized banks enjoy a higher profit ratio, which is considered to be resulted from the high level of market concentration and oligopoly. Out of expectation, the foreign banks do not show any advantage on profitability than the same-sized domestic banks. Rather than the bank ownership type, the relative bank size makes a more significant difference in terms of profitability.

Expense Ratio (Operating Expense)

Table 4.4 describes the change of expense ratio. It shows that the expense ratio of large-sized banks is lower than foreign bank UOB and CIMB, and also lower than TMB, which suggests a superior operation efficiency in large-sized banks. Similar to the outstanding performance on profitability, the small-sized foreign bank SCBT also keeps a relatively low expense ratio, which is almost equal to the average ratio of large-sized banks.

For the middle-sized banks, the expense ratio of UOB is very close to the same size domestic bank TMB, and significantly higher than CIMB. These facts seem to suggest that the foreign banks have not been more efficient than domestic banks, being contradict to the hypothesis that foreign bank is supposed to be more efficient due to their advantage on banking management experience and financial skills.

Table 4.4 The change of operating expense ratio (operating expense/total assets) of selected banks

Year	Operating expense ratio (operating expense/total assets)				
	Average of Big 4 (%)	TMB (%)	Standard chartered bank (%)	United overseas bank (%)	CIMB (%)
1999	2.0	1.8	4.2	2.0	
2000	2.0	1.8	4.2	2.4	
2001	2.0	1.7	4.0	2.5	
2002	1.9	1.8	4.2	2.6	
2003	1.7	2.0	4.1	2.4	
2004	1.9	1.2	4.6	2.6	
2005	2.0	1.6	2.4	2.0	
2006	2.2	2.5	2.4	2.7	
2007	2.2	4.8	2.1	2.8	
2008	2.1	2.5	1.6	2.7	
2009	2.2	2.8	1.7	2.5	3.5
2010	2.0	2.0	2.2	2.4	3.0
2011	1.9	1.9	1.8	2.2	2.6
2012	1.7	1.9	2.1	2.0	2.3
2013	1.8	1.8	1.9	1.9	1.8
2014	1.8	1.9	2.4	2.1	2.1
2015	1.9	1.9	2.6	2.1	1.9
2016	1.9	2.0	1.5	2.1	2.1

Both UOB and CIMB have showed an increase of expense ratio right after the entry, which is supposed to be related to the accruing cost on the integration of new business in the beginning, and a gradual decline afterwards.

Interest Rate Spread

Table 4.5 illustrates the change of interest rate spread of selected commercial banks. To begin with, the large-sized banks have a significant higher interest rate spread than TMB, which implies that Big 4 banks keep a relatively higher profitability through traditional lending operations. On one hand, it may be resulted from a lower founding cost due to the difference depending on bank size. As described in Chap. 1, the Big 4 banks have a significant market superiority in terms of total banking assets and nationwide branches networks,[3] which is supposed to be positively related to the overall fund-raising cost and thus contribute to a high interest rate spread. On the other hand, such a difference between Big 4 banks and middle-sized banks may also resulted from superior profit opportunities of the former due to the oligopolistic market structure.

In addition, UOB shows a higher interest rate spread than TMB and even close to the average ratio of Big 4, which implies its high competitiveness on lending business. As argued in many existing studies (De Haas, 2014; Claessens et al., 2001, etc.), it may be due to the foreign banks "cherry-pick" the premium clients.

Overall, the large-sized banks have a relatively superior profitability and operation efficiency, which implies their economies of scale and technological superiority in commercial banking sector. In regard to middle-size banks foreign banks, they show a higher interest rate spread as well as a similar expense ratio to the same size domestic banks, which finally resulted in a higher profitability of foreign banks than the same size domestic banks, while still lower than large-sized banks. It is found that the cost following market entry of foreign banks deteriorate operation efficiency to a large extent in an early phase. In general, as argued in existing studies (such as Claessens et al., 2001) that the foreign bank entry may result in the advancement of technology through financial technology transfer, this section barely finds any evidence in the case of Thailand in this regard.

To sum up this subsection, the gradual increase of non-interest income after the global financial crisis that follows a second upsurge of foreign bank entry, indicates the gradual improvement on banking services for fees and commissions in recent years. Nevertheless, the traditional lending operation is still the core profit source of commercial banks. In addition, it is found that commercial banks have shifted the focus of lending operations from traditional main sectors such as manufacturing and wholesale/retail commerce to personal consumption and finance sector.

[3] Table 1.2 of Chap. 1, "Number of Commercial Banks and Branches" list the detail branch numbers of Big 4 banks, and the branches ratio of Big 4 to total branches is keep on accruing from 57% in 1997 to 66% in 2014.

Table 4.5 The change of interest rate spread of selected banks

Year	Interest rate spread				
	Average of Big 4 (%)	TMB (%)	Standard chartered bank (%)	United overseas bank (%)	CIMB (%)
1999	1.0	0.6	0.8	0.9	
2000	1.8	0.6	1.8	1.7	
2001	2.1	1.0	2.8	2.1	
2002	2.1	1.4	4.8	2.2	
2003	2.2	1.7	5.3	2.2	
2004	2.7	1.6	6.5	2.4	
2005	3.2	2.0	3.9	2.2	
2006	3.4	2.0	4.7	3.3	
2007	3.4	2.6	4.0	3.1	
2008	3.3	2.7	2.5	3.4	
2009	3.0	2.4	2.7	3.0	3.5
2010	2.8	1.8	2.5	3.0	2.9
2011	2.9	2.0	2.8	2.6	2.5
2012	2.7	2.4	3.2	2.6	2.2
2013	2.8	2.7	3.4	2.7	1.9
2014	3.3	3.3	4.5	3.6	2.7
2015	3.2	3.4	3.9	3.4	2.8
2016	3.3	3.7	1.0	3.3	3.1

Source Tables (4.3–4.5) Revised and updated by the author based on Figs. 5.1 and 5.2 in Lu (2018) and Figs. 6–8, 9 and 10 in Mieno and Lu (2020), utilizing data from BankScope, Bureau van Dijk
Note Bank Thai was acquired by CIMB (Malaysia) to be CIMB (Thailand) in May 2009

4.5 Conclusions

For the past two decades since the AFC, the traditional commercial banking system has been changed dramatically. A long process of reorganization and financial reform is implemented through 2000s to 2010s, which places great emphases on strengthening market competition through new entries and improving market stability and soundness through continuous capital reinforcement. By means of a comprehensive observation on the structural evolvement of commercial banking sector, it is found that a number of traditional founding families losing the ownership control of the bank, while the foreign presence has increased to a significant level.

On one hand, new foreign bank players that mainly from ASEAN and East Asia, have entered Thai market mainly through the merges of small and medium-sized commercial banks. The accruing foreign bank entry, coupled with the establishment of small and medium-sized domestic banks, has resulted in an increase of total bank numbers that compared with the stable system of 15 banks for many decades before the AFC.

On the other hand, a large sum of foreign investment has flowed into large-sized commercial banks, the Big 4 banks in particular. This change has resulted in a further capital reinforcement in major banks. As a result, the overall market concentration condition gets strengthened, which is considered to deteriorate the overall market competition condition to a certain extent.

Under such a change of market structure and competitive environment, it is found that the commercial banks continue to depend on the traditional lending operations, as the net interest income remain as major profit source. The focus of bank credits has been shifted from manufacturing sector and wholesale/retail commerce sector to the finance sector and personal consumption.

In terms of banking performance, it is found that the large-sized banks have a generally higher profitability than the small and medium-sized banks, on account of their dominance position in the oligopoly market, and the economies of scale. Consequently, the major banks are more engaged in a mutual competitive condition among themselves, rather than competing with small and medium-sized banks, including foreign bank players.

In regard to the small and medium-sized banks, foreign banks have a higher interest rate spread as well as a similar operation efficiency compare with the same size domestic banks. The financial technological advance of foreign banks has hardly been proved, as the general performance of foreign banks is inferior to large-sized banks. In addition, the improvement of market competition condition through foreign bank entry is also found to be very limited due to their relatively small sizes.

Chapter 5
An Empirical Analysis of the Policy Impact of Foreign Investment Deregulation in the Banking Sector

Abstract This chapter is dedicated to the empirical examination of the long-term policy impacts of deregulation on foreign investment, initiated by reforms following the Asian Financial Crisis. It assesses the effects of increased foreign penetration in the banking sector by analyzing bank-level panel data from Thai commercial banks from 2000 to 2015. This analysis focuses on profitability, operational expenses, and risk management of commercial banks. By differentiating between the impacts of market-level entry of foreign banks and bank-level foreign ownership, the results indicate that increased foreign ownership at the individual bank level leads to higher interest rate spreads and operational expenses, while also improving loan quality. Conversely, the entry of foreign banks into the market correlates with higher returns on assets, increased non-interest income, wider interest rate spreads, and lower operational expenses. In summary, the presence of foreign banks significantly enhances long-term banking performance.

5.1 Introduction

Since late 2000s, the Association of Southeast Asian Nations (ASEAN) regional formation process has been accelerated on both business and political levels. On the one hand, along with the inauguration of the ASEAN Economic Community (AEC), the ASEAN Banking Integration Framework (ABIF) was endorsed in 2014, aiming to provide Qualified ASEAN Banks (QAB) with better access to regional markets, and more flexibility in their operations (Lu and Mieno, 2020). On the other hand, this regionalization boom has drawn more and more attention and participants, particularly investment from its neighboring countries. Either to follow their home customers, or to pursue local profit opportunities, foreign bank penetration, mainly from the East and Southeast Asia area, is forecasted to grow larger and larger in scale. For a typical example, in Thailand, among the nine foreign banks of the total nineteen commercial banks, seven are from the East and Southeast Asia area, and four entered the Thai banking market in the past four years. In order to examine the effects of foreign entry on the banking industry, this study focuses on the Thai

W. Lu, *Post-Asian Financial Crisis Reforms in Thailand*,
SpringerBriefs in Economics, https://doi.org/10.1007/978-981-97-3771-0_5

banking sector, by using a sample covering more than 95% of commercial banks over a relatively long term, since the financial deregulation after the Asian financial crisis (AFC) (Lu and Mieno, 2020).

Despite the onset of financial liberalization in Thailand in the early 1990s, entry regulations for foreign banks remained stringent prior to the 1997 financial crisis. These banks were prohibited from obtaining full commercial banking licenses, being permitted only to establish branches. (Chantapong, 2001). During this time, the regulatory oversight of commercial banks at the national level has faced criticism for perpetuating inadequate corporate governance and endorsing lending practices that are not only inefficient but also exhibit nepotism, alongside pervasive corruption. These practices are widely regarded as central catalysts for the AFC.

During the crisis, numerous financial firms and commercial banks declared bankruptcy, underwent nationalization, or were subjected to mergers and acquisitions by foreign entities. International financial assistance recommended financial restructuring and deregulation as means to facilitate economic reform and recovery, aiming to improve transparency, competitiveness, and discipline within financial markets and institutions, thereby enhancing efficiency (Lauridsen, 1998; Lu and Mieno, 2020). In this context, as noted in Chap. 1, Thailand's banking sector experienced substantial changes in ownership, including among those banks that remained operational. Notably, foreign ownership increased significantly, while the shares held by traditional, major founding families generally declined.

By 2016, twenty years after the market restructuring, the Asian economy had returned to its typical growth trajectory, predominantly driven by the export of manufactured goods and primary commodities. During this period, the banking sector in Thailand witnessed profound transformations: the overall configuration of banking institutions underwent dramatic changes, and there was a marked increase in foreign capital, facilitated by the establishment of new banking entities and substantial investments in existing banks.

However, against this backdrop, only a limited number of empirical studies have explored the impact of foreign entries on the Asian banking market, with the majority of these investigations concentrating on the short-term effects immediately following the AFC. This chapter aims to provide insights into the relatively long-term impacts of the rapid increase in foreign participation in the banking sector post-crisis. It seeks to assess whether the deregulatory measures on foreign investments have achieved the policy objectives outlined in the Financial Sector Master Plan. Additionally, this study tests the widely supported hypothesis that foreign entry enhances competition within the banking industry and improves its overall performance and functionality over the long term. Furthermore, it also explore the performance disparities between domestic and foreign banks, taking into consideration the market structure and scale effects.

This study includes six sections.[1] Section 5.2 reviews the literature related to the effects of foreign entry on the banking market. Section 5.3 provides the methodology used in this empirical study and attempts to establish a systemic and comprehensive set of measures for foreign entry. Section 5.4 contains a descriptive observation of the changes in the Thai banking sector since the 1997 AFC. Finally, empirical analysis and a conclusion are presented in Sects. 5.5 and 5.6.

5.2 Literature Review

The existing empirical studies on the impact of foreign bank entry on domestic banking markets can be generally divided into three genres: examining the effects of foreign entry across countries or focusing on a single country; examining the short term foreign entry effects, or long-term effects if we define long term as no less than a Juglar Cycle of seven to ten years[2]; examining the effect of restricted foreign bank entry, the effect of foreign ownership evolution, or both.

The assessment of the cross-country impacts of foreign bank entries utilizes panel data from the financial statements of banks, as demonstrated in studies by Claessens et al. (2001), Wu et al. (2017) and Uiboupin (2004), among others. These analyses offer a comprehensive view of the effects of international bank presence on local financial institutions in various countries. Most examinations of foreign entry's effects focusing on a particular country are related to European or Latin American or Asian countries, including those by Bhattacharaya (1993, 1997), Clarke et al. (1999), and Barajas et al. (2000), Unite and Sullivan (2003), Chantapong (2005), Okuda and Rungsomboon (2007) and Prasai (2016).

Wu et al. (2017) investigates the impact of foreign bank entries on the risk profiles of domestic banks in emerging markets. Utilizing bank-level data across 35 economies from 2000 to 2014. Their findings indicate that the risk exposure of domestic banks increases with the growing presence of foreign banks in these countries. This correlation was consistently observed across various robustness tests. In addition, the negative impacts were notably more pronounced in domestic banks that were less efficient and less engaged in traditional banking operations.

Uiboupin (2004) aims to empirically assess the immediate impacts of foreign bank entries on the performance of banks within Central and Eastern European (CEE) countries. Using a dataset that includes 219 banks across ten CEE nations (Bulgaria, Croatia, the Czech Republic, Estonia, Hungary, Latvia, Lithuania, Poland, Slovenia, Slovakia), this study investigates how these entries affect the financial health of local

[1] The methodology, data and empirical analysis presented in this chapter have been updated and revised by the author, utilizing the methodology, data, and empirical analysis from Lu and Mieno (2020) with the consent of all authors.

[2] The Juglar Cycle is one of the most widely acknowledged types of economic or business cycle. It is a fixed investment cycle of 7–10 years, identified in 1862 by Clément Juglar. There is a lack of formal and accurate definition for "long-term" in relation to economics. Generally, in practical applications, long term is considered to be no less than a Juglar Cycle of 7–10 years.

banks. The findings suggest that the presence of foreign banks generally reduces domestic banks' earnings from interest-bearing assets and non-interest income, as well as overall profitability. Moreover, the entry of foreign banks can temporarily elevate operational costs for local banks. The overarching conclusion is that foreign bank entries typically intensify market competition in the host countries, challenging local banks to adapt and innovate.

Unite and Sullivan (2003) and Alberto et al. (2018) analyze the impact of easing foreign entry regulations on Philippine banks, covering different periods (1990–1998 and 1994–2010, respectively). Unite and Sullivan observe that foreign bank entry initially reduces interest rate spreads and profits, particularly when these banks are part of domestic family businesses. They note a decrease in non-lending activities and an increase in operational costs due to higher foreign involvement, suggesting that increased foreign scrutiny prompts domestic banks to concentrate more on traditional banking, thereby raising intermediation and operational costs. Despite these challenges, they acknowledge that foreign entry generally enhances operational efficiencies but worsens risk control measures. Conversely, Alberto et al. (2018) uses an unbalanced panel of 34 banks and a fixed-effects model to show that foreign bank entry positively influences bank profitability based on net interest margin, although this effect diminishes with other profitability metrics. They conclude that the benefits of foreign bank liberalization, such as improved profitability and efficiency, manifest significantly only with substantial foreign ownership in the domestic banking sector.

Prasai (2016) investigates the influence of foreign bank participation through joint ventures on the performance of domestic banks in Nepal. It analyzes data from six joint venture banks and 15 non-joint venture commercial banks from 2008 to 2014, totaling 147 observations. The study employs a causal-comparative design to examine how various factors associated with joint venture banks affect the performance of non-joint venture banks. The performance metrics for non-joint venture banks include profitability, credit risk, and liquidity. The findings indicate that the presence of joint venture banks significantly impacts the performance metrics of non-joint venture commercial banks. In particular, the capital adequacy ratio and return on assets of joint venture banks are crucial in influencing the profitability of non-joint venture banks. Moreover, factors such as the foreign bank share in joint ventures, the number and age of joint venture banks, their capital adequacy ratio, and the real GDP growth rate play significant roles in affecting the credit risk faced by non-joint venture banks.

Chantapong (2005) and Okuda and Rungsomboon (2007) both analyze the Thai banking sector, focusing on different aspects influenced by external pressures and regulatory changes. Chantapong utilizes cross-bank time series data from 1995 to 2000, finding that Thai banks reduced credit exposure during the crisis and improved profitability post-crisis. Okuda and Rungsomboon extend their study period from 1990 to 2002, examining 17 domestic commercial banks to assess the impact of foreign ownership changes. Their analysis reveals that increased foreign bank presence heightens overhead expenses and interest spreads while reducing domestic banks' profits. Initially, foreign investment was minimal, with significant foreign bank entries beginning in 1998. They suggest that while short-term effects of foreign competition are negative for domestic banks, the long-term impact could improve domestic bank performance, aligning with findings from Claessens et al. (2001) and subsequent studies.

Despite numerous empirical studies on the effects of foreign bank entry, there remain significant gaps in the theoretical and empirical frameworks used. Both cross-country and single-country analyses struggle to fully account for or isolate the impacts of external and internal changes in the economic environment, political climate, and financial reforms. These include ongoing effects from regional integration initiatives, such as the endorsement of the ABIF and the establishment of the AEC, on local banking markets. The theoretical underpinnings and analyses of this topic are limited.

Levine (1996) offers one of the most comprehensive theoretical frameworks on the advantages and disadvantages of foreign bank entry. He suggests that foreign banks enhance connections between home countries and international financial markets, increase foreign investment, intensify market competition, and help local banks improve management skills and technology. They also facilitate more international transactions, which can promote the enhancement of financial supervisory and regulatory systems. However, foreign banks may also overpower local markets with their superior skills and capital, lead to capital flight due to stronger connections with international markets, typically focus on multinational enterprises and affluent individuals, struggle to maintain long-term cooperative relationships with host countries during crises, and potentially destabilize local financial markets due to inadequate supervisory and regulatory frameworks in the host countries.

5.3 Methodology and Data

This study employs panel data at the bank-level from commercial banks operating in Thailand over the period from 2000 to 2015. This dataset includes various bank types—local private banks, state-owned banks, joint-venture banks, and foreign subsidiaries[3]—which collectively represent more than 95% of the total assets in Thailand's commercial banking sector. The sources of this data include the Bank of Thailand, the World Bank, the Stock Exchange of Thailand, and Bank Scope. Historically, the number of commercial banks in Thailand has not exceeded 20, which allows for reduced sample heterogeneity given the uniform financial regulation and supervision across Thai provinces.

[3] According to the classification by the Financial Institution Business Act B.E.2551 in 2008, commercial banks in Thailand are comprised of Thai commercial banks, Foreign Commercial Bank Branches, and Foreign Commercial Bank Subsidiaries. Furthermore, Thai commercial banks can be divided into local private banks, state-owned banks, and joint-venture banks (with more than 50% foreign ownership). Besides these, there are Retail Banks that have a narrow business scope focusing on small and medium enterprises due to a limitation of bank license. In this study, our sample covers most Thai commercial banks and foreign commercial bank subsidiaries. Foreign Commercial Bank Branches and Retail Banks (because of their small size and limited business scope) and are outside of our consideration. If given without specific explanation, "all commercial banks" in this study covers the same range of Thai commercial banks and Foreign Commercial Bank Subsidiaries.

Following the AFC, Thailand implemented significant policy reforms concerning foreign investment regulations. These changes facilitated a substantial increase in foreign bank entries, contrasting with their minimal presence prior to 1998. To circumvent the immediate post-crisis instability, this analysis begins in the year 2000. The investigation aims to assess the impact of these foreign banks' entry, utilizing a theoretical framework consistent with Eq. (5.3.1) from Claessens et al. (2001), alongside insights from other earlier studies.

$$\Pi = \text{net interest income} + \text{non} - \text{interest income}-\text{overhead}-\text{loan loss provision} \quad (5.3.1)$$

This study assesses banking performance across three dimensions: profitability, operational efficiency, and risk management. To isolate the impacts of the intrinsic bank architecture and macroeconomic fluctuations, it incorporates bank-specific factors and broad market indicators. A primary focus of this analysis is the examination of foreign bank entry. We aim to engage in an exhaustive and meticulous discussion concerning the extent and quantification of this phenomenon.

5.3.1 Theories on Foreign Entry

Most empirical investigations reviewed primarily examine the impact of the presence or ownership of foreign banks, often utilizing measurement methodologies established by Claessens et al. (2001). These methodologies generally assess foreign bank entry based on the proportion of foreign-owned banks' numbers or assets relative to the overall commercial banking sector. Nevertheless, few studies, including Okuda and Rungsomboon (2007), explicitly adopt foreign ownership as a metric to quantify foreign bank entry. Comprehensive research that precisely delineates and assesses the scope of foreign bank operations is conspicuously scarce, both from empirical and theoretical standpoints (Lu and Mieno, 2020). In response to this gap, this paper advocates for the development of an exhaustive and structured analytical framework to systematically evaluate foreign bank integration.

Foreign banks' market entry involves incursions by both individual and institutional investors, often directly competing with domestic institutions. This conspicuous presence usually attracts increased regulatory scrutiny. Despite the liberalization of financial markets, foreign bank entry remains strictly regulated, leading to delays between their initial market entry and later changes in ownership levels. For example, in Thailand, foreign ownership stakes have been rising since the early 1990s, yet foreign banks were only allowed to enter post-AFC when these stakes exceeded 15%. Unite and Sullivan (2003) examined these dynamics in the Philippines under President Ramos during a period of increased foreign ownership in commercial banks.

Meanwhile, foreign bank entry is posited to influence the domestic market through distinct mechanisms, particularly foreign ownership, unlike broader foreign market penetration. Levine (1996) offers an extensive theoretical framework regarding foreign banks' impact on host countries. In contrast, theories on foreign ownership impacts are more sporadic and less elaborated. Furthermore, Li (2000) suggests that foreign participation may bolster corporate monitoring efficiency by diluting the influence of local ownership structures, which are often relation-based and prevalent in East Asian firms. This governance style has been extensively critiqued within Thailand's banking sector.

Overall, theories and hypotheses concerning foreign bank entry generally adopt a market-wide perspective, aiming to enhance financial competition, improve banking sector performance over the long term, and foster stronger regulatory and legal frameworks. Conversely, foreign ownership analyses are usually conducted from a micro, bank-specific viewpoint, focusing on bettering internal monitoring and mitigating negative managerial behaviors, thereby promoting governance modernization and operational advancements within banks. Some studies conflate these viewpoints, resulting in ambiguous interpretations of the impacts. Consequently, this study seeks to delineate the effects of foreign entry by exploring both macroscopic market and microscopic bank-specific impacts to comprehensively articulate its influence on the domestic banking environment.

5.3.2 Measures of Foreign Entry

The presence of foreign banks is commonly quantified using two ratios: the number of foreign banks relative to total banks (FOR#) and the proportion of assets held by foreign banks compared to total bank assets (FOR%). These measurements hinge on a precise definition of a "foreign bank," which, as per Claessens et al. (2001), generally identifies banks with at least 50% foreign ownership. While this definition is standard in academic studies, it presents challenges in practical applications.

For example, considering major Thai banks such as Siam Commercial Bank and TMB Bank as foreign based on this definition is problematic. Over a sixteen-year period, Siam Commercial Bank was classified as foreign for only five years based on the 50% ownership criterion. Despite this, the Bureau of the Crown Property and Group, its principal shareholder, continued to exert significant influence over its governance. Similarly, TMB Bank was above the 50% foreign ownership threshold for only one year in 2007, by a narrow margin of less than 3%, and the primary foreign stakeholder controlled just 25% of the shares, with the rest held by a diverse group of international investors. These instances underscore the inadequacies and potential misrepresentations of the foreign bank definition in capturing the true extent of foreign influence in cases where ownership does not straightforwardly indicate control.

Yeyati and Micco (2007) propose an alternative method for identifying foreign banks in their analysis of the Latin American banking landscape, defining them as entities where institutions from developed countries control at least 51% of the equity. This approach notably excludes banks under the control of developing country entities, which are often non-financial corporate subsidiaries lacking sophisticated financial expertise.

In contrast, in East and Southeast Asia, foreign-controlled banks frequently stem from adjacent developed nations like Japan, Singapore, China, and Malaysia, and are typically financial institution subsidiaries. Reflecting this regional variation, this study defines a foreign bank as an institution where a single foreign financial entity holds more than 50% ownership.

To validate our analysis of foreign bank entry, this study applies both the number ratio (FOR#) and assets ratio (FOR%) of foreign banks as evaluative metrics. These dual metrics are employed to diminish biases that might arise from using a singular measurement approach. Additionally, it engages in a comparative performance analysis of foreign versus domestic banks to better understand the impacts and mechanisms of foreign bank operations in these markets. This comprehensive methodological framework ensures the robustness of the findings and provides a detailed perspective on the influence of foreign banks.

5.3.3 Variables and Data

Therefore, this study formulates the empirical model as presented in Eq. (5.3.2), aligning it with Eq. (2) in Lu and Mieno (2020). This model utilizes F_{it} to evaluate bank performance, which encompasses aspects of profitability, operational efficiency, and risk assessment. MFP_t is employed to depict the extent of foreign bank entry and its market-level implications, while BFP_{it} serves as the metric for assessing the degree of foreign ownership at the individual bank level. Additionally, B_{it} captures bank-specific factors, and M_t includes various market indicators, notably macroeconomic variables, to provide a comprehensive view of the market's condition:

$$F_{it} = \alpha_0 + \beta_1 MFP_t + \beta_2 BFP_{it} + \beta_3 B_{it} + \beta_4 M_t + \varepsilon_{it} \tag{5.3.2}$$

In this setup, F_{it} quantifies the performance metrics of individual banks at time t, integrating financial robustness and efficiency measures. MFP_t and BFP_{it} are pivotal in evaluating the influence of foreign entities on both the broader market and specific banks, respectively. The inclusion of B_{it} and M_t allows for a nuanced analysis that considers both internal bank dynamics and external economic factors, facilitating a thorough investigation of the factors influencing bank performance within the context of increasing global financial integration. All the variables in this model are defined in Table 5.1.

Tables 5.2 and 5.3 delineates essential financial metrics for banks spanning from 2000 to 2015, covering return on assets (ROA), non-interest income, interest rate spread, operating expenses, and loan loss reserves. The non-interest income to total assets ratio serves as an indicator of non-lending financial activities, including investment banking operations. The interest rate spread is defined by the difference between the interest income ratio from loans and the interest expense ratio on deposits.

Table 5.1 Definition of dependent variables and independent variables

Variables	Definition
Dependent variables	
Profitability	
ROA	Ratio of annual net income to total assets of bank i at time t
Non-interest Income/ta (NII)	Ratio of non-interest income to total assets of bank i at time t
Interest Rate Spread (IRS)	The difference in lending rate on total loans and borrowing rate on total deposits of bank *i* at time *t*
Operating efficiency	
Overhead/ta (OE)	Ratio of operating expenses to total assets of bank *i* at time *t*
Risk control	
Loan Loss Reserve/ta (LLR)	Ratio of loan loss reserves to total assets of bank *i* at time *t*
Independent variables	
I. Foreign presence proxies	
Market-level Foreign Penetration (MFP)	
Ratio of Foreign Bank Numbers (FOR#)	Ratio of foreign bank numbers to total bank numbers at time t
Ratio of Foreign Bank Assets (FOR%)	Ratio of foreign bank assets to total bank assets at time *t*
Bank-level Foreign Penetration (BFP)	
Ratio of Foreign Ownership (FOW)	Ratio of foreign ownership of bank *i* at time *t*
Dummy of Foreign Bank (FD)	A dummy variable equals to 1 if a bank's foreign ownership is more than 50% and it is controlled by institutions with headquarters abroad
II. Bank specific factors	
Non-interest Earning Assets/ta (NIA)	Ratio of non-interest earning assets (cash, non-interest earning deposits at other banks, and other non-interest earning assets) to total assets of bank *i* at time t
Equity/ta (EQU)	Ratio of shareholders equity to total assets of bank *i* at time *t*
Overhead/ta (OE)	Ratio of operating expenses to total assets of bank *i* at time *t*
Relative Bank Size (RBS)	Ratio of one bank assets to all commercial banks' assets of bank *i* at time *t*
III. Market indicators	
Herfindahl–Hirschman Index (HHI)	A measure of internal market structure of market concentration, a higher index refers to a highly monopolistic market at time *t*

(continued)

Table 5.1 (continued)

Variables	Definition
Real GDP Growth Rate (GDP)	Real GDP growth rate on an annual basis and adjusted for inflation at time *t*
Real Interest Rate (RIR)	The nominal interest rate after allowing for inflation at time *t*
Inflation Rate (INF)	The annual percentage change in the consumer price index at time *t*

Note Revised by the author based on Table 4 in Lu and Mieno (2020)

Table 5.2 Descriptive statistics on dependent variables of banking performance of 2000–2008

	2000	2001	2002	2003	2004	2005	2006	2007	2008
ROA (return on assets)									
Average	−1.337	0.956	0.106	0.380	1.049	1.249	0.487	−0.442	0.636
St. dev	3.860	4.247	1.019	1.612	0.687	1.341	1.396	3.173	1.151
Minimum	−7.482	−2.395	−1.885	−3.712	0.141	−2.034	−2.686	−8.785	−2.441
Maximum	7.726	12.789	0.879	1.806	2.451	3.548	1.832	3.243	2.570
IRS (interest rate spread)									
Average	2.065	2.556	2.161	2.317	2.828	2.710	3.035	3.228	3.159
St. dev	2.783	3.009	1.180	1.217	1.450	1.231	1.117	1.119	0.976
Minimum	−0.781	0.025	0.396	0.576	1.345	0.248	0.692	1.705	1.642
Maximum	9.450	10.804	5.102	5.545	6.778	5.186	4.741	6.385	5.942
NII (noninterest-income/ta)									
Average	0.648	0.872	1.043	1.147	0.997	0.762	0.760	0.564	0.639
St. dev	0.428	0.681	0.493	0.297	0.528	0.894	0.409	0.977	0.532
Minimum	0.103	−0.016	0.409	0.658	0.232	−1.557	−0.067	−2.891	−0.661
Maximum	1.314	2.620	2.334	1.715	2.313	2.791	1.419	1.368	1.410
OE (overhead/ta)									
Average	2.303	2.303	1.930	1.999	1.953	1.698	2.338	2.754	2.153
St. dev	0.740	0.729	0.881	0.762	0.982	0.567	0.567	2.052	0.662
Minimum	1.786	1.694	0.924	1.367	0.927	0.405	1.553	1.396	1.308
Maximum	4.187	4.001	4.194	4.103	4.605	2.521	3.729	10.169	4.208
LLR (loan loss reserve/ta)									
Average	8.191	3.814	6.628	6.756	6.037	4.566	3.610	2.957	2.496
St. dev	11.584	2.020	3.578	2.892	2.912	3.403	2.324	1.775	1.825
Minimum	1.074	1.734	1.438	2.370	1.662	0.881	0.812	0.856	0.347
Maximum	37.383	7.310	12.119	9.971	10.355	14.683	10.305	8.170	8.376

Table 5.3 Descriptive statistics on dependent variables of banking performance of 2009–2015

	2009	2010	2011	2012	2013	2014	2015	16-year average
ROA (return on assets)								
Average	0.699	0.989	0.930	0.944	1.148	1.054	0.974	0.638
St. dev	0.580	0.489	0.570	0.687	0.613	0.496	0.472	1.706
Minimum	−0.917	0.311	0.079	−0.562	0.060	0.149	0.118	−8.785
Maximum	1.532	2.384	2.384	2.384	2.384	1.990	1.837	12.789
IRS (interest rate spread)								
Average	3.150	2.996	2.783	2.655	2.781	3.134	3.258	2.834
St. dev	0.574	0.829	0.860	0.881	0.976	0.843	0.923	1.276
Minimum	2.395	1.914	1.631	1.520	1.451	1.575	1.792	−0.781
Maximum	4.241	5.382	5.382	5.382	5.382	4.786	5.804	10.804
NII (noninterest-income/ta)								
Average	0.874	0.879	0.981	0.976	1.064	1.127	1.176	0.897
St. dev	0.388	0.425	0.463	0.486	0.526	0.542	0.571	0.581
Minimum	0.268	0.132	0.214	0.186	0.284	0.296	0.240	−2.891
Maximum	1.549	1.691	1.691	1.692	2.127	2.256	2.438	2.791
OE (overhead/ta)								
Average	2.236	2.056	1.942	1.933	1.830	1.901	1.909	2.065
St. dev	0.638	0.564	0.564	0.612	0.638	0.723	0.754	0.875
Minimum	1.296	1.167	1.073	0.926	0.744	0.725	0.781	0.405
Maximum	3.706	3.205	3.205	3.205	3.205	3.813	4.006	10.169
LLR (loan loss reserve/ta)								
Average	2.573	2.246	2.235	2.186	2.439	2.459	2.616	3.557
St. dev	1.473	1.154	1.033	0.910	0.900	0.782	0.934	3.386
Minimum	0.529	0.743	0.803	0.761	0.964	1.259	1.295	0.347
Maximum	6.628	4.301	4.301	4.301	4.301	3.951	4.475	37.383

Included in operating expenses are both interest-related and other operational expenditures. The loan loss provision ratio relative to total assets is applied as a measure of the banks' risk exposure. The dataset reveals pronounced trends and volatility: during the global financial crisis of 2007–2008, there was a significant downturn in ROA accompanied by a rise in operating expenses. Meanwhile, the interest rate spread initially increased consistently until 2007, followed by variable adjustments in subsequent years. This extensive dataset provides valuable insights into the responses of financial indicators to evolving economic scenarios and shifts within the banking sector over the studied interval.

5.4 Foreign Ownership Evolution in the Commercial Banking Market

Since the late 1980s, Thailand's economy experienced overheating due to capital flow deregulation, asset bubbles, and a fixed exchange rate system. This culminated in a significant financial crisis in 1997, leading to a shortage of foreign reserves, with one-third of commercial banks nationalized and another third bankrupt or acquired by foreign entities. In response, the Thai government, under international guidance from the World Bank and IMF, implemented stringent and transparent banking regulations. It also relaxed foreign ownership rules to rejuvenate the banking sector with necessary capital from beyond domestic business families (Lu and Mieno, 2020).

By 2003–2004, the banking institutions and non-performing loans had largely recovered. As noted in Chap. 2, the Thaksin government introduced the "Financial Master Plan" in 2004 aimed at creating a developed, competitive, and balanced financial system. This plan encouraged foreign bank entries and the establishment of "retail banks" to focus on small-sized lending while restricting domestic conglomerates. A second "Financial Master Plan" was unveiled in 2010, further promoting foreign bank involvement and enhancing financial infrastructure.

Despite these developments, foreign bank entry regulations remained stringent. The Financial Business Act B.E. 2551 (2008) limited foreign ownership in domestic banks, requiring approvals from the Bank of Thailand and the Ministry of Finance for significant stakes. However, by 2013, new policies allowed for increased foreign bank licensing, with recent entries from Japan, Australia, and China, demonstrating a gradual but cautious opening of Thailand's banking sector to international players.

The process of reorganization of commercial banks that occurred between 1997 and 2015 is pictured in Appendix 1. From 1997 to mid-2010s, Thailand's banking sector saw significant reorganization. The large banks like Bangkok Bank, Kasikorn Bank, Siam Commercial Bank, Ayutthaya Bank, and Krung Thai Bank remained stable even during the crisis, with Krung Thai absorbing some troubled banks as a state bank. In contrast, several mid-sized banks including First Bangkok City Bank and Bangkok Bank of Commerce were bankrupted and either nationalized or acquired by larger or foreign banks. Small banks such as Nakornthon Bank were typically purchased by foreign investors.

Post the first "Financial Master Plan" in the late 2000s, foreign bank entry increased; Standard Chartered and United Overseas Bank notably expanded by acquiring local banks. The 2010s saw further foreign entries, including Bank of Tokyo Mitsubishi acquiring Bank of Ayutthaya in 2013 and licenses granted to banks from Japan, Australia/New Zealand, and China in 2015.[4]

Despite these changes, market share and competition conditions between 1997 and 2013 remained relatively stable, with a trend towards market concentration. Interestingly, even large banks increasingly accepted foreign capital, with Bangkok Bank and Siam Commercial Bank having substantial foreign ownership in the 2000s.

[4] See more details on the market reorganization in Lu (2018), pp. 81–83; Lu and Mieno (2020).

This reflects diverse forms of foreign capital integration and suggests a multifaceted approach to analyzing the banking sector's function.

The evolution of foreign participation in Thailand's banking sector is detailed through various metrics in Fig. 4.1, highlighting changes in foreign bank numbers FOR# and assets FOR%. The foreign ownership to total market (FOWA) metric, a weighted average of each bank's foreign ownership based on assets, is also introduced to capture broader ownership trends. As illustrated in Chap. 4, the Thai banking sector is notably concentrated, with the top four banks holding about 65% of total commercial assets, reflected by an average Herfindahl–Hirschman Index (HHI) of 0.13 over 16 years. There was a significant increase in market concentration from 2002 to 2007, coinciding with financial reforms under the Thaksin government, including the creation of retail banks to support small and medium enterprises (SMEs).

Table 5.4 presents the evolution of foreign ownership in commercial banks from 2001 to 2016. Initially, foreign ownership averaged around 20%, primarily from European and Singaporean institutions. This increased to a peak of 45% by 2007–2008, before the global financial crisis, largely concentrated in the larger banks. Post-Lehman Brothers crisis, foreign ownership remained above 40%, with newer entries from Japanese and Chinese banks, marking a shift from earlier Western entrants. The period also saw acquisitions of small and medium banks by foreign entities during 1998–1999, but no new foreign bank entries occurred from 1999 to 2005. This pattern suggests that rising foreign ownership may enhance market concentration and strengthen the dominance of major banks in Thailand.

5.5 Empirical Results and Analysis

Table 5.5 analyzes the influence of foreign bank entry on the Thai banking sector from 2000 to 2015, focusing on both market-level and bank-specific effects attributable to foreign ownership. This assessment employs Eq. (5.3.2) to scrutinize key performance indicators such as return on assets, non-interest income, interest rate spread, operating expenses, and risk levels associated with banks.

Further insights are provided in Table 5.6, which contrasts the performance metrics of foreign banks with domestic banks. This comparison utilizes a 'foreign bank dummy' variable to distinguish between the two groups, enabling a targeted analysis of the differential impacts caused by foreign ownership.

The inquiry extends in Tables 5.7 and 5.8, which examine how the concentration of the market and the size of banks influence the interest rate spread and operating expenses, respectively, during the studied period. These analyses help elucidate the broader market dynamics shaped by the magnitude and density of banking operations.

All regression analyses in this research adopt a random effects model, chosen for its effectiveness in accounting for time-variant influences that a fixed effects model may overlook, including the time-invariant characteristics captured by the 'foreign bank dummy'. This methodological consistency across the datasets allows for a robust comparative analysis of findings from different tables. Additionally, a

Table 5.4 Foreign ownership evolution of commercial banks 2001–2016

ID	Symbol	2001	2002	2003	2004	2005	2006	2007	2008	2009	2010	2011	2012	2013	2014	2015	2016
1	BBL	48.8	48.7	48.3	48.3	48.3	48.1	46.9	44.6	44.0	43.6	43.0	42.9	42.5	35.0	30.7	29.5
		D	D	D	D	D	D	D	D	D	D	D	D	D	D	D	D
2	KTB	3.2	2.1	17.1	12.4	19.9	24.3	20.8	14.9	20.6	21.9	20.9	23.8	20.4	18.1	13.8	12.4
		D	D	D	D	D	D	D	D	D	D	D	D	D	D	D	D
3	KBANK	49.0	49.0	49.0	49.0	49.0	49.0	49.0	49.0	49.0	49.0	49.0	49.0	49.0	49.0	49.0	49.0
		D	D	D	D	D	D	D	D	D	D	D	D	D	D	D	D
4	SCB	41.6	56.3	60.8	52.7	55.5	56.4	56.1	41.3	35.9	34.8	36.0	38.3	37.0	37.3	35.6	32.6
		D	D	D	D	D	D	D	D	D	D	D	D	D	D	D	D
5	BAY	18.5	17.9	23.9	31.3	32.0	31.8	45.9	47.2	47.2	47.2	47.2	47.2	72.5	72.1	76.9	76.9
		D	D	D	D	D	D	D	D	D	D	D	D	F	F	F	F
6	TMB	4.9	4.3	6.6	26.8	39.6	42.4	52.8	47.5	43.7	36.1	34.6	35.1	35.6	39.0	36.8	33.5
		D	D	D	D	D	D	D	D	D	D	D	D	D	D	D	D
7	SCIB	0.0	0.0	4.8	24.0	25.0	25.0	24.9	21.8	22.5	0.0	–	–	–	–	–	–
		D	D	D	D	D	D	D	D	D	D	–	–	–	–	–	–
8	UOBT	1.1	0.9	1.0	97.0	98.6	99.6	99.6	99.7	99.7	99.7	99.7	99.7	99.7	99.7	99.7	99.7
		F	F	F	F	F	F	F	F	F	F	F	F	F	F	F	F
9	SCBT	75.0	75.0	75.0	75.0	99.8	99.8	100.0	100.0	99.9	100.0	100.0	100.0	100.0	100.0	100.0	100.0
		F	F	F	F	F	F	F	F	F	F	F	F	F	F	F	F

(continued)

Table 5.4 (continued)

ID	Symbol	2001	2002	2003	2004	2005	2006	2007	2008	2009	2010	2011	2012	2013	2014	2015	2016
10	CIMBT	0.0	3.9	0.7	5.8	6.0	0.5	37.1	88.2	97.2	97.2	97.2	96.8	96.8	96.8	95.7	95.7
		D	D	D	D	D	D	D	F	F	F	F	F	F	F	F	F
11	TBANK	–	0.1	0.0	0.1	0.0	0.0	25.0	25.0	N.a	N.a	N.a	N.a	N.a	N.a	N.a	N.a
		–	D	D	D	D	D	D	D	N.a	N.a	N.a	N.a	N.a	N.a	N.a	N.a
12	TISCOB	–	–	–	–	44.5	48.6	48.9	40.1	47.3	48.2	47.8	49.0	42.5	48.1	47.0	47.9
		–	–	–	–	D	D	D	D	D	D	D	D	D	D	D	D
13	KKP	–	–	–	–	42.9	44.0	38.8	38.4	32.8	43.2	33.6	38.5	33.6	32.7	34.6	38.4
		–	–	–	–	D	D	D	D	D	D	D	D	D	D	D	D
14	ICBCT	–	–	–	–	38.4	30.0	29.7	26.0	18.1	97.4	97.7	97.7	97.7	97.7	97.7	97.7
		–	–	–	–	D	D	D	D	D	F	F	F	F	F	F	F
15	LHBANK	–	–	–	–	N.a	N.a	N.a	N.a	N.a	N.a	0.2	0.3	0.8	0.9	0	0
		–	–	–	–	N.a	N.a	N.a	N.a	N.a	N.a	D	D	D	D	D	D
16	TCRB	–	–	–	–	–	–	N.a	N.a	N.a	N.a	N.a	N.a	N.a	N.a	N.a	N.a
		–	–	–	–	–	–	N.a	N.a	N.a	N.a	N.a	N.a	N.a	N.a	N.a	N.a
17	MICB	–	–	–	–	N.a	N.a	N.a	N.a	N.a	N.a	N.a	N.a	N.a	N.a	N.a	N.a

(continued)

Table 5.4 (continued)

ID	Symbol	2001	2002	2003	2004	2005	2006	2007	2008	2009	2010	2011	2012	2013	2014	2015	2016
		–	–	–	–	N.a	N.a	N.a	N.a	N.a	N.a	N.a	N.a	N.a	N.a	N.a	N.a
18	BMB	0.0	–	–	–	–	–	–	–	–	–	–	–	–	–	–	–
		0	–	–	–	–	–	–	–	–	–	–	–	–	–	–	–
19	DTDB	58.1	59.7	60.9	–	–	–	–	–	–	–	–	–	–	–	–	–
		1	1	1	–	–	–	–	–	–	–	–	–	–	–	–	–
20	UOBR	75.0	78.8	78.8	83.8	–	–	–	–	–	–	–	–	–	–	–	–
		1	1	1	1	–	–	–	–	–	–	–	–	–	–	–	–
21	AIG	–	–	–	–	–	–	N.a	N.a	N.a	N.a	N.a	N.a	N.a	N.a	N.a	N.a
		–	–	–	–	–	–	N.a	N.a	N.a	N.a	N.a	N.a	N.a	N.a	N.a	N.a
22	GE	–	–	–	–	–	N.a	N.a	N.a	N.a	N.a	N.a	N.a	N.a	N.a	N.a	N.a
		–	–	–	–	–	N.a	N.a	N.a	N.a	N.a	N.a	N.a	N.a	N.a	N.a	N.a

Source Compiled by the author utilizing datasets from the Stock Exchange of Thailand and various annual reports

Note 1. "BBL" = Bangkok Bank, "KTB" = Krung Thai Bank, "KBANK" = Kasikornbank, "SCB" = Siam Commercial Bank, "BAY" = Bank of Ayudhya, "TMB" = TMB Bank, "SCIB" = Siam City Bank, "UOBT" = United Overseas Bank (Thailand), "SCBT" = Standard Chartered (Thailand), "CIMBT" = CIMB Bank (Thailand), "TBANK" = Thanachart Bank, "TISCOB" = Tisco Bank,"KKP" = Kiatnakin Bank, "ICBCT" = Industrial and Commercial Bank Of China (Thailand), "LHBANK" = Land and Houses Bank, "TCBR" = Thai Credit Retail Bank, "MICB" = Mega International Commercial Bank, "BMB" = Bangkok Metropolitan Bank, "DTDB" = DBS Thai Danu Bank, "UOBR" = UOB Radanasin Bank, "AIG" = AIG Retail Bank, "GE" = GE Money Retail Bank

2. According to the Stock Exchange of Thailand, each listed company may have restriction on foreign ownership limit (Foreign Limit). Foreign investors are allowed to convert local shares to foreign shares as long as the Foreign Limit has not yet been reached. In the event that Foreign Limit has been reached, foreign investor conversion request will be placed on a queue (Foreign Queue), and their local shares will be automatically converted to foreign shares if the foreign room becomes available (Foreign Available > 0). Therefore, the foreign ownership share is calculated as the percentage of the Foreign Limit ratio minus Foreign Available ratio. If data of Foreign Limit ratio and/or Foreign Available ratio is not available, the foreign ownership share is calculated as the ratio of the total holding foreign shares to total shares.
3. The foreign shareholding in Thanachart bank increased from 0.02 to 25% in 2008. Subsequently, no further data on foreign shareholdings has been available from the Stock Exchange of Thailand

Table 5.5 The baseline results of commercial banks

	(1) ROA		(2) IRS		(3) NII		(4) OE		(5) LLR	
Market level effect										
FOR#		0.105*** (3.43)		0.0411* (2.52)		0.0181* (2.09)		−0.0223* (−2.47)		−0.260*** (−3.33)
FOR%	0.169*** (3.30)		0.0994*** (3.74)		0.0238 (1.64)		−0.0336* (−2.22)		−0.371** (−2.82)	
Bank level effect										
FOW	−0.00242 (−0.51)	−0.00276 (−0.58)	0.00686** (2.81)	0.00723** (2.91)	0.00152 (0.94)	0.00127 (0.79)	0.00461* (2.49)	0.00479** (2.58)	−0.0246* (−2.13)	−0.0228* (−1.99)
Market condition										
RBS	0.0483* (2.05)	0.0483* (2.05)	0.0359** (3.00)	0.0368** (3.08)	0.0406*** (4.11)	0.0407*** (4.12)	−0.0188 (−1.33)	−0.0187 (−1.33)	0.0251 (0.46)	0.0249 (0.46)
HHI	36.15 (1.16)	−42.44 (−0.99)	−28.79 (−1.78)	−53.60* (−2.33)	20.46* (2.32)	5.966 (0.49)	−24.05** (−2.67)	−6.796 (−0.53)	181.7* (2.26)	384.5*** (3.50)
Control variable										
NIA	−0.0247 (−1.27)	−0.0250 (−1.29)	0.0631*** (6.25)	0.0605*** (5.84)	0.0110 (1.95)	0.0112* (1.99)	0.0172** (2.94)	0.0171** (2.93)	0.0756 (1.52)	0.0739 (1.50)
EQU	0.110** (3.15)	0.110** (3.15)	0.0656*** (3.64)	0.0700*** (3.81)	0.0467*** (4.19)	0.0462*** (4.16)	−0.0182 (−1.48)	−0.0177 (−1.44)	0.122 (1.41)	0.126 (1.46)
OE	0.122 (0.52)	0.140 (0.60)	1.033*** (8.51)	1.030*** (8.26)	0.0393 (0.57)	0.0466 (0.67)			1.067 (1.80)	0.984 (1.67)
GDP	−0.0491 (−0.79)	−0.0544 (−0.89)	−0.00176 (−0.05)	−0.0234 (−0.72)	0.0000218 (0.00)	0.00204 (0.12)	0.00387 (0.21)	0.00373 (0.21)	0.0242 (0.15)	0.00985 (0.06)
RIR	−0.744*** (−9.33)	−0.757*** (−9.41)	−0.245*** (−5.92)	−0.236*** (−5.46)	−0.0570* (−2.52)	−0.0619** (−2.71)	0.0515* (2.20)	0.0553* (2.34)	0.819*** (3.99)	0.875*** (4.25)

(continued)

Table 5.5 (continued)

	(1) ROA		(2) IRS		(3) NII		(4) OE		(5) LLR	
INF	−0.390** (−3.18)	−0.424*** (−3.40)	−0.141* (−2.21)	−0.134* (−2.00)	−0.0512 (−1.48)	−0.0602 (−1.72)	−0.0152 (−0.42)	−0.00652 (−0.18)	0.547 (1.73)	0.660* (2.06)
Intercept	−2.564 (−0.62)	6.018 (1.17)	3.134 (1.45)	5.921* (2.14)	−2.544* (−2.14)	−0.978 (−0.66)	5.135*** (4.28)	3.241* (2.08)	−23.97* (−2.25)	−45.91*** (−3.49)
Obs	193	193	193	193	193	193	193	193	193	193
R^2	0.4563	0.4588	0.5939	0.5789	0.2291	0.235	0.2719	0.2764	0.2454	0.2531

Note The regressions are estimated by a random effects model with a sample that covered more than 95% of all commercial banks in Thailand. All variables are defined in Table 5.1. *denotes 10% level of significance, **denotes 5% level of significance, and ***denotes 1% level of significance

Table 5.6 Comparative analysis of foreign banks and domestic banks

	(1) ROA		(2) IRS		(3) NII		(4) OE		(5) LLR	
Market level effect										
FOR#		0.103***		0.0524**		0.0211**		−0.0233*		−0.266***
		(3.56)		(3.19)		(2.61)		(−1.98)		(−3.88)
FOR%	0.166***		0.108***		0.0299*		−0.0246		−0.384***	
	(3.46)		(4.04)		(2.22)		(−1.24)		(−3.33)	
Bank level effect										
FD	0.0964	0.0749	0.648**	0.651**	0.0866	0.0734	0.0467	0.0807	−1.157	−1.071
	(0.29)	(0.23)	(2.96)	(2.95)	(0.71)	(0.60)	(0.24)	(0.41)	(−1.49)	(−1.39)
Market condition										
RBS	0.0491*	0.0496*	0.0278	0.0291	0.0424***	0.0425***	−0.0205	−0.0199	0.0218	0.0199
	(2.22)	(2.24)	(1.75)	(1.83)	(4.53)	(4.55)	(−1.26)	(−1.22)	(0.42)	(0.39)
HHI	22.19	−55.40	−47.74**	−82.81***	16.33	−0.333	−36.40**	−16.09	185.6*	395.1***
	(0.72)	(−1.31)	(−2.80)	(−3.46)	(1.91)	(−0.03)	(−2.96)	(−0.94)	(2.52)	(3.94)
Control variable										
NIA	−0.0188	−0.0187	0.0680***	0.0658***	0.00906	0.00931	0.0229**	0.0218**	0.107*	0.104*
	(−0.98)	(−0.98)	(6.23)	(5.93)	(1.63)	(1.68)	(2.83)	(2.70)	(2.35)	(2.29)
EQU	0.0369	0.0383	−0.00187	0.000710	0.0226**	0.0229**	0.00274	0.00330	0.0365	0.0340
	(1.66)	(1.72)	(−0.13)	(0.05)	(2.94)	(2.99)	(0.22)	(0.27)	(0.69)	(0.65)
OE	−0.471**	−0.450**	0.418**	0.431**	0.00989	0.0166			0.0987	0.0371
	(−3.22)	(−3.07)	(4.80)	(4.86)	(0.22)	(0.36)			(0.28)	(0.11)
GDP	−0.0444	−0.0505	−0.00202	−0.0193	0.000272	0.00138	0.0209	0.0146	0.0163	0.00419
	(−0.74)	(−0.86)	(−0.06)	(−0.58)	(0.02)	(0.09)	(0.86)	(0.62)	(0.11)	(0.03)
RIR	−0.721***	−0.729***	−0.253***	−0.247***	−0.0619**	−0.0655**	0.0658*	0.0729*	0.878***	0.919***
	(−9.15)	(−9.22)	(−5.78)	(−5.51)	(−2.82)	(−2.98)	(2.06)	(2.29)	(4.64)	(4.88)

(continued)

Table 5.6 (continued)

	(1) ROA		(2) IRS		(3) NII		(4) OE		(5) LLR	
INF	−0.411*** (−3.49)	−0.443*** (−3.69)	−0.177** (−2.71)	−0.178** (−2.62)	−0.0572 (−1.75)	−0.0663* (−2.00)	−0.0248 (−0.52)	−0.00914 (−0.19)	0.582* (2.06)	0.695* (2.43)
Intercept	0.798 (0.20)	9.228 (1.86)	7.650*** (3.47)	11.52*** (4.08)	−1.733 (−1.56)	0.0567 (0.04)	6.551*** (4.17)	4.362* (2.17)	−23.11* (−2.44)	−45.69*** (−3.88)
Obs	217	217	217	217	217	217	217	217	217	217
R^2	0.4208	0.4227	0.4002	0.3882	0.2138	0.2196	0.118	0.1209	0.246	0.2594

Note The regressions are estimated by a random effects model with a sample that covered more than 95% of all commercial banks in Thailand. All variables are defined in Table 5.1. * denotes 10% level of significance, ** denotes 5% level of significance, and *** denotes 1% level of significance

Table 5.7 The regression results of interest rate spread

	Benchmark		(3)	(4)	(5)	(6)
	(1)	(2)				
Market level effect						
FOR%	0.0994*** (3.74)	0.108*** (4.04)	0.0928*** (3.56)	0.117*** (4.44)	0.101*** (3.96)	0.101*** (3.80)
Bank level effect						
FOW	0.00686** (2.81)					
FD		0.648** (2.96)	0.994** (3.09)	1.171*** (3.66)	−8.167* (−2.15)	−8.766* (−2.23)
Market conditions						
RBS	0.0359** (3.00)	0.0278 (1.75)	0.0264 (1.59)	0.0276 (1.66)		0.0294 (1.83)
RBS*FD			−0.179 (−1.70)	−0.226* (−2.18)		
HHI	−28.79 (−1.78)	−47.74** (−2.80)		−53.31** (−3.20)	−64.68*** (−3.74)	−64.31*** (−3.57)
HHI*FD					68.96* (2.32)	74.04* (2.40)
Control variable						
NIA	0.0631*** (6.25)	0.0680*** (6.23)	0.0651*** (5.96)	0.0688*** (6.45)	0.0675*** (6.44)	0.0662*** (6.15)
EQU	0.0656*** (3.64)	−0.00187 (−0.13)	−0.00238 (−0.16)	−0.0149 (−1.00)	−0.0124 (−0.87)	−0.000764 (−0.05)
OE	1.033*** (8.51)	0.418*** (4.80)	0.460*** (5.33)	0.398*** (4.61)	0.316*** (3.57)	0.360*** (4.06)
GDP	−0.00176 (−0.05)	−0.00202 (−0.06)	−0.0482 (−1.65)	0.0000940 (0.00)	−0.000387 (−0.01)	−0.00243 (−0.08)
RIR	−0.245*** (−5.92)	−0.253*** (−5.78)	−0.268*** (−6.12)	−0.256*** (−6.04)	−0.250*** (−6.07)	−0.251*** (−5.86)
INF	−0.141* (−2.21)	−0.177** (−2.71)	−0.108 (−1.79)	−0.183** (−2.90)	−0.182** (−2.97)	−0.180** (−2.81)
Intercept	3.134 (1.45)	7.650*** (3.47)	1.705*** (3.40)	8.462*** (3.92)	10.38*** (4.59)	9.928*** (4.23)
Obs	193	217	217	217	217	217
R^2	0.5939	0.4002	0.3871	0.4018	0.3861	0.4158

Note The regressions are estimated by a random effects model with a sample that covered more than 95% of all commercial banks in Thailand. All variables are defined in Table 5.1. *denotes 10% level of significance, **denotes 5% level of significance, and ***denotes 1% level of significance

Table 5.8 The regression results of operating expenses

	Benchmark		(3)	(4)	(5)	(6)
	(1)	(2)				
Market level effect						
FOR%	−0.0336* (−2.22)	−0.0246 (−1.24)	−0.0413* (−2.12)	−0.0225 (−1.12)	−0.0322 (−1.65)	−0.0322 (−1.67)
Bank level effect						
FOW	0.00461* (2.49)					
FD		0.0467 (0.24)	0.0601 (0.22)	0.177 (0.65)	−10.79*** (−3.82)	−10.58*** (−3.79)
Market condition						
RBS	−0.0188 (−1.33)	−0.0205 (−1.26)	−0.0222 (−1.34)	−0.0194 (−1.18)		−0.0145 (−0.91)
RBS*FD			−0.0253 (−0.31)	−0.0573 (−0.70)		
HHI	−24.05** (−2.67)	−36.40** (−2.96)		−37.41** (−3.02)	−53.79*** (−4.22)	−52.46*** (−4.16)
HHI*FD					85.53*** (3.87)	83.51*** (3.81)
Control variable						
NIA	0.0172** (2.94)	0.0229** (2.83)	0.0215** (2.60)	0.0229** (2.82)	0.0194* (2.42)	0.0186* (2.35)
EQU	−0.0182 (−1.48)	0.00274 (0.22)	0.00918 (0.74)	0.00123 (0.10)	0.00705 (0.62)	0.00646 (0.54)
GDP	0.00387 (0.21)	0.0209 (0.86)	−0.0133 (−0.61)	0.0210 (0.87)	0.0189 (0.80)	0.0186 (0.79)
RIR	0.0515* (2.20)	0.0658* (2.06)	0.0596 (1.83)	0.0650* (2.03)	0.0639* (2.04)	0.0640* (2.07)
INF	−0.0152 (−0.42)	−0.0248 (−0.52)	0.0276 (0.61)	−0.0257 (−0.54)	−0.0270 (−0.58)	−0.0256 (−0.55)
Intercept	5.135*** (4.28)	6.551*** (4.17)	2.034*** (5.41)	6.669*** (4.22)	8.675*** (5.31)	8.624*** (5.34)
Obs	193	217	217	217	217	217
R^2	0.5939	0.4002	0.3871	0.4018	0.3861	0.4158

Note The regressions are estimated by a random effects model with a sample that covered more than 95% of all commercial banks in Thailand. All variables are defined in Table 5.1. *denotes 10% level of significance, **denotes 5% level of significance, and ***denotes 1% level of significance

robustness check using a fixed effects model was conducted for the regressions in Table 5.5 to ensure the stability of the results across different modeling assumptions. This comprehensive approach strengthens the credibility of the conclusions regarding the effects of foreign bank entry on the banking industry in Thailand.

The principal results of the baseline empirical analysis are detailed below, focusing on several critical financial metrics: (1) ROA, which measures overall profitability; (2) interest rate spread, indicating the difference between the interest income generated and the interest paid out; (3) non-interest income, reflecting revenue from alternative financial services outside of traditional interest-earning activities; (4) operational efficiency, assessing the effectiveness of bank management in controlling costs relative to its operations; and (5) loan loss reserves, a key indicator of future expected losses and financial robustness. These metrics collectively provide a comprehensive overview of the financial health and operational performance of banks.

5.5.1 Baseline Empirical Analysis

(1) Table 5.5 demonstrates that the ROA is significantly and positively correlated with foreign bank entry, a result consistent across two analytical models. This outcome is in stark contrast to the findings of Claessens et al. (2001), which suggested that a higher presence of foreign banks is associated with decreased profitability. The discrepancy between these studies may be explained by the beneficial impacts of foreign bank penetration on increasing non-interest income, widening interest rate spreads, and reducing operating expenses. These factors collectively contribute to the observed positive effect on ROA.

Furthermore, fluctuations in the degree of foreign ownership (FOW) do not appear to significantly impact the ROA, a finding that is consistent with the observations made by Unite and Sullivan (2003). Additionally, the analysis identifies a positive correlation between the capital adequacy ratio and ROA. This suggests that banks with higher levels of equity are better positioned to enhance their profitability over the long term, likely due to improved financial stability and lending capacity.

(2) In terms of the interest rate spread, the empirical results shows that both the presence and the degree of foreign ownership are positively associated with the interest rate spreads in commercial banks.

According to Feldstein (2002), foreign bank entry is associated with negative impacts on interest rate spread, which is theorized to arise from foreign banks' tendency to "cherry-pick" the most creditworthy borrowers, relegating riskier and less profitable loans to domestic banks. This strategy forces domestic banks to adopt conservative lending practices and diligently manage their loan portfolios against foreign competition. Consequently, domestic banks might see reduced interest income and heightened interest expenses as they intensify deposit attraction efforts, which should logically compress the interest rate spread.

However, despite expectations that foreign bank entry (quantified by FOR% and FOR#) would intensify market competition, the findings in Table 5.5 suggest it may actually diminish it, leading to increased interest income while domestic banks continue to excel in deposit acquisition. The greater presence of foreign banks could lessen overall market competition by promoting product differentiation, leveraging brand value, and utilizing the implicit support of parent companies, thereby creating a less competitive industry (Yeyati & Micco, 2007). This complex dynamic challenges the traditional assumption that increased market concentration deteriorates competition, proposing instead that foreign bank entry may cultivate a distinctively competitive landscape with diverse banking products and services.

Meanwhile, Table 5.5 also indicates that an increase in foreign ownership (quantified by FOW) is positively correlated with an increase in the interest rate spread, which can be attributed to a combination of higher interest income and reduced interest expenses. Notably, foreign investments predominantly target larger banks within the Thai banking sector (as indicated in Table 5.4), which may lead to enhanced market concentration. This concentration enables larger domestic banks to predominate in deposit absorption, effectively lowering their interest expenses. Additionally, elevated foreign ownership levels are likely to bolster a bank's perceived creditworthiness, consequently decreasing the costs associated with deposit attraction due to the enhanced perception of financial stability.

Furthermore, the analysis demonstrates a positive correlation between the relative bank size (RBS) and the interest rate spread, indicating that larger banks typically enjoy higher spreads. This finding contrasts with the observations of Unite and Sullivan (2003), who did not identify a similar pattern within the Philippine banking sector. This variance underscores how distinct market structures and regulatory environments influence the operational dynamics and competitive strategies of commercial banks in Thailand. Specifically, it illustrates the manner in which large-sized banks interact with the market through their pricing strategies. These banks often exploit their scale and the perceived stability offered by foreign ownership to adjust interest rates favorably, thus widening their interest rate spreads compared to smaller institutions. This strategic differentiation in pricing not only reflects the banks' competitive tactics but also their adaptive responses to the concentrated market conditions enhanced by foreign investment in the post-crisis era.

Additionally, Table 5.6 indicates that foreign banks consistently achieve higher interest rate spreads than domestic banks, deriving greater benefits from core banking operations. Overall, the baseline findings, both from Tables 5.5 and 5.6, highlight the diverse effects of bank size and foreign ownership on Thailand's financial sector, illustrating a dynamic and significant interaction between these elements that profoundly shapes market dynamics. This interaction involves not just competitive advantages in terms of financial performance but also strategic positioning within the market. To delve deeper into this complexity and better understand how foreign ownership combined with relative bank size influences competitive strategies—specifically regarding pricing and market positioning—an extended analysis is undertaken in the next subsection, presented in Table 5.7.

(3) Regarding the non-interest income, the analysis reveals a positive correlation between the presence of foreign banks and the ratio of non-interest income to total assets. This supports the hypothesis that greater foreign bank presence enables local banks to innovate more effectively, adopt advanced banking technologies, and expand their expertise in investment banking, brokerage, and consultancy services (Levine, 1996). It is also suggested that local banks might branch into non-banking sectors to alleviate losses incurred in traditional banking due to intensified competition in lending from foreign banks. Meanwhile, the influence of foreign ownership on non-interest income is found to be negligible in Thailand, providing a stark contrast to the Philippine scenario (Unite and Sullivan, 2003) where greater foreign involvement has spurred technological advancements in non-banking functions.

Additionally, the analysis reveals a substantial positive correlation between bank size and non-interest income in Table 5.5. It underscores that larger banks excel in deploying non-traditional banking services such as asset management, investment banking, and wealth management. This relationship highlights the critical role of scale in facilitating banks' ability to diversify their offerings and succeed in a broad spectrum of financial services, moving beyond conventional banking paradigms. This diversification enables these institutions to tap into new revenue streams, illustrating the strategic benefits of expansive operational scale in the banking industry.

Moreover, contrary to expectations, Table 5.6 shows that foreign banks, despite their extensive experience and capabilities in non-banking areas, do not achieve higher non-interest income than domestic banks. This discrepancy might be due to foreign banks' focus on traditional lending, particularly to serve expatriates from their originating countries, or the comparatively higher profits from interest-earning activities.

(4) Table 5.5 compellingly shows that as the presence of foreign banks increases, there is a notable reduction in operating expenses, establishing a negative correlation. This relationship underscores the transformative influence of foreign bank entry on the operational cost structures of domestic banking institutions. Echoing the findings of Bayraktar and Wang (2004) from their study on developing countries, the increased proportion of foreign banks correlates inversely with cost metrics, fostering more streamlined and cost-efficient operational practices among commercial banks. These enhancements often include the integration of advanced technological systems and the refinement of operational processes, which not only cut costs but also bolster the competitive edge of these banks.

Interestingly, the analysis also indicates a positive correlation between foreign ownership degree and operating expenses, supporting the theory that higher foreign stakes in banks are associated with increased costs related to personnel and equipment. This rise in expenses is typically aimed at modernizing operations to better prepare for market challenges and opportunities, as well as includes significant investments in non-lending sectors such as the development of internet banking and new financial products. Additionally, the result may suggest that enhanced foreign ownership leads to increased spending on internal monitoring mechanisms, reflecting a commitment to maintaining high standards of oversight and compliance, thereby further elevating operational costs.

In addition, operating expenses are positively correlated with the ratio of non-interest earning assets (NIA). This observation leads to the inference that an uptick in non-interest earning assets typically results in heightened non-interest expenses, primarily due to the expansion of non-lending activities. These activities could include investments in technological advancements, infrastructure development, and service diversification, which do not directly generate interest income but are essential for broadening the bank's operational capabilities and service offerings.

Contrary to expectations, Table 5.6 indicates that foreign banks do not consistently demonstrate greater cost efficiency than domestic banks. This is diverging from the findings of several existing studies, including Poghosyan and Poghosyan (2010), who observed superior cost management in foreign banks. This variation highlights that the operational efficiencies often associated with foreign banks may not be universally applicable, especially in the Thai context. This anomaly necessitates a deeper examination of the operational tactics and market dynamics influencing cost efficiency differences between foreign and domestic banks, as explored in Sect. 5.5.2.

(5) Concerning loan loss reserves, Table 5.5 indicates that credit default risk and associated costs are generally lower in environments with a significant presence of foreign banks. Furthermore, the analysis reveals that the proportion of foreign ownership at the bank level is significantly inversely related to loan loss reserves, implying that higher foreign participation tends to reduce the reserves needed for potential loan defaults. This relationship supports the view that foreign ownership enhances a bank's monitoring capabilities, promoting a more meticulous and risk-averse management style. Such enhancements in risk management are pivotal in bolstering the financial stability of banks, demonstrating the beneficial impact of foreign capital on the robustness of banking operations and their ability to manage risks effectively.

Furthermore, the analysis shows that market concentration is significantly positively correlated with loan loss reserves. This finding aligns with prevailing theories suggesting that banks in more concentrated markets tend to engage in riskier behaviors, necessitating higher reserves to cover potential loan defaults. In an environment where a few banks dominate (Big 4 banks), these institutions might exploit their market power to take on greater risks, anticipating higher returns while also increasing their exposure to potential defaults.

Additionally, the analysis indicates that the relationship between loan loss reserves and the dummy variable of foreign/domestic banks is represented by a negative coefficient in the model in Table 5.6; however, this relationship is statistically insignificant. This suggests that there is no substantial evidence to conclude that foreign banks engage in less risk-taking than domestic banks. Such a finding challenges the assumption that foreign banks inherently adopt more conservative financial practices compared to their domestic counterparts.

5.5.2 Extended Analysis

Building on the foundational empirical analysis, this subsection extends the study to scrutinize the intricate effects of market conditions and the roles of foreign versus domestic banks on interest rate spread and operational efficiency, as detailed in Tables 5.7 and 5.8. Columns (1) and (2) extract results from Tables 5.5 and 5.6 respectively, serving as benchmarks for subsequent comparative analysis.

In Columns (3) and (4), an interaction term is introduced between bank size and a foreign bank dummy variable. This is intended to test how the impact of bank size on interest rate spread and operational efficiency varies between foreign and domestic banks. This analysis aims to uncover if larger foreign banks experience different financial dynamics compared to their domestic counterparts under similar conditions.

Columns (5) and (6) incorporate another interaction term, this time between the HHI, which is a measure of market concentration, and the foreign bank dummy. This aspect of the study examines how market concentration impacts the financial metrics of interest rate spreads and operational efficiency differently in foreign banks compared to domestic banks. The purpose of this additional layer of analysis is to ascertain whether foreign banks leverage market concentration differently to affect financial performances. The major findings are summarized as follows:

(1) The impacts on interest rate spread (Table 5.7)

In the initial comparison in Table 5.7, Column (1), a significant positive association is found between RBS and interest income when including FOW, implying that in larger banks where foreign ownership is more prevalent (as indicated in Table 5.4), bank size plays a crucial role in enhancing interest income. However, the significance of this relationship diminishes in Column (2) when FOW is replaced by the foreign bank dummy. This finding implies that after accounting for foreign ownership share (FOW), which is predominantly observed in large-sized banks, the size of a bank remains a significant factor for interest income. Essentially, bank size plays a critical role in driving interest income among smaller institutions once the variable of foreign ownership is controlled.

Further examination in columns (3) and (4) with an interaction term between FD and RBS reveals a significant and negative interaction, indicating that while larger bank size generally contributes to higher interest income, this trend inversely affects foreign banks. In foreign banks, it is the relatively smaller institutions that surprisingly register higher interest income. This counterintuitive finding suggests that small, foreign-owned banks may be more agile in adopting reforms that bolster profitability, despite their smaller scale which typically would not confer significant market control power. This phenomenon underscores the complex dynamics where market power and size interact differently within foreign-owned banks compared to domestic or larger banks.

In Column (5) and (6), the HHI demonstrates a significant negative correlation with interest rate spread, suggesting that increased market concentration tends to result in lower interest income. Conversely, the interaction between HHI and the foreign bank dummy (FD) is positively related to interest rate spread. This indicates that, for foreign banks, the detrimental effects of high market concentration on interest income are mitigated. In essence, while higher concentration generally suppresses interest rate spreads, foreign banks experience a less pronounced decrease, potentially due to their different operational strategies or competitive advantages in concentrated markets.

(2) The impacts on operating expenses (Table 5.8)

The results in Column (3) and (4) implies that bank size is not significantly related to operating expenses. Meanwhile, there is no difference in the effects of bank size on operation efficiency between foreign banks and domestic banks.

On the other hand, an unexpected inverse relationship is observed between HHI and operating expenses. It is hypothesized that although greater market concentration enables large banks to retain market dominance, this could foster complacency, leading to potential operational inefficiencies as these banks face less competitive pressure to streamline operations. This situation could normally result in increased operational costs; however, these dominant banks might instead strategically reduce costs to prepare for future market challenges and competition, ostensibly improving operational efficiency.

Contrary to this hypothesis, the findings in Table 5.8 show that an increase in market concentration, as reflected by a higher HHI, actually correlates with enhanced operational efficiency. This suggests that the reduced competitive pressures in more concentrated markets enable banks to optimize their cost structures more effectively, contrary to the expected outcome of complacency-induced inefficiency.

Furthermore, an intriguing aspect of the analysis is the positive correlation found between the interaction term of the Herfindahl–Hirschman Index (HHI) and the foreign bank dummy with operating expenses. This relationship may reflect X-inefficiency within foreign banks, which appears more pronounced in highly concentrated markets. Here, foreign banks might incur higher operational costs due to inefficiencies in their administrative practices. This observation suggests that foreign banks, unlike their domestic counterparts, may not streamline their operations effectively in less competitive environments, potentially due to a misalignment between their global operational strategies and the local market dynamics. This increased cost burden could stem from maintaining broader administrative structures or possibly due to less motivation to optimize resources in a market where competitive threats are minimized.

5.6 Conclusions

This research distinguishes between the mechanisms of market-level foreign bank entry and bank-level foreign ownership to investigate the long-term impacts of foreign entry, which resulted from the deregulation of foreign investment in the post-AFC financial reforms, on the banking performance in Thailand from 2000 to 2015. The focus is on examining changes in profitability, operational expenses, and risk management.

The regression analysis reveals that market-level foreign bank entry, which typically introduces increased competition, prompts domestic banks to enhance their operational efficiency. This is achieved through innovations and advancements that expand non-lending activities. However, foreign entry also tends to reinforce oligopolistic market structures, which leads to higher interest rate spreads and increased profitability for the banks.

Consequently, the anticipated outcome of creating a competitive banking market through financial liberalization—a common assumption in policies advocated by scholars like Claessens et al. (2001)—is only partially realized.

Bank-level foreign entry, on one hand, characterized by partial capital investments in local banks, has notably increased the interest rate spread. This rise in spread is likely attributable to the banks' oligopolistic advantages in the market. However, this entry has concurrently led to a decline in operational efficiency, implying that substantial operational reforms were not undertaken. These findings suggest that these banks prioritized aggressive long-term investments over immediate, comprehensive operational overhauls, resulting in increased expenditure.

This strategy indicates a preference for strengthening market position and revenue streams through significant capital injections into core business areas, rather than engaging in cost-cutting or efficiency-enhancing reforms. Such decisions reflect a strategic choice to solidify competitive standing at the potential cost of higher operational expenses, highlighting a trade-off between short-term efficiency and long-term investment goals in the banking sector.

The impact of bank-level foreign entry, on the other hand, specifically through the full acquisition of local banks by foreign entities, remained ambiguous. Nonetheless, it was observed that these fully acquired banks managed to secure relatively high interest rates, attributed to their prominent brand presence.

During the post-AFC era, it's observed that the pattern of foreign investments primarily targeting large local banks via partial capital stakes significantly increased market concentration. This strategic choice bolstered the market dominance of well-established local banks, intensifying the oligopolistic nature of the market.

Overall, this study elucidates the complex effects of foreign involvement in the banking sector, indicating that while certain aspects are positively transformed, others do not necessarily benefit. These findings challenge the prevalent belief that foreign capital injections automatically confer advantages to the banking industry, a sector often targeted by financial reforms aimed at attracting such investments.

The mixed outcomes of foreign capital entry call for a more discerning approach to financial reforms that not only encourage foreign investment but also address the potential complexities introduced by such capital inflows. Future policies should therefore be crafted with an awareness of these nuances, ensuring that they foster a banking environment that is both competitive and robust. These insights urge policymakers and stakeholders to reconsider simplistic narratives about the benefits of foreign capital in the banking sector and to formulate strategies that capitalize on its advantages while mitigating its downsides.

It's also notable that the complex dynamics of foreign investment in the banking sector necessitate further empirical and theoretical exploration to fully grasp its extensive impacts. Future research should especially focus on the differential effects of various types of foreign entry—from partial investments to complete acquisitions—on the banking industry's financial and operational metrics. By examining how different models of foreign involvement affect market competition, operational efficiency, and financial stability, policymakers can better understand the trade-offs involved and potentially recalibrate regulatory frameworks to optimize the benefits of foreign capital while mitigating its risks.

Chapter 6
Ownership and Business Practice of the Thai Banking Sector After the Asian Financial Crisis: A Case Study of a Family Business

Abstract In the two decades following the Asian Financial Crisis, Thailand's financial landscape has seen profound changes. This chapter delves into the effects of these extensive regulatory and financial environmental shifts on the Thai commercial banking sector after the crisis, from an organizational perspective. Through an analysis of Kasikornbank, a leading bank initiated by families with Chinese heritage, the study specifically examines the key elements of family business progression, ownership changes, management control, and business practices. Concerning ownership, the founding family became minor shareholder post-crisis, while foreign ownership saw a considerable increase. Predominantly financial sector-based major foreign investors emerged as significant shareholders, maintaining a stable shareholding ratio since their initial investment. In terms of management control, the founding family holds a consistent, senior board position, along with executive roles, underscoring their ongoing influence in management. The study's analysis of post-crisis management reforms reveals that the increased proportion of foreign investors has not markedly affected the bank's top management. Additionally, the continuous control exerted by the founding family ensures internal stability in decision-making, especially in long-term strategic corporate projects. This stability ultimately grants the bank a significant competitive advantage.

6.1 Introduction

In the development of Thailand's financial sector during the past several decades, few events have had as much of an impact as the Asian Financial Crisis (AFC). Before the crisis, Thailand's commercial banking sector used to be a highly closed[1] and concentrated market due to the "no exit, no entry" policy after the 1960s (Chantapong, 2005). The total assets of the Thai Big 4 banks—Bangkok Bank, Siam Commercial Bank, Krung Thai Bank, and Kasikornbank—consisted of around 60% of this

[1] The Thai government permitted only two new banks to enter the market in the four decades from the 1950s until the Asian Financial Crisis: One is the Thai Military Bank Public Company Limited that was established in 1957.

W. Lu, *Post-Asian Financial Crisis Reforms in Thailand*,
SpringerBriefs in Economics, https://doi.org/10.1007/978-981-97-3771-0_6

market. Another major characteristic of the Thai banking industry was its family-run business style. The ownership and/or management control of most commercial banks were dominated by the founding families or several cooperative families before the AFC. For instance, three of the top five large commercial banks—Bangkok Bank, Kasikornbank, and Bank of Ayudhya—were all family-run enterprises affiliated with financial conglomerates owned by their founding families.

The previously closed banking system was positively related to the high levels of concentration in the banking market. Its structure was criticized as having undermined the efficiency of resource allocation, created connected lending and corruption, and weakened banking governance, which is considered as a major cause of the AFC.

The essential characteristics of the structural changes of the Thai banking market since the AFC were summarized in previous chapters: (1) further strengthening of market oligopoly, (2) deregulation of market entry from a "no exit no entry" banking system, and (3) significantly high foreign ownership shares in large-sized commercial banks, which are in sharp contrast to the characteristics of family-run businesses in the sector before the AFC.

Beyond the financial reforms and the ensuing shifts in Thailand's financial landscape, commercial banks have experienced substantial transformations in their internal ownership structures and have been exposed to a changing competitive environment in the external market. This is particularly true of ethnically Chinese family-run bank groups (Pipatpokaisri, 2003). This sharp increase in foreign ownership has culminated in multi-faceted effects on domestic banks. For instance, on the one hand, foreign participation enhances domestic links to the international financial market, results in more foreign investment, and provides local banks with advanced management skills and technology (Levine, 1996). On the other hand, it leads to a decrease in non-lending activities and business diversification (Unite & Sullivan, 2003), and an increase in operational costs (Okuda & Rungsomboonv, 2007). In addition, foreign participation is also linked to higher interest rate spread and lower default risk (see Chap. 5). The effects of foreign participation on the ownership evolution in banks, which includes management control, leadership, and banking governance, still need further investigation.

Consequently, this study seeks to examine the evolution of ownership in the Thai banking sector following the financial reforms post-AFC and to assess their effects on banking management and business practices at the organizational level. By conducting a case study of Kasikornbank, this research delves into the long-term evolution of the banking sector, focusing on structural changes post-AFC. This analysis is pivotal in highlighting the adaptive strategies employed by Thai family-owned banks during economic downturns, offering nuanced insights into the relationship between financial reforms and institutional performance. It also lays a groundwork for future research on the post-crisis era. Moreover, this study distinguishes itself from predominantly empirical existing research by adopting a business history research approach, thereby providing a more detailed and comprehensive understanding of how shifts in ownership influence business practices.

Kasikornbank was chosen as the object of this study for the following reasons: (1) it is one of the Big 4 banks in Thailand, (2) it is one of the few domestic banks that accepted large foreign investments in the early stages after the AFC, and (3) the bank is very well known for being owned by an ethnically Chinese family. Kasikornbank was founded by the Lamsam family, one of the three largest ethnically Chinese family business groups in the Thai financial sector, as well as the most successful Hakka family business group[2] in Thailand. Thus, we can expect to observe the effects of ownership change on banking governance and banking performance by tracing the development process of Kasikornbank, which has a typical family-run business style as well as a high ratio of foreign ownership.

The study committees organized as follows: Sect. 6.2 is a literature review that examines general theories on family-run businesses and other major findings in Thai markets. Section 6.3 is a descriptive study on the development history of the family-run business that is Kasikornbank. Section 6.4 examines Kasikornbank's structural ownership changes since the AFC. Section 6.5 investigates the impact of the AFC on Kasikornbank's management structure and Sect. 6.6 analyzes its management reforms and banking performance. Finally, conclusions are presented in Sect. 6.7.

6.2 Literature Review

6.2.1 Theories on Family-Run Businesses

As defined in Suehiro (1993, 378), a family-run business model is characterized by both ownership and management being vested in family members, whether from a nuclear or extended family. The benefits generated by the enterprise are retained within the family and distributed among its members in some manner.

Accordingly, the following questions arise: (1) what is the nature of a family business? and (2) What kind of roles do founding families play in the development of family-run businesses?

In general, the characteristics of family business management in existing studies on "family-run businesses" can be classified into two approaches.[3] The first approach is to explore family-run business growth and management style from a sociological viewpoint, with a particular focus on the indigenous structures of founding families and their interpersonal relationships. For example, Yu (1991) studied ethnically Chinese networks as community resources in the enterprise development process.

The second approach examines family business development from a corporate control perspective and the changes of ownership control and management control in family-run businesses alongside company development. For example, Herman

[2] The main five sub-ethnic Chinese communities, also known as the five largest dialectal groups of overseas Chinese in Southeast Asia, are the Hokkien, Teochew, Hakka, Cantonese, and Hainanese groups (Gomez & Hsin-Huang, 2013).

[3] See a detail summary on "family capitalism" and "the sociological approach" in Suehiro (1993) "Family business reassessed: Corporate structure and late-starting industrialization in Thailand," 381–384.

(1982) comprehensively examines the ownership control and management control of 200 companies in the United States (US) in the 1970s. The study finds a deconcentrating trend of family ownership resulting from an increase in capital, business expansion, and the diffusion of shareholdings among family members. In addition, he found that despite a decrease in their ownership shares, founding families are still in a dominant position of management control.

Regarding ownership structure, compared to Herman (1982), studies on developing economies revealed that this view on ownership structure is not necessarily applicable to all cases. Hattori (1984) argues, in his case study on Korea, that the ownership control of major families has strengthened rather than deteriorated alongside business expansion. Suehiro (1989) found the same evidence for Thailand's financial and insurance business groups.

However, regarding management structure, business performance, and the role founding families play in the development of family-run enterprises, Useem (1986) observes the prosperous growth and management improvement of large family-run business groups. He interprets that instead of focusing on the preservation of family fortune and social position, more attention is paid to the "preservation of the profits of the enterprises that now control the family's economic destinies." This alters managerial personnel's positions, making them an important asset for the preservation of company wealth.

6.2.2 *Family Business in Thailand*

Suehiro (1993) is a representative study on Thai family business, which investigates the ownership structure and management structure of family business groups in Thailand. Regarding ownership structure, he found that until the late 1980s, Thai-owned large corporations continue to primarily depend on individual ownership instead of adopting corporate ownership models, and they show no substantial inclination towards widespread stock distribution. However, this situation has changed drastically since the AFC. Many large-sized commercial banks in Thailand have accepted a large portion of foreign capital while the shareholdings of founding family members have decreased by a large extent.

In addition, regarding management structure, Suehiro (1993) points out that in family business corporations, most CEOs are not only appointed due to their specialized managerial skills but also because of nepotism or connections with other families who are affiliated with the organization. Further, he argues that large family-run business groups in Thailand are more interested in expanding their business through quickly adapting to the changing economic conditions both domestically and internationally, with a focus on capitalizing on the profit opportunities presented by later stages of industrialization. This leads them to actively carry out internal reform and business innovation and introduce professional management personnel.

Regarding the role played by founding families in the development of family-run businesses, Tasaka (1996) surveyed specific changes in family-run banking businesses, such as equity capital structure, major shareholders, and the shareholding ratio of commercial banks in Thailand in the 1970 and 1980s. He concluded that the commercial bank played a crucial role in the whole family business group, and in turn, the family business group has played a generally active role in the expansion of bank's market shares in the early stages of the Thai banking market (1970–1980s). This was predominantly achieved through bank loans from the commercial bank to family-affiliated companies. However, the lending relationship between family group companies and others also increased the number of non-performing loans, which helped cover family group companies' losses during overseas expansion or hide and transfer profits to family group companies through the processing of bad debt.[4]

As mentioned above, few existing studies have examined the family business development over the past two decades after the AFC. In this regard, this study aims to identify the transformations in ownership structure for the family business groups in Thailand after the AFC. In particular, by analyzing the modernization reforms by Banthoon Lamsam, the fifth generation of the founding family, this study contributes to the research and discussion on the historical development and management modernization of banking and family businesses in Southeast Asia during the post-crisis period.

Furthermore, the existing studies on the impacts of increasing foreign ownership have mainly focused on empirical analyses using microdata, making it difficult to elucidate the mechanisms behind these effects. In addition to an empirical analysis, this study interprets the mechanism of the impact using the business history research method by combining the two approaches used in extant family business studies through an examination of the following: (1) the indigenous structures of founding families and (2) the changes in ownership control and management control in family-run businesses. It thus provides a more specific interpretation of this subject and paves the way for future research.

This study uses ownership data on founding families and domestic and foreign shareholders, as well as balance sheet and income statement data from Kasikornbank and other Thai commercial banks from 1997 to 2016, to investigate family business development history, transformation of ownership structure, management control, and business practice during the two decades after the AFC. The data on ownership and business practice were obtained from Kasikornbank Annual Reports (various versions), Commercial Banks in Thailand (Bangkok Bank, vol. 1997–2017), official documents from the Bank of Thailand, and interviews with the following institutions: Information Services Department of Stock Exchange of Thailand, Thai Bond Market Association, and Money & Banking Research Department of Kasikorn Research Center in 2015–2018. The data on banking performance were acquired from BankScope and Stock Exchange of Thailand.

---

[4] See Fig. 1 and Table 8 of Tasaka (1996, 107–108).

6.3 Kasikornbank: A Family-Style Business

Kasikornbank has been a family business since its establishment. In other words, its family-run approach is one of its most significant characteristics. However, currently, the founding family are minority shareholders due to the boom in foreign participation after the AFC. Therefore, as a case study on family-run banking business, examining Kasikornbank's family-run development history is valuable. This section presents a descriptive analysis of its family history, including the indigenous structure of the founding families, to determine the major characteristics of its deep-rooted family-run business style.

Since the 1940s, several influential and powerful family business groups have entered the banking market. For instance, on June 8, 1945, Mr. Choti Lamsam and his Thai-Chinese relatives established Thai Farmers Bank,[5] which focused mainly on banking services for farmers and retail businesses. The Lamsam family group had businesses in Thailand dating as far back as 1901 or earlier, thus making them one of the oldest existing family business groups in Thailand (comparable to the Wanglee family[6]).

In this subsection, the history of the bank's head office relocation and expansion is presented to capture the main characteristics of the corporate development of an ethnically Chinese business network at various time points over the past several decades. In other words, this subsection develops a descriptive study on the family-run business model, its network of connections to other ethnically Chinese and local Thai business groups, and the evolution of ownership structure, including leadership changes.

Kasikornbank's first head office was located in a predominately ethnically Chinese business and trade area on Sua Pa Road, Bangkok. In addition, the Lamsam family was appointed the leader of the local Hakka community in the early nineteenth century, which is significant to their predominant social status.

Similar to other successful ethnic Chinese family-run businesses, Kasikornbank also features business networks of significant mutual intimacy and complexity. The Lamsam family are Hakka immigrants from the Guangdong province in China, which is a minority ethnically Chinese Thai area.[7] However, the marriage between Ng Yuk Long (the second-generation leader[8]) and Thongyu Wanglee built a close relationship with one of the most influential Thai-Chinese families (the Wanglee family) for the Lamsams. The Wanglee family lead the Teochew ethnically Thai people and

[5] The bank name was changed from Thai Farmers Bank to Kasikornbank in 2003.

[6] The establishment of the Lamsam family's first company documented from 1901, according to Suehiro (1991).

[7] The word "Lamsam" is an alias invented by Ung Miao Ngian, the first generation of the family who moved to Thailand. The family used it as a Thai surname since their third generation. As a result, the first and second generations have a different surname.

[8] As defined by Early (2001, 4), "The second-generation leader is given his title as head of the organization at a point when the founder feels he is ready to take on new, more formal responsibilities as head of the organization."

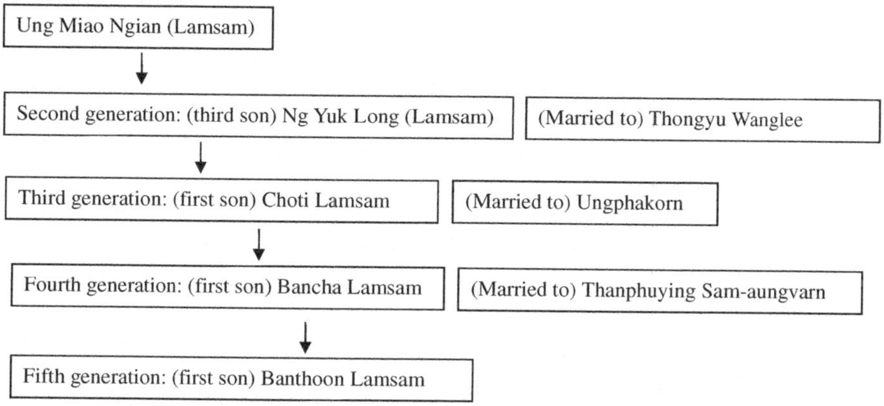

Fig. 6.1 The Lamsam family leaders of Kasikornbank. *Source* "Zaibatsu in Thailand" Suehiro (1991), Kasikornbank Annual Report of Kasikornbank, various versions

owned the largest *zaibatsu* (conglomerate) rice businesses.[9] As Useem (1986) argues, "family capitalism equates kinship relations with the control and ownership of a business enterprise and is a system consisting of business mergers via descent and marriage."

From around the third generation, the Lamsam family also expanded their network of connections to include the local upper class. Figure 6.1 depicts the Lamsam family leaders of each generation and several influential marriages that had a significant effect on the development of the Lamsam family business group.[10]

For instance, the fourth-generation leader, Bancha Lamsam, married Thanphuying Sam-aungvarn, who is related to the royal family. This marriage in particular afforded the Lamsam family extraordinary business opportunities[11] which extended beyond the local Thai–Chinese merchant community. To a large extent, since the fourth and fifth generation, the family has gradually transcended the limitations of their initial Chinese ethnic identity, thus being somewhat perceived as locally Thai within the business world. Overall, their strong network of personal contacts within the

---

[9] The leader of the second generation of the Lamsam family, Ng Yuk Long, married Thongyu Wanglee, who is the sister of Tan Lip Buay, the leader of the second generation of the Wanglee family. In addition, to deepen the relationship between two families, Ng Yuk Long's daughter married the leader of the third generation of the Wanglee family. This close relationship between them benefited the two families with a firm business foundation and cooperation thereafter.

[10] The leader of the third generation, Choti Lamsam, married Puey Ungphakorn's sister, who was a famous economist appointed as the former Governor of the Bank of Thailand in the 1960s and played an important role during its economic development and regional financial cooperation.

[11] The leader of the fourth generation, Bancha Lamsam, married Thanphuying Sam-aungvarn, the daughter of Prince Pridipheppong Devakula and Rajawongse Sa-ang Pramoj. Pridiyathon Thewagun, Thanphuying Sam-aungvarn's brother, then became the vice president of Thai Farmers Bank. Due to this connection, Bancha Lamsam took part in business cooperation related to the Bureau of the Crown Property. In addition, he was invited as a board member of the Siam Cement Group, which is one of largest cement manufacturing companies funded by the Bureau of the Crown Property.

Thai-Chinese merchant community and local upper classes is considered the most important factor in their tremendous business success.

As business in Thailand gradually saw stable expansion during the 1970s, Kasikornbank opened a new head office on Silom Road, which later became the central business district of Bangkok.[12] In addition to participating in domestic business expansion, Kasikornbank also participated in the overseas market by establishing branches in Hong Kong, Hamburg, New York, and Los Angeles. The Hong Kong branch, in particular, later became a strategic node of Kasikornbank regarding its business expansion in the East and Southeast Asian areas. Further, it played an important role in providing networking opportunities with overseas Chinese businessmen and Chinese family business groups in Southeast Asia, thus benefiting regional family business cooperation greatly.

In the late 1980s, the Silom head office moved to Phahon Yothin Road, which was expected to become the new central business and finance district. Due to the Thai economy's rapid expansion and financial liberalization, Kasikornbank was able to establish branches in all 73 provinces in Thailand, placing its new head office on Rat Burana Road.[13] As a financial institution, Kasikornbank is sensitive to changes in the domestic economic environment and has actively taken advantage of the opportunities of financial liberalization and globalization at home and abroad. Therefore, Kasikornbank is considered a top tier commercial bank with nationwide and global branch networks.

6.4 Ownership Evolution After the Asian Financial Crisis

The AFC engulfed domestic markets and greatly altered the landscape of Thailand's banking sector. Most large banks, including Kasikornbank, suffered an immense loss of foreign currency debt exposure, and their shareholder composition changed significantly through reforms and recapitalization. As a result, State Street Bank and Trust Company from the US became shareholders in Kasikornbank while the Lamsam family dropped to a minority shareholder position. Figure 6.2 illustrates the evolution of the ownership structure since the AFC.

The polylines show a comparison of foreign ownership shares between Kasikornbank and the banking sector as a whole. Directly after the crash, Kasikornbank introduced a large ratio of foreign investment into the company more rapidly than the average market level, with a high and stable foreign ownership share of close to 49% since 2002. The steady long-term participation of large-scale foreign capital is a primary characteristic of the overall structural changes in ownership at the bank.

The cumulative bar chart in Fig. 6.2 depicts the ownership evolution of major shareholders (top 10 largest shareholders). Overall, the foreign ownership average

[12] According to Kasikornbank's company background (https://kasikornbank.com/en/about/Information/Pages/company-background.aspx).

[13] According to the Kasikornbank company background.

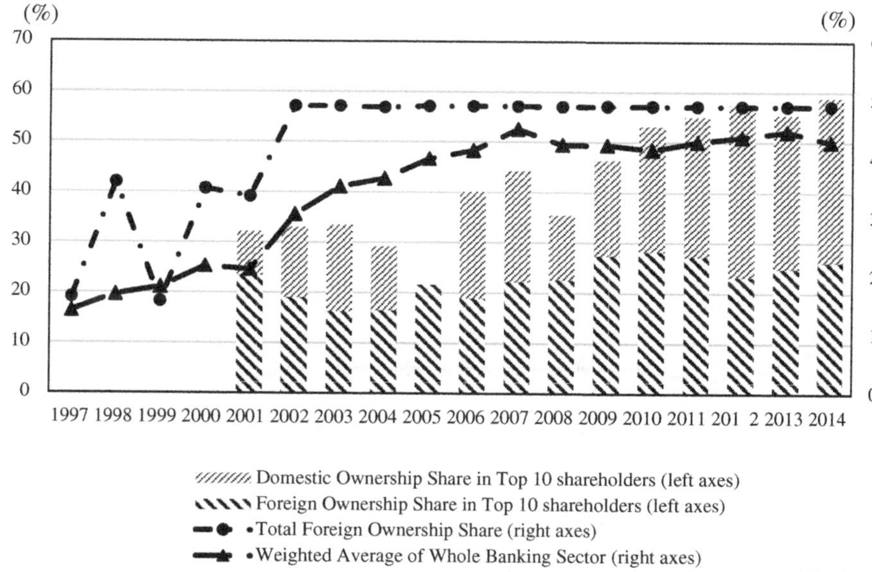

Fig. 6.2 Kasikornbank ownership evolution. *Source* Stock Exchange of Thailand, Kasikornbank Annual Report 2001–2014. *Note* FOWA is the weighted annual average of foreign ownership in the whole banking sector by bank assets

of major shareholders is 22.7%, which is almost half of the total foreign participation since the 2000s. In addition, the number of foreign shareholders among the top 10 largest shareholders also has stayed stable around an average of 7.5 seats, mainly from the US, Great Britain (GB), and Singapore.

Further, foreign ownership among major shareholders increased by more than one third after the global financial crisis, from an average of 19.1% during 2002–2007 to 26.2% during 2009–2014.

In addition, domestic ownership shares among major shareholders also increased sharply by 86.1% after 2008, from an average of 15.1% during 2002–2007 to 28.2% during 2009–2014. In general, the total shares of the top 10 largest shareholders increased from an average of 33.6% during 2002–2007 to 54.4% during 2009–2014. Unlike the fluctuation before 2008, there is a notable concentration trend in the overall ownership structure of Kasikornbank. Figure 6.3 illustrates major domestic shareholder changes at a micro-level.

As noted above, domestic shareholders of the top 10 largest shareholders also kept an average of 2.5 seats since the 2000s. Regarding the proportion of shareholdings, Thai Non-Voting Depository Receipts[14] (NVDR) ranked as the largest domestic Kasikornbank shareholders, but also the overall largest Kasikornbank shareholders

[14] According to the Stock Exchange of Thailand (SET), the Thai NVDR is "responsible for executing the purchase or sale of those listed company shares whose investors wish to trade through NVDRs." SET is its largest shareholder, holding 99.99% of the total shares (https://www.set.or.th/nvdr/en/nvdr.html).

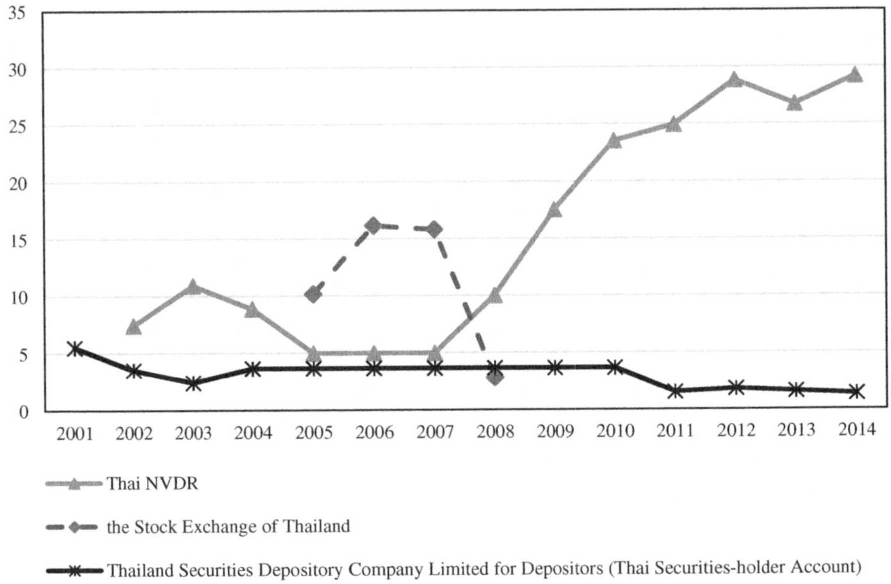

Fig. 6.3 Change in major domestic shareholders (Unit: %). *Source* Stock Exchange of Thailand, Kasikornbank Annual Report of 2001–2014. *Note* The three shareholders are selected from the top 10 largest shareholders each year since the 2000s. The rest of the domestic shareholders in the top 10 were not selected due to small scale and/or short-term holding

after 2008. Shareholders that trade through NVDRs are entitled to the same financial benefits as when investing directly. However, NVDR holders are not entitled to any voting rights, which can have a limiting impact on banking governance. Table 6.1 shows changes in major foreign shareholders and further examines the major characteristics of ownership evolution after the crisis.

First, Kasikornbank went through two upsurges of major foreign shareholder entries following the financial crisis. After the 2000–2014 period (post the AFC), the bank accepted more foreign shareholders during the global financial crisis. Other major shareholders, Bank of New York Mellon (US), N.C.B. Trust Limited (GB), and Nortrust Nominees Limited (GB), emerged around 2008. This study focuses on the two post-crisis periods to investigate the influence of ownership change on banking management and banking performance.

Second, aside from foreign investment being significantly high and maintaining a stable ratio since 2002 (Fig. 6.2), the table also suggests that major foreign investors have continued investing from a relatively stable position since their initial investments. For example, State Street Bank and Trust Company (including branch investments) maintained their investment for a long period (at least until 2014) after first appearing in the early 2000s, even accruing a major shareholder position. A similar trend can be seen in HSBC (Singapore), Chase Nominees Limited (GB), and Bank of New York Mellon (US).

Table 6.1 Kasikornbank major foreign shareholders (%)

Major foreign shareholders	2002	2005	2008	2011	2014
State Street Bank and Trust Company (US) ①	2.80	3.56	6.99	8.44	4.62
State Street Bank Europe Limited (branch) ②	0.00	0.00	0.00	4.74	9.45
State Street Bank and Trust Company for Australia (branch) ③	0.00	0.00	1.58	1.88	N.a
Sum ① + ② + ③	2.80	3.56	8.57	15.06	14.07
HSBC Nominees PTE Limited (Singapore)	3.36	3.09	2.92	2.31	2.41
Chase Nominees Limited (GB)	1.89	2.16	1.43	1.82	2.08
GIC Private Limited–C (Singapore)[a]	3.03	1.58	N.a	N.a	1.70
The Bank of New York Mellon (US)	0.00	0.00	1.56	1.45	1.21
N.C.B. Trust Limited (GB)	0.00	0.00	1.50	2.25	N.a
Nortrust Nominees Limited (GB)	0.00	0.00	2.34	3.11	N.a
Etc.					

Source Stock Exchange of Thailand, Kasikornbank Annual Report 2001–2016
Note 1. "N.a." refers to no available data
2. The shareholders above are selected from the top 10 largest shareholders each year since the 2000s. The rest of the foreign shareholders in the top 10 were not selected due to small scale and/or short-term holding
3. [a]Formerly named the Government of Singapore Investment Corporation C

Despite some significant structural ownership changes at Kasikornbank since the AFC, the bank has maintained a relatively stable composition of major shareholders. Its stable partnership between the founding family and major foreign shareholders in turn facilitates long-term stability in banking management. In addition, it is also significantly related to overall banking performance.

Lastly and most importantly, most major foreign shareholders belong to financial services or investment business sectors. In other words, this study suggests that the increase of foreign participation in the banking market of developing countries is positively related to financial innovation and the improvement of management skills.[15]

However, the impact of foreign capital participation on banking operation efficiency is unclear and requires further investigation.

[15] From a market-level perspective, foreign entry should be associated with a reduction in operating expenses as foreign presence may inspire domestic banks to operate more efficiently to strengthen the competition (Claessens et al., 2001). In contrast, it has also been argued that foreign entry might result in the strengthening of market concentration and deteriorate the overall competitive environment, as has happened in Thailand. From a bank-level perspective, the increase in foreign ownership should accompany an improvement in banking management and increase operating costs, as was found with Kasikornbank in the following analysis.

6.5 Management Structure

As described and analyzed in the previous section, Kasikornbank's ownership evolution after the AFC can be interpreted in several ways, as seen in Hattori (1984), Suehiro (1989), and Suehiro (1993). Overall, the members of the founding family turned out to be relatively small shareholders after the recapitalization process post the AFC. Thus, the following sections conduct a comprehensive survey of the bank's corporate governance transformation process synchronized with its ownership evolution to examine the theory of "the transition of family-run business from ownership control to management control" (Herman, 1982). Furthermore, these sections explore the impact of changes in management structure on banking governance and performance.

Kasikornbank's foreign ownership shares soared to 48.98% in 2002. In addition to major foreign shareholder entry, changes at the top management level occurred. After 2001, the economy showed signs of recovering from the AFC, and the commercial banking sector started to record, albeit minor, positive improvements in banking performance. Thus, Tables 6.2 and 6.3 depicts detailed information on the changes in management structure and control post the AFC.

Regarding the influence of ownership evolution on top management positions, this section examines the characteristics of board directors and executive changes at the bank with two main focus areas:

(1) Changes in top management positions and ownership transformation in the recapitalization process post-AFC, especially regarding the large influx of major foreign shareholders.
(2) The founding family's persistent management control and leadership as means of ensuring stability in decision-making processes. Ultimately, this should play a crucial role in upholding long-term development strategy during management reforms.

6.5.1 Changes in Top Management Positions and Large-Scale Foreign Entry

Kasikornbank's major change of ownership structure post the AFC was mostly completed around 2001–2002, and since then, major foreign shareholders have remained fairly constant. Thus, this subsection begins with an examination of the changes in top management positions in the most crucial phase of the organizational restructuring process from 1997 to 2001. Tables 6.2 and 6.3 summarize the board of directors and executives during the periods of 2001–2012 and 2013–2016.

Table 6.2 lists the board of directors from 2001 to 2012. Among the 16 directors in 2001, nine of them were appointed after the crisis. Other than one founding family member, three of the nine aforementioned directors had experience working in top management positions for foreign financial institutions. One was at a bank

Table 6.2 Kasikornbank's top management and shareholders from 2001 to 2012

	Board of directors	Holding of Kasikornbank shares					Experience as board member of KB since	Key experience before the AFC
		2001	2004	2007	2010	2012		
Chairman								
1	Mr. Banyong Lamsam	0.14%	0.14%	0.14%	0.14%	0.14%	Chairman since 1992	
Vice Chairman								
2	Police General Pow Sarasin	0.01%	0.01%	0.01%	0.01%	0.02%	Vice Chairman since 1992	
Directors								
3	Mr. Banthoon Lamsam	0.00%	0.00%	0.19%	0.19%	0.07%	1992	
4	Ms. Sujitpan Lamsam	0.00%	0.00%	0.00%	0.00%	0.12%	1999	
5	Mr. Sukri Kaocharern	○	○	○	○	○	1981	
6	Mr. Sarisdiguna Kitiyakara	○	○	○	○	×	1985	
7	Mr. Yongswasdi Kridakon	○	○	○	×	×	1991	
8	Mr. Somchai Bulsook	○	○	○	○	○	1993	
9	Dr. Khunying Suchada Kiranandana	○	○	○	○	○	2000	Professor, Chulalongkorn University
10	Dr. Yongyuth Yuthavong	○	○	×	○	○	2000	The Council of Trustee; Thailand Development Research Institute Foundation
11	Dr. Abhijai Chandrasen	○	○	○	○	○	2000	Director, Siam Motors Parts Company Limited
12	Mr. Charles L. Coltman, III	○	○	○	×	×	2000	Global Corporate Banking First Union Corporation; CoreStates Financial Corporation

(continued)

Table 6.2 (continued)

	Board of directors	Holding of Kasikornbank shares					Experience as board member of KB since	Key experience before the AFC
		2001	2004	2007	2010	2012		
13	Mr. William Mark Evans	○	×	×	×	×	2000	Chairman and Managing Director, Goldman Sachs Asia, Hong Kong
14	Ms. Elizabeth Sam	○	○	○	○	○	2001	Deputy President, Overseas Chinese Banking Corporation
15	Mr. Chaisak Saeng-Xuto	○	○	○	×	×	2001	President, Siam Pulp and Paper Public Company Limited
16	Dr. Schwin Dhammanungune	○	○	○	○	×	2001	President, Business Intelligence & Creativity Company, etc.
17	Dr. Prasarn Trairatvorakul	N.a	○	○	×	×	2004	President 2004–2010
18	Prof. Dr. Pairash Thajchayapong	N.a	N.a	○	○	○	2007	
19	Mr. Hiroshi Ota	N.a	N.a	N.a	○	○	2009	
20	Ms. Kobkarn Wattanavrangku	N.a	N.a	N.a	N.a	○	2011	
21	Ms. Chantra Purnariksha	N.a	N.a	N.a	N.a	○	2012	
22	Sqn. Ldr. Nalinee Paiboon, M.D	N.a	N.a	N.a	N.a	○	2012	
23	Mr. Saravoot Yoovidhya	N.a	N.a	N.a	N.a	○	2012	
Total number		16	16	16	14	16		

Source Kasikornbank Annual Report, survey by the author

*Note*1. The table lists ownership information of the founding family members, the chairman, and the vice chairman of the board. Kasikornbank's holding shares are the total share of spouse and minor children

2. ○refers to the position of board members × refers to the position of non-board members
3. Kasikornbank established the position of Chief Executive Officer (CEO) in 2004
4. Regarding family relationship, Mr. Banyong Lamsam and Ms. Sujitpan Lamsam are cousins. Further, he is uncle to Mr. Banthoon Lamsam, Mr. Krisada Lamsam, and Mr. Sara Lamsam

Table 6.3 Kasikornbank's top management and shareholdings (2013–2016)

	Board of directors	Holding of Kasikornbank shares				Background
		2013	2014	2015	2016	
Chairman						
1	Mr. Banthoon Lamsam	**0.07%**	**0.07%**	**0.07%**	**0.00%**	President 1992–2004 & 2010–2013, CEO 2004–present
2	Mr. Somchai Bulsook	**Vice Chair (0.01%)**	**Vice Chair (0.01%)**	×	×	
3	Mr. Krisada Lamsam	**Vice Chair (0.00%)**	**Vice Chair (0.00%)**	**Vice Chair (0.00%)**	×	Senior Executive Vice President, KB, 2010–2013
4	Professor Dr. Khunying Suchada Kiranandana	**Director (0.00%)**	**Director (0.00%)**	**Vice Chair. (0.00%)**	**Vice Chair (0.00%)**	
5	Ms. Sujitpan Lamsam	**Director (0.13%)**	**Director (0.13%)**	**Director (0.13%)**	**Vice Chair (0.13%)**	
Directors						
6	Mr. Predee Daochai	○	○	○	○	Senior Executive Vice President 2010–2013, President 2013-present
7	Mr. Teeranun Srihong	○	○	○	○	Senior Executive Vice President 2010–013, President 2013-present
8	Dr. Piyasvasti Amranand	○	○	○	○	President, Thai Airways International PCL, 2009–2012; Chief Advisor to Chief Executive Officer, KB, 2008–2009

(continued)

Table 6.3 (continued)

	Board of directors	Holding of Kasikornbank shares				Background
		2013	2014	2015	2016	
9	Mr. Somkiat Sirichatchai	○	○	○	×	Senior Executive Vice President, KB, 2010–2013
10	Mr. Rapee Sucharitakul	○	○	×	×	Executive Chairman, Kasikorn Asset Management, 2009–2011
11	Mr. Sara Lamsam	×	×	×	○	President, The Thai Life Assurance Association, 2012–2016
Etc.						

Source Kasikornbank Annual Report, survey by the author
Note 1. The table lists ownership information of the founding family members, the chairman, and the vice chairman of the board. Kasikornbank's holding shares are the total share of spouse and minor children
2. The table lists the board members that are either related to the founding family or appointed as top-level executives
3. ○refers to the position of board members; × refers to the position of non-board members

holding company in the US, one at a restricted licensed bank called Goldman Sachs Asia in Hong Kong, and the other at the Overseas Chinese Banking Corporation in Singapore. Two of the three are located in East and Southeast Asia and affiliated with highly ranked multinational financial groups. These appointments may be an attempt to improve banking governance as a result of a skilled and experienced foreign management team.

In sum, drastic changes in ownership structure during the recapitalization phase do not seem to have a significant impact on top management positions. Further, the newly appointed foreign management personnel are not affiliated with the new major foreign shareholders. Finally, although the founding family became a minority shareholder, one more Lamsam family member was selected for the board of directors in 1999.

Furthermore, this study also conducted a thorough survey on the list of executives in 2001, which included the positions of seven executive vice presidents, two first senior vice presidents, and two senior vice presidents. This survey found the same results regarding the change of personnel on the board as summarized above.

Table 6.4 The expansion of overseas service network of Kasikornbank

	2001	2004	2008	2012	2016	Established after 2012
① **Locally Incorporated Institution**						
KASIKORNTHAI BANK (Lao PDR)	×	×	×	×	○	In 2014
② **Branch and Sub-Branch**						
Shenzhen Branch	○	○	○	○	○	
Hong Kong Branch	○	○	○	○	○	
Chengdu Branch	×	×	×	×	○	In 2013
Shenzhen, Longgang Sub-Branch	×	×	×	×	○	In 2014
Los Angeles International Branch	○	○	○	○	○	
Cayman Islands Branch	○	○	○	○	○	
Phenom Penh Branch -Cambodia	○	×	×	×	×	
Vientian– Branch - Lao P.D.R.	○	×	×	×	×	
③ **Representative Office**						
Shanghai Representative Office	○	○	○	○	○	
Beijing Representative Office	○	○	○	○	○	
Kunming Representative Office	○	○	○	○	○	
Tokyo Representative Office	×	×	×	○	○	
Yangon Representative Office	×	×	×	○	○	In 2012
Hanoi Representative Office	×	×	×	×	○	In 2014
Ho Chi Minh Representative Office	×	×	×	×	○	In 2014
Phnom Penh Representative Office	×	×	×	×	○	In 2014
Jakarta Representative Office	×	×	×	×	○	In 2015
New York Representative Office	○	×	×	×	×	
London Representative Office	○	×	×	×	×	
total number	**11**	**7**	**7**	**9**	**16**	

Source Kasikorn Research Center, Annual Report of Kasikornbank
Note The three main organizational forms of Kasikornbank in foreign banking business, (1) Locally Incorporated Institution, which has the qualification of legal entity and a broad licenses for banking transaction; (2) Branch and Sub-Branch, which has no qualification of independent legal entity and is qualified for the general banking business; (3) Representative Office, which is a junior form in overseas banking expansion and not qualified for deposit and loan business

6.5.2 Persistence of Management Control by the Founding Family

In the above summary of previous studies on family-run businesses, one major theory by Herman (1982) is the transition of the role of founding families from ownership control to management control along with family business expansion. Other studies that focused on developing countries before the AFC found a different pattern to Herman's regarding family business development. Accordingly, this subsection investigates management control in Kasikornbank during the post-crisis period, with a particular focus on the founding family's leadership.

Thus, Tables 6.2 and 6.3 also list the ratio of shareholdings by major founding family members on the board. The survey found that the former chairman, Mr. Banyong Lamsam (2001–2012), chairman Mr. Banthoon Lamsam (2005–2011), and vice chairman Ms. Sujitpan Lamsam (2012) hold or used to hold a total share of no more than 0.15%, while the rest of the family members hold less or none.

According to the executives' survey, the most important executive positions at the bank have been dominated by the founding family members thus far. While the above survey depicts board directors and executive changes over the past two decades, it also illustrates the founding family's persistent management control, which was not influenced by losing ownership control.

For instance, Banyong Lamsam had served as the chairman of the board from 1992 to 2012 and he is Bancha Lamsam's (leader of the fourth generation) brother. During the same period, Police General Pow Sarasin had served as vice chairman. The newly established (2004) position of CEO was overtaken by then-president Banthoon Lamsam. This "chairman of the board–vice chairman–CEO" triangle at the top management level was steadily maintained for around two decades since 1992 until a major change of personnel in 2013. This consistency of management control played an important role in the bank's response to the AFC.

More importantly, however, the major personnel change in 2013 demonstrates the continuity of management control by the founding family more concretely as it is the most significant personnel change of the past two decades. In 2013, Banyong Lamsam and Police General Pow Sarasin resigned as chairman and vice chairman, respectively. Thereafter, Banthoon Lamsam took over as chairman of the board and kept his position as CEO. Another family member, Krisada Lamsam, was appointed as the vice chairman (the first time he was appointed as a board member). The Lamsam family has held the position of chairman, CEO, and one vice chairman since 2013. In 2016, after Krisada Lamsam's resignation, Sujitpan Lamsam took over the vice chairman position. In addition, one more family member (Sara Lamsam) was elected as a director of the board the same year.

Overall, regarding the personnel appointments over the past two decades, the family has held at least three seats on the board of directors since 1992. Noteworthily, every time one family member left the board, another family member took a seat. Thus, overall, this case study supports Herman's theory that the founding family underwent a transition from ownership control to management control as the scale of the family-run business expanded.

Generally speaking, personnel at a top management level make strategic decisions for long-term enterprise development, and their decision-making has a great influence on the organizational performance of the business (Amason, 1996). Therefore, one can infer that the Lamsam family's consistent management control of Kasikornbank ensured stability in decision-making. This should also ensure the complete enforcement of management reforms and long-term strategic programs.

6.6 Management Reforms and Banking Performance

From the perspective of Kasikornbank's ownership structure and management control, this subsection observes the bank's management reforms and the impact of these reforms on banking performance according to the following three phases: (1) the organizational restructuring and management reforms as a result of the AFC until 2006, (2) the further adjustment of business development strategy from 2007 to 2012, and (3) a phase of regional business expansion since 2013.

6.6.1 Organizational Restructuring Post the AFC

In response to the drastic changes in the financial environment post the AFC, Kasikornbank made an important adjustment in the enterprise's organizational structure from 2001 to 2003.

In 2001, the bank's management structure consisted mainly of six departments: the Board of Directors, the Advisers to the Board of Directors, the Audit Committee, the Remuneration Committee, the Advisory Board to the Management Committee, and the Management Committee. Since then, the Corporate Governance Committee (CGC) and the Human Resources Committee were established in 2002 and the Risk Management Committee (RMC) was set up in 2003. This organizational management structure was maintained for a long period until 2013, when the Independent Directors Committee was established.

The establishment of the aforementioned three new committeeees from 2002 to 2003 suggests an emphasis on management reform after the crisis.[16] The CGC focuses on the supervision and improvement of business practices, realization of good corporate governance, and compliance with various kinds of regulations. The RMC focuses on the management of personnel expenses and the introduction of talents. In

[16] Police General Pow Sarasin, the vice chairman of the board of directors, was appointed as the chairman of Corporate Governance Committee; Mr. Charles L. Coltman, III, the independent director of the board, was appointed as the chairman of the Human Resources Committee; and Mr. Banthoon Lamsam, the executive director of the board and the president of Kasikornbank, was appointed as the chairman of the Risk Management Committee.

addition, it places great emphasis on developing an efficient risk management system to identify, evaluate, and manage various risks, including operational risk, market risk, liquidity risk, and credit risk[17] (the largest risk for banks).

In addition to the management reform post the AFC, Kasikornbank also implemented a series of strategic programs to ensure long-term sustainable profitability. In sum, the eight strategic programs could be concluded into four aspects: (1) improve credit approval management and strengthen customer relationships, (2) enhance non-interest income (fee income), (3) develop information technology that applies to financial services, and (4) improve human resources management and internal supervision. This section makes a detailed analysis on the enforcement of (1) strengthening non-interest income and (2) development of financial information technology in order to examine the role of the aforementioned management structure in the reforms.

Regarding the enhancement of fee income, to begin with, it exploits multiple strategies to fulfill the increase of fee-based income from credit cards. On the one hand, it strengthens business cooperation with allies to expand its client base, such as major direct sales companies, universities, and state-owned companies. On the other hand, it places significant emphasis on market campaigns, media publicity, and "brand awareness building" to promote the total card spending amount.

Furthermore, the bank develops various financial services and products to meet and expand customer demands to increase fee-based income through cooperation with multiple financial business partners, especially partner companies affiliated with the Lamsam family business group, such as bancassurance with the Muang Thai Life Assurance Company and long-term fund products for the investment of corporate debentures with Kasikorn Asset Management.[18]

Regarding the development of financial information technology, Kasikornbank was ahead of most other domestic banks. This gave the bank a significant advantage as it exploits the Fee-based Business Development Program, E-Approach Development Project, and IT Infrastructure Development Program, to meet the rapidly changing market environment and customer requirements. Moreover, Kasikornbank gained an advantage for potential digital banking market opportunities in the future. For instance, Kasikornbank placed great focus on constructing Internet-based banking transaction systems. Its full-time online electronic banking system enables customers to engage in various transactions (including a foreign exchange service), which realize the improvement of fee income.

Overall, an observation of the reforms in this phase finds that the founding family's management control plays a significant role in the business, especially regarding cooperation between family business group affiliated enterprises. Further,

---

[17] Operational risk is the risk of loss resulting from errors, interruptions, or damages caused by people, systems, or processes. Market risk results mostly from banks' investment, sales, and trade in capital markets. Liquidity risk refers to banks' ability to access cash to meet funding obligations. Credit risk refers to the loss resulting from creditors default.

[18] For further details on the "Changes in Operating Environment and Business Operations," see columns in MD&A reports and annual reports for each year.

the family's persistent management control impacts strategic decision-making significantly, especially regarding substantial investment in financial information technology innovation and in the construction of related infrastructures, such as KBANK e-Mobile Phone Banking, KBANK e-ATM, and KBANK e-Internet Banking systems.

That being said, the bank's management reforms place great emphasis on the innovation of financial products. In addition, these reforms have introduced successful foreign ventures, such as the "marketing campaigns, credit card design and size changes" (Annual Report 2003, 34–35) in the competitive credit card market. It is also likely that foreign shareholders or foreign board members introduce advanced financial technologies into domestic companies.

Figure 6.4 describes the change in the non-interest income ratio (non-interest income/total assets), operating expense ratio (operating expense/total assets), and return on Kasikornbank assets, and compares these with another four selected banks. Two of them are Big 4 banks, Bangkok Bank and Krung Thai Bank (the last Big 4 bank, Siam Commercial Bank, is mainly owned by the Bureau of the Crown Property and is known for superior banking performance), while the other two are medium-sized foreign banks, one from an Association of Southeast Asian Nations (ASEAN) country and one affiliated to a multinational financial group from western countries, being the most representative competitors of Kasikornbank in the Thai banking market.

Kasikornbank's non-interest income ratio has accrued steadily since 2004 and has outperformed other large-sized banks and foreign banks since 2006–2007. The advantage of fee-income business has been further enlarged since 2010. Such a change suggests the positive impact of management reforms relating to the enhancement of fee income.

In other words, except for the aforementioned increase in operational fee income and financial service income, the gains from investments in bonds and security also contribute significantly to increasing non-interest income and the overall recovery of the domestic economy and buoyant capital market. In addition, Kasikornbank closed four foreign branches and representative offices during this period.[19] Gains on exchange from closing also make a large contribution to the rise of non-interest income.

As expected, Kasikornbank's operating expenses accrued steadily during this phase. In addition to the reforms to improve human resources management, the bank's personnel expenses increased, including annual pay, provisions for bonuses, staff retirement funds, and employee wages. Moreover, the bank also saw an increase in expenses relating to promotions, public relationship management, expanded life insurance transactions, and premises and equipment costs due to rapidly growing

[19] They include the Phenom Penh Branch in Cambodia, Vientiane Branch in Laos, New York Representative Office in the US, and the London Representative Office in GB. Refer to Table 6.4. The Expansion of Overseas Service Network of Kasikornbank for more details on the closing of foreign branches since 2001.

(a)

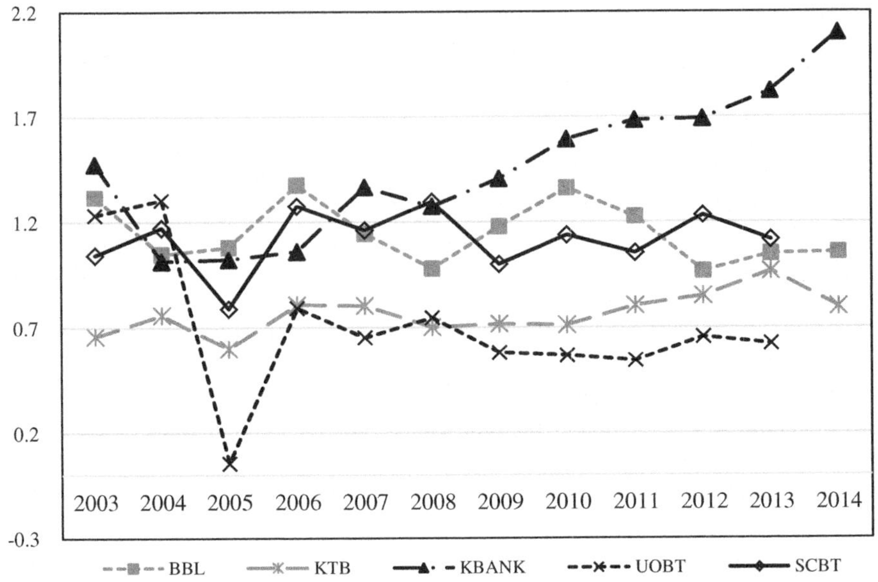

(b)

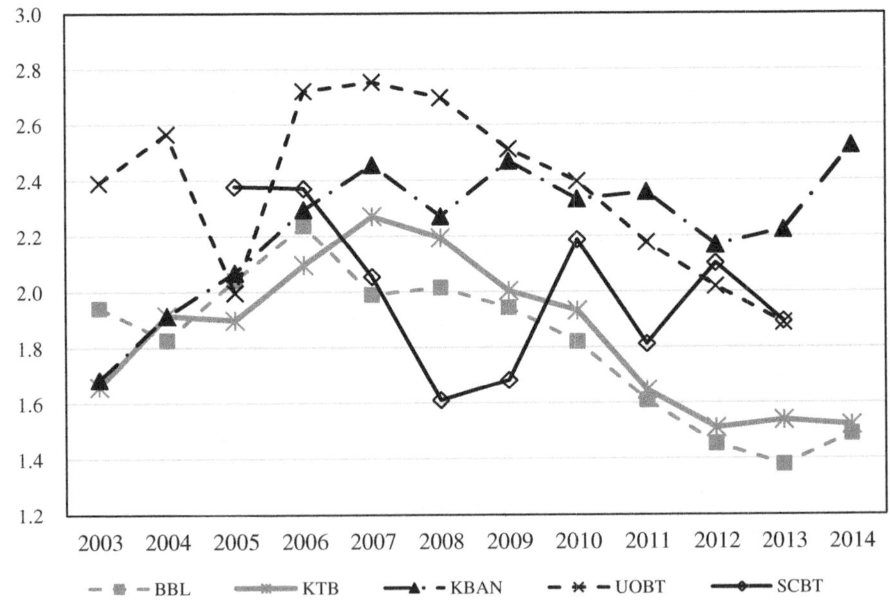

Fig. 6.4 **a** Change in non-interest income ratio. **b** Change in operating expense ratio. **c** The change in return on assets. *Source* Stock Exchange of Thailand; BankScope, Bureau van Dijk.
Note BBL = Bangkok Bank, KTB = Krung Thai Bank, KBANK = Kasikornbank, UOBT = United Overseas Bank Thai, SCBT = Standard Chartered Bank Thai

(c)

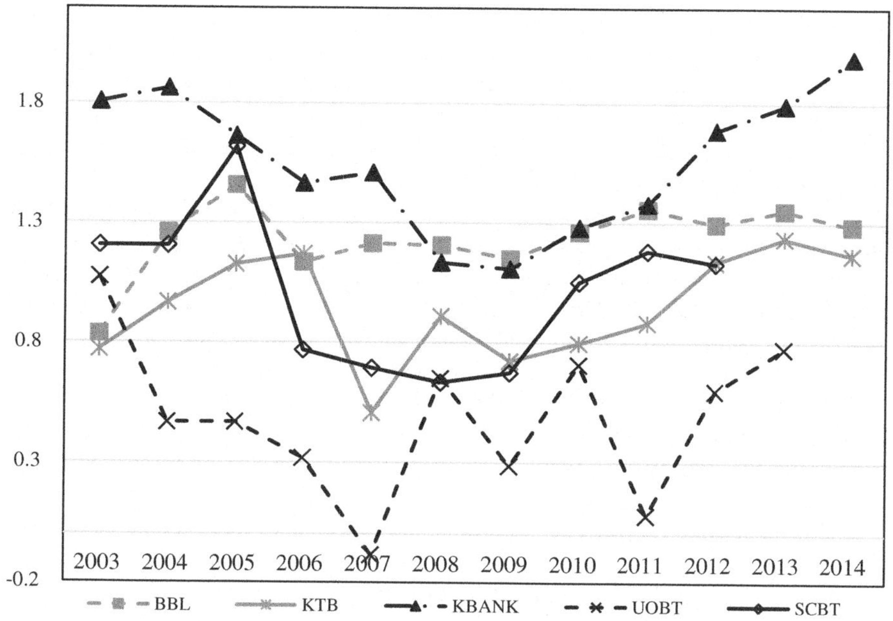

Fig. 6.4 (continued)

branch networks and IT infrastructures. All of the above contributed to the accruing operating expense ratio.

In the years that followed the implementation of the Customer Relationship Management Development Program, Kasikornbank continued to expand greatly. The branches in the Bangkok area increased by 40.9% from 2003 to 2007, which is far quicker than the average growth ratio (20.1%) of the other Big 4 banks. Further, branches in other provincial areas increased by 43.2% in the same period, which is also more rapid than the average growth ratio (34.1%) of the other Big 4 banks.

Overall, in addition to the organizational restructuring process and management reforms after the AFC, the costs for premises and equipment, media publicity, sales promotions, as well as the bank's information technology (IT) program increased the overall operating expenses, while the return on assets declined continually during this period.

6.6.2 Further Adjustments in Business Development Strategies from 2007 to 2012

From the global financial crisis in 2008 to the severe Thailand floods in 2011, the Thai market experienced unprecedented economic turbulence and its real GDP growth rate fluctuated violently during this time. Due to domestic political uncertainty, global economic woes, and major regulatory changes,[20] Kasikornbank took further adjustments in its business development strategy. The bank continued to emphasize the implementation of strategic projects, especially regarding the technological advancement and innovation of financial products. Moreover, the bank focused on improving the quality of financial services for customer satisfaction rather than rapid branch expansion as in the last phase.

In comparison to branch expansion during the aforementioned phase, in the Bangkok area, Kasikornbank's presence increased by 33.6% from 2007 to 2012, which is similar to the average growth ratio (33.7%) of the other Big 4 banks during the same period. In other provincial areas, it increased by 34.2%, which is the same as the average growth ratio (34.2%) of the Big 4 banks. Subsequently, rather than focusing on the development of business facilities and branch networks, the bank prioritized financial service excellence through the "customer-centric" strategy during this period. A key project, the "K-Transformation Project," was implemented to improve the quality of financial services by expanding the bank's capacity to handle increasing business needs.

The project aimed to provide solutions and products to meet the needs of each customer segment and the "Know Our Customer" program conducted several studies on customers' needs and behavior patterns by using in-depth data analysis. The goal was to re-categorize customer segments, identify the characteristics of their customer behavior, and target their potential financial service needs.

Thereafter, the bank also introduced programs to enhance the efficiency and effectiveness of responding to customers' needs, for instance, the "IT Capital" program and the "Financial Information System" program. These projects promote the development of financial technology to expand the bank's capacity for "computing workloads" and the expansion of electronic service channels.

Furthermore, by collecting customer opinions, the project also emphasized the improvement of the bank's operational procedures. It aimed to provide multiple convenient channels for product sales and financial services.

Overall, these programs played an important role in reaching potential customers, expanding the capacity to handle banking transactions, realizing the convenience of multiple services, and responding to the requirements and needs of clients in various segments, all of which made Kasikornbank a competitor in the financial services market despite the global economic slowdown.

As shown in Fig. 6.4, the bank's non-interest income ratio continued accruing significantly throughout this phase. Besides continued customer growth, which may have stemmed from the rapid expansion of nationwide branch networks in the previous phase, the implementation of the "customer-centric" strategy that provides customers with more efficient and convenient channels for their financial needs

---

[20] Except for the implementation of the "Financial Sector Master Plan Phase II," which emphasized the improvement of operation efficiency and enhancement of market competitiveness, several financial regulatory reforms with a focus on risk management and accounting standards were effective during this period.

may have contributed significantly to the strong and stable increase of non-interest income. This includes the fee-income sales and other financial services income from bancassurance, credit card business, and mutual fund management.

Regarding operational efficiency, the operating expense ratio has gradually declined since 2007, which contrasts with its sharp increase during the last phase. Further, the operating expense ratio is positively related to improving financial technology and advancing management following the programs above, which aim to enhance operational effectiveness.

In sum, despite a range of nationwide negative factors and a global economic recession, Kasikornbank was still highly profitable. For instance, although its return on assets declined until 2008, it increased steadily thereafter. Regarding management reforms and banking performance during these two phases, the bank's quick response to the changing global financial environment played an important role in its profitability. The shift of strategic emphases on business expansion, branch network expansion, and quality improvement of financial services ensured a stable increase in income while avoiding an increase in operational expenses. One could argue that the bank's response to the global financial crisis was more beneficial than its response to the AFC.

6.6.3 Regional Business Expansion Since 2013

In 2013, Kasikornbank went through major personnel changes to the board of directors and the top-level management team (Tables 6.2 and 6.3). The chairman of the board, Mr. Banyong Lamsam, and vice chairman, Police General Pow Sarasin, who were appointed in 1992, resigned in the same year. Along with Mr. Banthoon Lamsam becoming the chairman, some other founding family members were appointed to key positions in 2013, including vice chairman of the board and senior executive vice president. During this phase, Kasikornbank adopted a business expansion strategy both at home and abroad. This subsection makes a comprehensive analysis of banking practices from two perspectives: one focuses on projects aimed at reaching more customers in the domestic market and the other focuses on business expansion in ASEAN countries and three other regions (Japan, China and Korea). The latter was implemented for the bank to build a broad base of clients in the ASEAN Economic Community.

Domestically, the bank (once again) focused on business expansion in strategic provinces based on predictions of increasing business opportunities and economic growth potential due to ASEAN regional economic integration. In the previous phase (2007–2012), the bank's annual average branch growth rate was 6.74%, which is slightly lower than the average ratio (6.87%) of Big 4 banks. However, the ratio climbed to 9.24% during 2013–2016, which is far higher than the average ratio (4.14%) of Big 4 banks. In particular, the domestic branch numbers increased by 29.57% and the overseas branch numbers increased by 50% in 2014.

Except for the expansion of nationwide branch networks mentioned above, there was also a significantly rapid expansion of multiple service channels since 2013. As per the "customer-centric" strategy of the previous phase, the bank increased branding and marketing to reach new customers in strategic provinces that were under urbanization. The bank also established special departments in various provinces, as SME Business Centers and THE WISDOM centers, to respond to the financial needs of corporate and individual local customers with better efficiency.

Furthermore, the bank played an active role in introducing customers (the private individual customer in particular) to multiple digital banking service channels to satisfy their various requirements.

To enhance electronic banking services, the bank established 1113 ATMs, 580 cash deposit machines, and 190 passbook update machines during 2014, which increased with an annual growth rate of 12.7, 26.4, and 17.0%, respectively. Consequently, as shown in Fig. 6.5, retail and SME loans increased steadily during this phase despite the economic slowdown and the slow recovery afterward.

Through the continuous investment to enhance the bank's information technology systems, the bank has gradually become the leader in the digital banking business in Thailand and benefited significantly from expanding its capacity to handle increasing operations. In 2015, this leadership brought about a total of 1135 million THB annual transactions, which accounted for 39% of the domestic digital banking market. Many banks are working to promote mobile banking services, and 50% of Kasikornbank

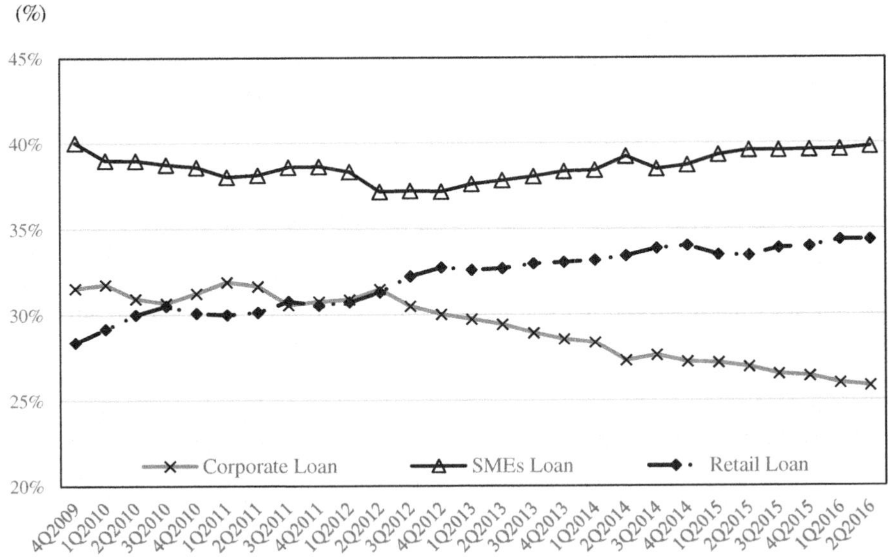

Fig. 6.5 Kasikornbank's change in bank credits since 2008. *Source* Kasikorn Research Center, survey by the author. *Note* The percentage is calculated as the ratio of corporate loan to total loan, the ratio of SMEs loan to total loan, and the ratio of retail loan to total loan

customers use mobile banking, which is the highest among the Big 4 banks (15% higher than the bank in second place).

In addition, as the financial technology upsurge becomes more influential across regional markets and the globe, the bank also established the Kasikorn Business-Technology Group (KBTG) in 2016. The KBTG focuses on technological innovation and related business support to retain its leadership position and technological competitiveness in the upcoming technology-led business environment.

Overall, the thorough and continuous implementation of information technology (IT) programs since 2003 has leveraged the bank significantly as not just a competitor but a leader in one of the most promising fields. The founding family's persistent management control and strong leadership are considered the most important factors for maintaining the enforcement of large-scale investments and long-term strategic projects, particularly during the first two phases, when the digital banking market was still under development.

In addition, the bank placed significant emphasis on reaching the overseas markets since 2013, especially in ASEAN countries. In 2014, the number of overseas branches increased by 50%. Table 6.4 illustrates the expansion of Kasikornbank's overseas service network.

Compared to previous stages, the bank expanded by 120% in terms of the total number of overseas networks during this stage. In addition, except for one representative office in Jakarta, all of the new overseas networks are concentrated in fast-growing CLMV countries (Cambodia, Laos, Myanmar, Vietnam) and China. This indicates a deliberate move toward overseas business development that aims to build a local customer base and provide trade and investment services for domestic customers in those areas.

Nevertheless, the bank acted with great caution during this regional expansion. Only newly established overseas networks in Laos and China were locally incorporated or foreign branches (including sub-branch) that were qualified for universal banking business including deposits and loans. Laos has an abundance of business opportunities for Thai domestic investors due to its geographic proximity and similar language background. Meanwhile, China is a major player in the Thai export market and regional trade and investment, which should accompany growing bilateral business opportunities. Other overseas networks in CLMV countries are all representative offices (junior forms) and mainly focus on collecting local information to prepare for market entry in the future.

In sum, the aforementioned measures reflect Kasikornbank's outstanding rapid responsiveness to the domestic and global changing economic climate. This is especially true regarding the enhancement of its fee-income business model after the AFC, the strategic shift from branch network business expansion to improving the quality of its financial services during the global financial crisis, the thorough and continuous implementation of IT programs during the period, and a rapid overseas expansion in ASEAN countries and three other regions. Thus, this case study's findings are consistent with Suehiro (1993). Concerning large family-run businesses in Thailand, he argued that a prompt response to the changing economic environment resulted in increasing profitability through business expansion and internal management improvement. In addition, this success can be attributed to strong leadership in top management positions, which, in this case, refers to the founding family's persistent management control which includes board members and executive seats at the company.

6.7 Conclusions

Following the AFC, Thailand witnessed a significant influx of foreign investment in its banking sector, predominantly targeting larger banks rather than small and medium-sized institutions. This influx led to heightened market concentration, evidenced by the substantial increase in market share held by the Big 4 banks post-1997. This case study focuses on a major family-owned commercial bank, representative of Thailand's common banking structure, to explore how ownership changes driven by extensive regulatory and financial environmental shifts at the bank level influence management control. This study additionally delves into the subsequent effects on business practices and overall banking performance, offering a detailed perspective on the manifestation of financial reforms' impacts at the organizational level.

This descriptive study found that the bank underwent two upsurges of foreign entry, both following financial crises (the AFC and the global financial crisis). Its total foreign ownership shares are significantly high and have maintained a stable ratio since 2002. In addition, major foreign investment has persisted in a relatively stable fashion since the initial investment. Furthermore, most of the bank's major foreign shareholders belong to the global financial services sector or investment business. This suggests that an increase in foreign participation is positively related to financial innovation and improvement of management skills.

Regarding management structure, this study found that drastic ownership evolution post financial crises did not have a significant impact at a top management level. In other words, no major personnel changes were a consequence of new major foreign institutional shareholders. This implies that accruing foreign ownership did not compromise the founding family's strong leadership.

On the contrary, regardless of a decrease in the founding family's ownership shares, they still maintained stable board members and the executive seats. This is especially true of significant positions such as chairman of the board and CEO. This illustrates the founding family's transition from ownership control to management control, which is consistent with the findings of Herman (1982) that despite a deconcentrating trend of family ownership resulting from an increase in capital and business expansion, founding families still maintain their dominance in corporate governance.

In addition, it implies that the founding family has maintained consistent management control, which ensures the stability of decision-making. Moreover, this management structure contributes significantly to the complete enforcement of management reforms and long-term strategic programs.

Finally, this study examines the mechanism by which management control continuity and decision-making stability influence business practice and banking performance. Throughout Kasikornbank's three phases of management reforms, the thorough implementation of corporate long-term strategic projects benefited the bank with a significant competitive advantage.

In particular, its IT strategy to strengthen the bank's IT infrastructure played an important role in realizing its market leadership potential in digital banking. Kasikornbank was ahead in capitalizing on this field and its continuous efforts to invest in technology and innovation stemmed from the bank's consistent management control and stable decision-making. Similarly, its human capital strategy and "customer-centric" strategy resulted in superior customer service and obtaining new customers. These findings provide an explanation to existing empirical studies, such as those by Unite and Sullivan (2003) and Lu and Mieno (2020) on why and how foreign participation is linked to business diversification and higher operating expenses.

Therefore, alongside Kasikornbank's strategy for expanding its operations both within Thailand and internationally since the 2010s, its capacity for innovative and swift adaptation to evolving economic conditions can be attributed to the strategic leadership of its top management team. This case study also presents an analysis of the growth of ethnically Chinese family-owned enterprises in the post-crisis era, examining aspects such as ownership evolution, corporate governance, and management reforms. While Kasikornbank's experience provides valuable insights into the dynamics of ownership changes at the bank level, it is noted that Kasikornbank, as a typical example of Thai family-run commercial banks, does not encapsulate the entire spectrum. Hence, cross-country comparative studies and further theoretical elaboration are necessary to assess the impacts of regulatory changes post-crisis, particularly the ramifications of growing foreign involvement in the sector.

Chapter 7
Conclusion

Abstract This chapter outlines the principal conclusions of this study, which conducted a longitudinal, evidence-based policy analysis of the financial reforms following the Asian Financial Crisis. In the Thai commercial banking sector, the aftermath of the crisis saw the continuation of a strong oligopoly, characterized by intense competition among large local banks. The entry of mainly Asian-origin foreign banks introduced a medium-sized banking segment and, along with the rise of small banking groups funded by both local and foreign capital, restructured the banking hierarchy. Despite the diverse impacts of foreign capital, large traditional family-owned banks retained robust leadership and management structures, mitigating the effects of reduced family ownership and maintaining their competitive edge. Overall, it appears challenging to assert that Thailand's post-crisis financial reforms—aimed at enhancing competition and advancing technological progress—have been explicitly successful. This analysis suggests that while structural changes have occurred, the intended policy goals have not been fully realized.

Prior to the late 1990s, foreign banks were restricted to branch operations in Thailand due to stringent regulations. Leading up to the AFC, this lack of foreign participation contributed to poor governance and competition in the domestic banking industry, exacerbating issues like connected lending and internal corruption factors, factors later deemed crucial to the crisis. In response, post-crisis, the Thai government implemented initiatives such as the "Financial Sector Master Plan Phase I and II" to encourage both foreign and domestic bank entry, aiming to improve market competition and promote financial technology development. The AFC led to significant financial distress among Thai financial companies and banks, particularly affecting smaller banks, which faced bankruptcy or restructuring through government interventions such as capital injections, temporary nationalization, or acquisition by foreign entities. Concurrently, larger banks attracted substantial foreign investments after the crisis, reflecting a shift towards more open banking regulations.

Set against this backdrop of a shifting domestic financial landscape, this study offers a thorough analysis of the financial reform processes and their significance post-AFC. It places special emphasis on the regulatory adjustments concerning

W. Lu, *Post-Asian Financial Crisis Reforms in Thailand*,
SpringerBriefs in Economics, https://doi.org/10.1007/978-981-97-3771-0_7

foreign investments in the banking sector and their ensuing impacts, seeking to elucidate the policy intentions behind the "Financial Sector Master Plan." Additionally, this research delves into the evolution of ownership structures following banking market reorganization, examines ensuing shifts in market competition dynamics, business methodologies, and the profit-cost framework, and provides an assessment of these financial reforms. The principal conclusions of this study are outlined below.

Initially, this research undertakes a thorough analysis of the financial reorganization process in the early 2000s, which notably reshaped Thailand's financial landscape. It delves into the regulatory reforms and various phases of the "Financial Sector Master Plan," deducing that the overhaul in financial regulations primarily focused on enhancing market efficiency, stability, and competitiveness. This included the deregulation of foreign investments to foster improved market competition conditions. Moreover, the study highlights efforts to address systemic weaknesses and structural challenges, notably in improving corporate governance and risk management within financial institutions.

Concurrent with these financial restructurings, the study identifies a fundamental shift in the market structure of the commercial banking sector.

(1) There was a marked decline in ownership by traditional founding families in the banking sector. Additionally, numerous such families and their majority-owned business conglomerates exited the banking market. Concurrently, foreign involvement in the banking industry has consistently escalated since the AFC. By 2014, the aggregate foreign ownership stake in the banking sector exceeded 40%, with foreign banks accounting for over 15% of the total assets across the entire banking sector.
(2) There has been a notable influx of both foreign and domestic entities entering the market, particularly in the segment of small and medium-sized banks. Notably, since the Lehman Shock, multinational banks from neighboring Asian countries have been more active than well-known Western financial groups in this space.
(3) The research indicates that increased foreign involvement has primarily targeted the large-sized commercial banks rather than small and medium-sized ones. In the wake of this shift, the total asset share of Thailand's Big 4 banks surged rapidly post-AFC. Although the market concentration initially declined due to new entrants during the Thaksin financial reforms, it began to climb steadily from 2006, showing consistent and significant growth. This persistently high market concentration level suggests that the oligopolistic structure of Thailand's commercial banking sector has not substantially improved, despite being a key objective of the financial reforms. The study also explores the alterations in the profit–cost structure and business models corresponding to these changes in ownership and the competitive landscape of the market.

The study finds that commercial banks continue to predominantly depend on traditional lending practices, with net interest income constituting the main source of profits. A notable shift is observed in the primary customer segments of these banks, moving from sectors like manufacturing and wholesale/retail commerce to finance and personal consumer loans.

When examining banking performance, the analysis reveals that large-sized banks outperform their smaller counterparts, including foreign banks, in terms of profit ratios, interest rate spreads, and operational efficiency. This superior performance of large-sized banks is attributed to their dominant position in an increasingly oligopolistic market and the benefits derived from economies of scale. As a result, the study notes a trend where major banks primarily compete among themselves, rather than with smaller or foreign bank entities.

In the context of small and medium-sized banks, foreign banks demonstrate higher interest rate spreads and comparable operational efficiency to domestic banks of similar size. However, their overall performance still falls short of that of larger banks. At this stage, significant advancements in financial technology by foreign banks have not been observed, and their contribution to enhancing market competition is limited due to their relatively smaller scale.

Additionally, the research delves into the effects of the evolving financial landscape in East and Southeast Asia, especially within the framework of regional financial integration. It concludes that although Thailand has made considerable strides in financial accessibility compared to its regional counterparts, its larger banks still face a disparity in scale and overseas expansion compared to leading banks in Singapore and Malaysia.

Secondly, this study undertakes an empirical analysis with bank-level panel data from 1999 to 2014 to investigate the effects of foreign capital entry on the cost and profit structures of commercial banks, distinguishing between market-level and individual bank-level impacts.

At the bank level, an elevation in foreign ownership within domestic banks correlated with higher interest rate spreads and reduced default risks, but also elevated operating expenses. This suggests that operational reforms were somewhat limited, with banks opting for long-term investment strategies over immediate operational overhauls, incurring higher costs in the process.

At the market level, the presence of foreign banks is associated with increased interest rate spreads and non-interest income, alongside a reduction in operating expenses, culminating in higher asset returns. The entry of foreign banks intensified market competition, propelling domestic banks to enhance their operational efficiency and expand their non-lending activities through innovation. Simultaneously, this influx led to a stronger market concentration, which drove up interest rate spreads and profitability. Overall, the entry of foreign banks appears to significantly improve banking performance over the long term.

In conjunction with earlier findings, this research uncovers how these reforms, notably the heightened foreign bank involvement, have paradoxically degraded market competition while also not fully achieving their intended policy goals in financial technology advancement. This nuanced understanding challenges us to reconsider the effectiveness of policies and to better comprehend market dynamics within the sphere of emerging markets.

Ultimately, this study, by merging macroeconomic trends with micro-level analysis, investigates how these regulatory impacts materialize at the corporate level. In

Thailand and across Southeast Asia, family business groups are often viewed as structurally weak in developing long-term entrepreneurial dynamism due to their entwined ownership and control, a characteristic widely criticized post-AFC. Existing literature has not thoroughly examined how familial corporate control, extending beyond mere ownership, influences long-term business practice and competitiveness. This research, through a case study of Kasikornbank, assesses the impact of shifting ownership dynamics—increased foreign and decreased family ownership—on governance and performance in banking. It crucially sheds light on the adaptation strategies of Thai family-owned banks during economic crises and provides a more intricate view of the interplay between financial reforms and institutional performance.

In the immediate aftermath of the Asian financial crisis, Kasikornbank family owners were among the earliest to embrace foreign investments into the bank to maintain business stability. Diverging from conventional Thai family business groups' business practices on diluting family shareholding mainly for financial reasons, the family owners went further by relinquishing their ownership control from the early 2000s but maintained management control through board and management representations.

With respect to ownership control, it was observed that the founding family transitioned to a minority shareholder status following the Asian Financial Crisis, while there was a marked increase in foreign ownership. Notably, major foreign investors, primarily from the financial sector, have maintained a consistent shareholding ratio since their initial investments. Concerning management control, despite the reduced ownership stake of the founding family, they continue to occupy stable and prominent positions within the board and executive team.

This transformation in ownership and management control suggests that the significant ownership changes post-AFC have not notably altered the upper echelons of management. There are a lack of major personnel shifts attributable to new major foreign institutional shareholders, which implies that the growing foreign ownership has not undermined the dominant leadership of the founding family. Furthermore, this shift indicates a transition from direct ownership control to a more pronounced management control by the founding family, highlighting their continued influence over the bank's management decisions and maintaining internal stability in its governance.

The analysis of key management reforms post-crisis indicates that the rising proportion of foreign investors has not markedly influenced the upper management echelons of banks. Meanwhile, the internal stability through the family's continued management control and reforms in corporate governance in turn, provided secured decision-making processes with its new and foreign shareholders on various long-term investments, such as digital banking business. This resulted in Kasikornbank's market leadership in Thailand's digital banking, which became a significant competitive advantage over its rivals currently.

Consequently, this research also enriches the discourse on family business and emerging market business history, providing a more detailed perspective on how entrepreneurship within family business groups in emerging markets intertwines with evolving social and economic landscapes.

In conclusion, through longitudinal and evidence-based analyses of the impact of post-AFC financial regulatory reforms, this study deepens the understanding of policy impact mechanisms at the micro-level. Following these reforms, the commercial banking sector in Thailand has evolved into a distinct segment-based structure. The substantial market concentration among large banks has driven competitive dynamics in this segment. Medium-sized banks are mainly composed of foreign banks from neighboring Asian countries, and the latest group of domestic and foreign banks constitutes the small bank segment. Despite reduced ownership by founding families and increased foreign participation in larger banks, the continued dominance of these families in management control correlates with significant competitive advantages. However, both descriptive and data-driven analyses reveal that deregulation in foreign investment strengthens the market power of larger banks, enhancing their profitability. The clear realization of policy goals, particularly in enhancing market competition and advancing financial technology, remains inconspicuous.

Crucially, this study highlights areas that necessitate additional research for an expanded understanding of this topic in future studies. Firstly, Thailand's experience reveals that foreign entry into the commercial banking sector is characterized by complex effects. Notably, the growing presence of foreign capital has intensified market concentration, as a substantial portion of this capital targeted large local banks. This observation challenges the conventional belief that foreign participation inherently enhances banking market performance, suggesting a need for more comparative studies and theoretical refinement in the future.

Secondly, the Kasikornbank case study illustrates the founding family's sustained control over management, unaffected by the entrance of significant foreign institutional shareholders. Yet, the precise dynamics enabling the founding family to maintain such dominant governance in the banking sector require further elucidation.

Appendix 1
Reorganization of Thai Commercial Banks (1997–2017)

W. Lu, *Post-Asian Financial Crisis Reforms in Thailand*, SpringerBriefs in Economics, https://doi.org/10.1007/978-981-97-3771-0

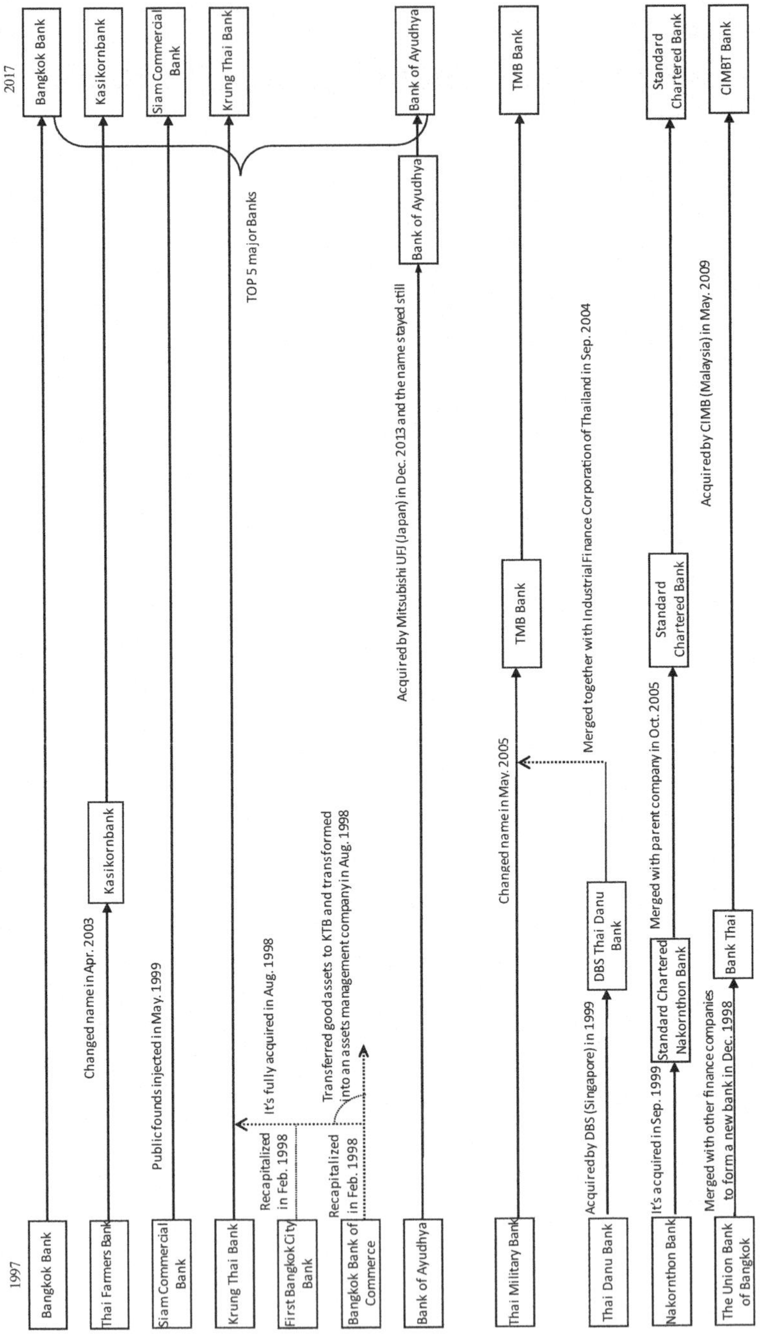
1997
2017
Bangkok Bank
Thai Farmers Bank
Siam Commercial Bank
Krung Thai Bank
First Bangkok City Bank
Bangkok Bank of Commerce
Bank of Ayudhya
Thai Military Bank
Thai Danu Bank
Nakornthon Bank
The Union Bank of Bangkok
Changed name in Apr. 2003
Kasikornbank
Public founds injected in May. 1999
Recapitalized in Feb. 1998
It's fully acquired in Aug. 1998
Recapitalized in Feb. 1998
Transferred good assets to KTB and transformed into an assets management company in Aug. 1998
Acquired by Mitsubishi UFJ (Japan) in Dec. 2013 and the name stayed still
Changed name in May. 2005
TMB Bank
Acquired by DBS (Singapore) in 1999
DBS Thai Danu Bank
Merged together with Industrial Finance Corporation of Thailand in Sep. 2004
It's acquired in Sep. 1999
Standard Chartered Nakornthon Bank
Merged with parent company in Oct. 2005
Standard Chartered Bank
Merged with other finance companies to form a new bank in Dec. 1998
Bank Thai
Acquired by CIMB (Malaysia) in May. 2009
TOP 5 major Banks
Bangkok Bank
Kasikornbank
Siam Commercial Bank
Krung Thai Bank
Bank of Ayudhya
TMB Bank
Standard Chartered Bank
CIMBT Bank

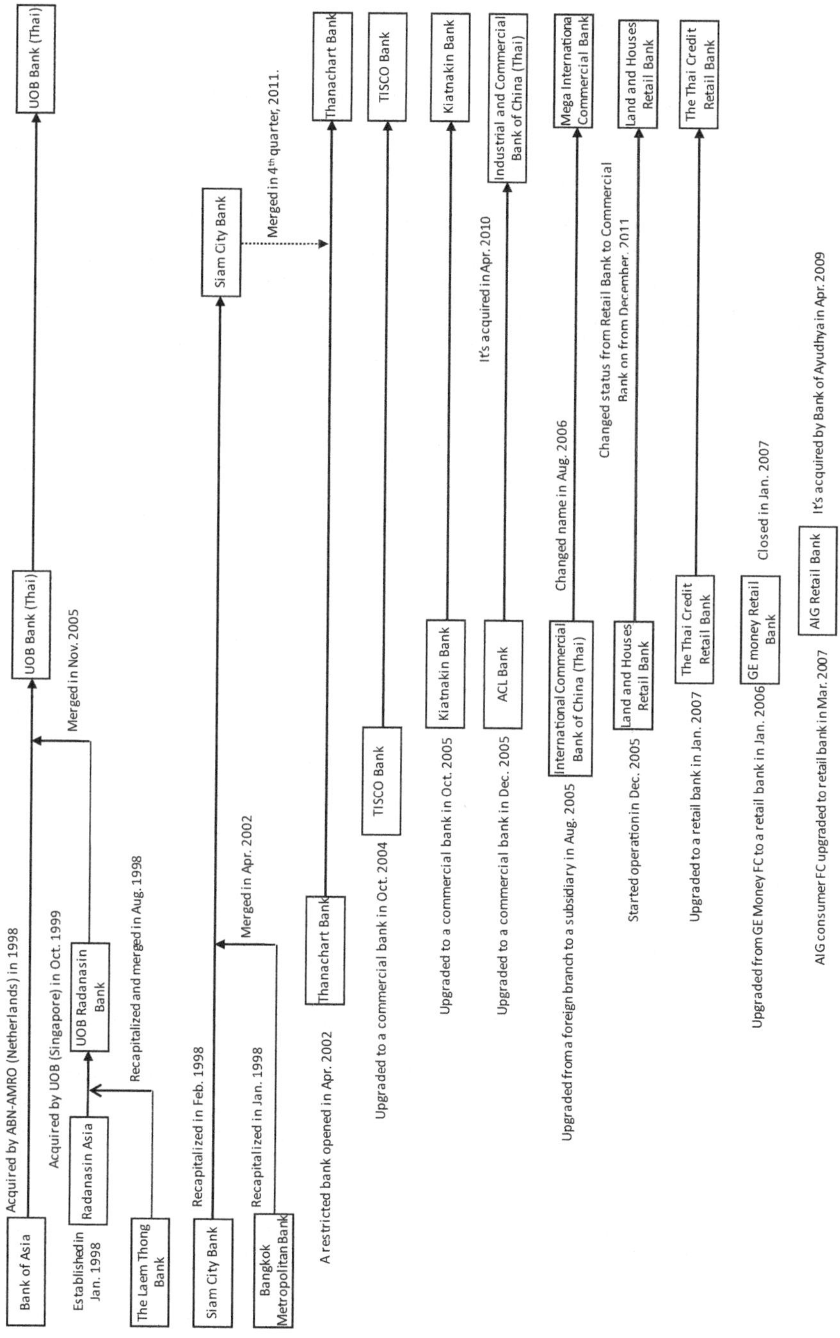
Bank of Asia
Acquired by ABN-AMRO (Netherlands) in 1998
UOB Bank (Thai)
UOB Bank (Thai)
Established in Jan. 1998
Radanasin Asia
Acquired by UOB (Singapore) in Oct. 1999
UOB Radanasin Bank
Merged in Nov. 2005
The Laem Thong Bank
Recapitalized and merged in Aug. 1998
Siam City Bank
Recapitalized in Feb. 1998
Siam City Bank
Merged in 4th quarter, 2011.
Bangkok Metropolitan Bank
Recapitalized in Jan. 1998
Merged in Apr. 2002
A restricted bank opened in Apr. 2002
Thanachart Bank
Thanachart Bank
Upgraded to a commercial bank in Oct. 2004
TISCO Bank
TISCO Bank
Upgraded to a commercial bank in Oct. 2005
Kiatnakin Bank
Kiatnakin Bank
Upgraded to a commercial bank in Dec. 2005
ACL Bank
It's acquired in Apr. 2010
Industrial and Commercial Bank of China (Thai)
Upgraded from a foreign branch to a subsidiary in Aug. 2005
International Commercial Bank of China (Thai)
Changed name in Aug. 2006
Mega International Commercial Bank
Started operation in Dec. 2005
Land and Houses Retail Bank
Changed status from Retail Bank to Commercial Bank on from December, 2011
Land and Houses Retail Bank
Upgraded to a retail bank in Jan. 2007
The Thai Credit Retail Bank
The Thai Credit Retail Bank
Upgraded from GE Money FC to a retail bank in Jan. 2006
GE money Retail Bank
Closed in Jan. 2007
AIG consumer FC upgraded to retail bank in Mar. 2007
AIG Retail Bank
It's acquired by Bank of Ayudhya in Apr. 2009

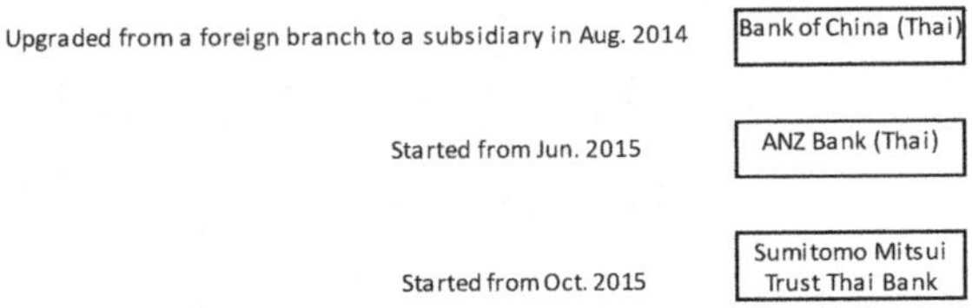

Note Updated by the author based on Appendix Fig. 1 in Lu (2018) and Fig. 1 in Lu and Mieno (2020), utilizing data from Commercial Banks in Thailand (1997–2017); the Bank of Thailand (statistical data from 1997 to 2017); and annual reports of commercial banks incorporated in Thailand.

References

Books and Articles

Alberto, M., Tan, L., Regalado, K., & Reyes, M. (2018). The Effect of Foreign Bank Entry on the Performance of Philippine Domestic Banks. In DLSU Research Congress.

Amason, A. C. (1996). Distinguishing the effects of functional and dysfunctional conflict on strategic decision making: Resolving a paradox for top management teams. *Academy of Management Journal*, *39*(1), 123–148. https://doi.org/10.5465/256633

Barajas, A., Steiner, R., & Salazar, N. (2000). The impact of liberalization and foreign investment in Colombia's financial sector. *Journal of Development Economics*, *63*,157–196. https://doi.org/10.1016/S0304-3878(00)00104-8

Bayraktar, N., & Wang, Y. (2004). Foreign bank entry, performance of domestic banks, and sequence of financial liberalization. *Performance of Domestic Banks, and Sequence of Financial Liberalization (August 8, 2004)*. https://ssrn.com/abstract=625293

Bhattacharaya, J. (1993). The role of foreign banks in developing countries: A survey of evidence. Unpublished manuscript, Cornell University.

Bhattacharaya, A., Lovell, C. A. K., & Sahay, P. (1997). The impact of liberalization on the productive efficiency of Indian commercial banks. *European Journal of Operational Research*, *98*, 332–345. https://doi.org/10.1016/S0377-2217(96)00351-7

Chantapong, S. (2001). *What happened to the banking sector in the aftermath of financial crisis: The case of Thailand*. Kiel Institute of World Economics Working Paper. https://doi.org/10.2139/ssrn.310179

______. (2005). Comparative study of domestic and foreign bank performance in Thailand: The regression analysis. *Economic Change and Restructuring*, *38*(1), 63–83. https://doi.org/10.1007/s10644-005-4523-5

Claessens, S., Demirguc-Kunt, A., & Huizinga, H. (2001). How does foreign entry affect the domestic banking market? *Journal of Banking and Finance*, *25*, 891–911. https://doi.org/10.1016/S0378-4266(00)00102-3

Clarke, G., Cull, R., D'Amato, L., & Molinari, A. (1999). *The effect of foreign entry on Argentina's domestic banking sector*. World Bank Policy Research Working Paper, 2158.

De Jesus, F. L. B., & Torres, E. A. (2017). Analysis of the ASEAN Banking Integration Framework: The Philippines as a looking glass for consumer preference. *Journal of Global Entrepreneurship Research*, *7*(1), 24. https://doi.org/10.1186/s40497-017-0082-2

W. Lu, *Post-Asian Financial Crisis Reforms in Thailand*, SpringerBriefs in Economics, https://doi.org/10.1007/978-981-97-3771-0

Feldstein, M. S. (2002). Economic and financial crises in emerging market economies: Overview of prevention and management. https://doi.org/10.3386/w8837

Hattori, T. (1991). Kankoku keizai no kōgyōka katei ni okeru sho mondai 5. Gendai Kankoku kigyō no shoyū to keiei [Issues in the industrialization process of the Korean economy 5. Ownership and management of contemporary Korean companies]. Japan External Trade Organization Institute of Developing Economies.

Herman, E. S. (1982). Corporate control, corporate power. Cambridge Books.

Imaizumi, S. (2007). Tai [Thailand]. In Kin'yū-chō itaku Ajia kinyū seka- no kisei kanwa ni kansuru hōseido kenkyū [Research on the deregulation of the financial sector in Asia commissioned by the Financial Services Agency]. Japan External Trade Organization Institute of Developing Economies.

Lauridsen, L. S. (1998). The financial crisis in Thailand: Causes, conduct and consequences? *World Development*, 26(8), 1575–1591. https://doi.org/10.1016/S0305-750X(98)00069-2

Levine, R. (1996). Foreign banks, financial development, and economic. International financial markets: Harmonization versus competition, 224.

Lu, W. (2018). Tai shōgyō ginkō seka- to ginkō seka- e no gaishi sannyū [Thai commercial banking sector and foreign capital entry into the banking sector]. In Mieno, F. (Ed.), Tōnan Ajia ni okeru shōgyō ginkō bumon no hen'yō to genjō kenkyūkai hōkokusho [Transformation and current status of the commercial banking sector in Southeast Asia] (pp. 77–95). Japan External Trade Organization Institute of Developing Economies.

Lu, W., & Mieno, F. (2020). Impact of foreign entry into the banking sector: The case of Thailand in 1999–2014. *Pacific-Basin Finance Journal*, *64*. https://doi.org/10.1016/j.pacfin.2020.101424

Menkhoff, L., & Suwanaporn, C. (2007). 10 years after the crisis: Thailand's financial system reform. Discussion Paper 356, 1–25. https://doi.org/10.1016/j.asieco.2006.12.002

Mieno, F., & Lu, W. (2020). Tai shōgyō ginkō no shoyū ・ shūeki kōzō no hen'yō [The transformation of ownership and profit structure of Thai commercial banks]. In Hen'yō suru ASEAN no shōgyō ginkō [Transforming commercial banks in ASEAN]. Japan External Trade Organization Institute of Developing Economies.

Moore, J. D. (2017). Varieties of capitalism in Southeast Asia. Springer. https://doi.org/10.1007/978-3-319-53700-9

Muscat, R. J. (1994). The fifth tiger: A study of Thai development policy (pp. 267–268). Armonk, NY: ME Sharpe.

Nomura Research Institute, Ltd. (2015). Tai ni okeru kinyū infra seibi shien no tame no kisoteki chōsa [Preliminary survey for the support of financial infrastructure development in Thailand]. Nomura Research Institute, Ltd.

Okuda, H., & Rungsomboon, S. (2007). The effects of foreign bank entry on the Thai banking market: Empirical analysis from 1990 to 2002. *Review of Pacific Basin Financial Markets and Policies*, *10*(01), 101–126. https://doi.org/10.1142/S0219091507000970

Pipatpokaisri, O. (2003). A historical study of Thai business conglomerates and their business strategy. *Keio business review*, 41, 23–42.

Poghosyan, T., & Poghosyan, A. (2010). Foreign bank entry, bank efficiency and market power in Central and Eastern European Countries. *Economics of transition*, 18(3), 571–598. https://doi.org/10.1111/j.1468-0351.2009.00378.x

Prasai, A. (2016). Impact of foreign banks entry on the performance of Nepalese Banks. *Nepalese Journal of Finance*, 13.

Suehiro, A. (1989). Capital accumulation in Thailand, 1855–1985. Tokyo, the Centre for East Asian Cultural Studies.

______. (1993). Family business reassessed: Corporate structure and late-starting industrialization in Thailand. *Developing Economies*, *31*, 378–378. https://doi.org/10.1111/j.1746-1049.1993.tb00032.x

Suehiro, A., & Nanbara, M. (1991). Tai no zaibatsu [Thai conglomerates]. Tōbunkan Shuppan.

Takayasu, K. (2008). Tai ni okeru kinyū kaikaku no hyōka to seisaku kadai [Evaluation of financial reforms and policy issues in Thailand]. Ajia Kenkyū, 54(2), 33–47.

Tasaka, T. (1996). Tai no shōgyō ginkō to dōzokuteki keiei [Thai commercial banks and family-based management]. Kikan Keizai Kenkyū, 19(1), 95–122.

Uiboupin, J. (2004). Effects of foreign banks entry on bank performance in the CEE countries. University of Tartu Faculty of Economics and Business Administration Working Paper (33-2004). https://doi.org/10.2139/ssrn.679995

Unite, A. A., & Sullivan, M. J. (2003). The effect of foreign entry and ownership structure on the Philippine domestic banking market. *Journal of Banking & Finance*, *27*(12), 2323–2345. https://doi.org/10.1016/S0378-4266(02)00330-8

Useem, M. (1986). The inner circle: Large corporations and the rise of business political activity in the US and UK. Oxford University Press. https://doi.org/10.2307/2150884

Wu, J., Chen, M., Jeon, B. N., & Wang, R. (2017). Does foreign bank penetration affect the risk of domestic banks? Evidence from emerging economies. *Journal of Financial Stability*, 31, 45–61. https://doi.org/10.1016/j.jfs.2017.06.004

Yeyati, E. L., & Micco, A. (2007). Concentration and foreign penetration in Latin American banking sectors: Impact on competition and risk. *Journal of Banking & Finance*, *31*(6), 1633–1647. https://doi.org/10.1016/j.jbankfin.2006.11.003

Yutani, H. (2014). Tai no kinyū shisutemu kaikaku no shinten: Shikin junkan kara no hyōka [Progress in Thailand's financial system reform: An evaluation from the perspective of fund circulation]. Shōgaku Ronsan [Journal of Commerce], Chūō University, 55(3).

Official Documents

Bangkok Bank. Commercial Banks in Thailand, various issues.

Bank of Thailand, 2004. Foreign-owned Financial Institutions under Financial Sector Master Plan.

______. 2006. Thailand's Financial Sector Master Plan Handbook.

______. 2009. BOT News No. 54/2552 Re: The Financial Sector Master Plan Phase II.

______. 2016a. Financial Stability Report

______. 2016b. Executive Summary of Financial Sector Master Plan Phase III.

______. Annual Economic Report, Bangkok, various issues.

______. 1998. Financial Institutions and Markets in Thailand.

______. Financial Stability Report, Various issues.

______. Quarterly Bulletin, Bangkok, various issues.

______. Supervision Report, Bangkok, various issues.

Kasikornbank, Annual Report, various issues.

Newspapers, Magazines and Leaflets

Asia Times.

Bangkok Post.

BBC News.

Bloomberg: Business News.

Financial Times.

Forbes Asia.

New York Times.

Thailand News.

The Economic Times.

The Economist.

The Nation Thailand.

The Thaiger.
The Wall Street Journal.

Interviews

Interview with the Chattawat Yanopas, Senior Officer from Information Services Department, Stock Exchange of Thailand. March 20, 2015, Bangkok, Thailand.

Interview with Saithip Konggiatnarong, a former Senior Researcher from Money & Banking Research Department, Kasikorn Research Center. October 8, 2016, Bangkok, Thailand.

Interview with Thai Bond Market Association. December 18, 2017, Bangkok, Thailand.

Interview with Thanyalak Vacharachaisurapol, Deputy Managing Director of Kasikorn Research Center. November 1, 2018, Bangkok, Thailand.

The manufacturer's authorised representative in the EU is Springer Nature Customer Service Centre GmbH, Europaplatz 3, 69115 Heidelberg, Germany. If you have any concerns regarding our products, please contact ProductSafety@springernature.com

Printed and bound by CPI Group (UK) Ltd, Croydon, CR0 4YY
01/10/2026
02225839-0010